"This timely volume integrates a[n] experience, and theological exper[...] and a renewed biblical discremen[...] ...ering. The authors offer a needed call for a deeper Christian understanding and rearticulation of the fight against illness worldwide. Their compelling metanarrative provides a practical theology of medical care grounded in intelligent love and active mercy."

**–James K. Bruckner**, Professor, North Park University, and author of *Healthy Human Life*

"Jesus' way of ministry highlighted in this book remains our example. He gave of himself rather than providing a service. He taught, modeled, and made disciples, then made his disciples his coworkers. He delegated tasks and responsibilities with authority. Then he handed over the ministry before departing, ensuring sustained and multiplied impact. This evidenced transformational strategy of missions is what God is blessing in our times. As recipients become owners, take over, and multiply the initial work: dignity is built, dependency is broken, and the whole person and environment are served."

**–Florence Muindi**, President and CEO, Life in Abundance International

"This valuable publication underscores that theologians, pastors, and church leaders can also be effective 'health workers' in their own right by engaging in health matters to inform and empower their communities to espouse beliefs, values, and practices that promote health and wellness, and to deny those that militate against life. The pandemic has underscored that health belongs to all sectors."

**–Mwai Makoka**, Program Executive for Health and Healing, World Council of Churches, and author of *Health-Promoting Churches*, vols. 1–2

"This book is an important contribution, bringing the theological and medical perspectives into one place. This will lay a good foundation for 'healing' and 'wholeness' as a theological and missiological agenda."

**–Wonsuk Ma**, Dean, Professor, Oral Roberts University, and former executive director, Oxford Centre for Mission Studies

"This multidisciplinary volume will be a tremendous resource not only to missionaries, but to pastors, students, missions committees, and teams that want to do the work of the church in places impacted by disease. I can easily see this work becoming required reading for those working especially in a majority-world contexts where health systems are fragile and missionary involvement is complex."

**—Jerry M. Ireland**, Chair, Department of Ministry, Leadership and
Theology and Department of Intercultural Studies,
University of Valley Forge

"This remarkable collection of essays addresses from a variety of biblically sound perspectives the troubling phenomenon of why evil, disease in particular, exists in a world created by a loving God who once declared it to be 'good.' The authors plead for getting actively involved in alleviating the havoc brought about by evil on all of creation, not just humans. A stimulating book that encourages God's people to engage in this *missio Dei* whole heartedly."

**—Christoffer H. Grundmann**, Professor, Tübingen, Germany

"The vast majority of people tend to think of disease, epidemics, famines, and disasters as an expression of great divine judgement. All suffering is not punitive . . . . Suffering aids in healing and building the kingdom of God, and in this area, we Christians have been given the privilege to work in partnership with him. Some of the best minds are at work in this book."

**—Vinod Shah**, Senior Surgeon, St. Thomas Hospital, Chetpet, India

"A needed resource to strengthen the competence of public health professionals in addressing the multiple determinants of health, including the spiritual. I appreciate the focus the authors have taken in placing the spiritual as foundational in understanding the physical and social determinants of health rather than neglecting these aspects of disease."

**—Jason Paltzer**, Assistant Professor of Epidemiology, Baylor University

"Ralph D. Winter never stopped trying to identify specific issues and problems that impede the flow of the gospel. . . . This book draws on like-minded scholars from a wide range of disciplines just as Winter would have. As you read this book, your perspective will be challenged in new ways. And perhaps we will see new approaches to solving the right problems."

**–Greg H. Parsons**, Director, Ralph D. Winter Research Center,
Pasadena, California


"There are few real-world issues that impact the lives of more people than disease. . . . We need to think theologically about how engaging with it—seeking to understand diseases, mitigating their effects, combatting or even eradicating them—is an expression of the kingdom of God and contributes to the church's mission in the world."

**–Andrew Sloane**, Director of Research, Morling College, Australia


"In my missions experience, I am often saddened by the church's relegation of health matters to healthcare professionals as opposed to seeing health as part of the gospel message and an integral part of *missio Dei*, and therefore to be included in the role of the church. . . . Addressing the topic of disease from a theological perspective is a welcome addition to nursing literature."

**–Grace Tazelaar**, Medical Surgical Nursing, Missions Director,
Nurses Christian Fellowship

# All Creation Groans

# All Creation Groans

Toward a Theology of Disease and Global Health

EDITED BY

## Daniel W. O'Neill

AND

## Beth Snodderly

FOREWORDS BY

Michael J. Soderling

AND

Rebecca Winter Lewis

PICKWICK *Publications* · Eugene, Oregon

ALL CREATION GROANS
Toward a Theology of Disease and Global Health

Pickwick Publications
An Imprint of Wipf and Stock Publishers
199 W. 8th Ave., Suite 3
Eugene, OR 97401

www.wipfandstock.com

PAPERBACK ISBN: 978-1-7252-9011-2
HARDCOVER ISBN: 978-1-7252-9010-5
EBOOK ISBN: 978-1-7252-9012-9

*Cataloguing-in-Publication data:*

Names: O'Neill, Daniel W., editor. | Snodderly, Beth, editor. | Soderling, Michael J., foreword writer. | Lewis, Rebecca Winter, foreword writer.

Title: All creation groans : toward a theology of disease and global health / edited by Daniel W. O'Neill and Beth Snodderly ; forewords by Michael J. Soderling and Rebecca Winter Lewis.

Description: Eugene, OR: Pickwick Publications, 2021 | Includes bibliographical references and index.

Identifiers: ISBN 978-1-7252-9011-2 (paperback) | ISBN 978-1-7252-9010-5 (hardcover) | ISBN 978-1-7252-9012-9 (ebook)

Subjects: LCSH: Diseases—Religious aspects—Christianity | Church work and the sick | Diseases—Religious aspects | Medical care—Religious aspects—Christianity | Religion and Medicine—Christianity

Classification: BV4460 O54 2021 (print) | BV4460 (ebook)

05/14/21

Permission granted by Gregory H. Parsons, on behalf of Frontier Ventures, holder of the rights to Ralph D. Winter's writings, to republish excerpts from Ralph Winter's original writings for chapter 2, "The Biblical Context for a Theology of

Disease," and chapter 18, "A Missiology that Includes Fighting Disease."

Dedicated to the editors' mentors, Daniel Fountain and Ralph D. Winter, and to those who would build on their legacy of life-giving and engaging application of the *missio Dei* to the pathologies of this life.

We know that the whole creation has been groaning as in the pains of childbirth right up to the present time.

(Rom 8:22)

And we know that in all things God works together with those who love him to bring about what is good—with those who have been called according to his purpose.

(Rom 8:28; text is from a footnote in the NIV)

# Contents

# Contributors

**Lizette Acosta**, PhD, Health Care Chaplain, Orlando Health Dr. P. Phillips Hospital.

**Gregory A. Boyd**, PhD, Senior Pastor, Woodland Hills Church, St. Paul, Minnesota; Adjunct Professor, Northern Theological Seminary; Adjunct Professor, Bethel University.

**Giuseppe Cinà**, MI, former president of Camillianum Istituto Internazionale di Teologia Pastorale Sanitaria, Rome, Italy.

**Daniel Fountain**, MD, Medical missionary in the Democratic Republic of the Congo; Medical Director, Vanga Evangelical Hospital; Founder and Medical Director, Vanga Medical Training Institute.

**Richard S. Gunasekera**, PhD, Associate Dean of Academic and Research Affairs and Professor of Biochemistry, Biola University.

**Jim Harries**, PhD, Missionary in East Africa; Chairman, Alliance for Vulnerable Mission; Adjunct Faculty, William Carey International University.

**Daniel Isgrigg**, PhD, Reference Librarian and Director of the Holy Spirit Research Center, Oral Roberts University.

**Stephen Ko**, MD, MPH, MDiv, Senior Pastor, New York Chinese Alliance Church; Adjunct Professor, Boston University; Adjunct Professor, Alliance Theological Seminary.

**Rebecca Winter Lewis**, MA International Development, field practitioner in Africa and Asia for thirty years.

**Kalemba Mwambazambi**, PhD, Registrar, Université Protestante au Coeur du Congo; Dissertation and Thesis Supervisor, University of South Africa.

**Daniel W. O'Neill**, MD, MTh, Associate Professor of Family Medicine, University of Connecticut School of Medicine; Founder and Managing Editor, *Christian Journal for Global Health*; Founding Board Member, Health for All Nations.

**Beth Snodderly**, DLitt et Phil, Editor, Ralph D. Winter Research Center; Editor, *William Carey International Development Journal*; past president of William Carey International University.

**Keith So**, MD, MPH, Attending physician, Lawndale Christian Health Center; Lecturer in Internal Medicine, Pyongyang University Science and Technology Medical College.

**Michael J. Soderling**, MD, MBA, Director, Health for All Nations; former medical missionary in Guatemala; co-catalyst for Lausanne Health for all Nations issue network.

**Sigve K. Tonstad**, MD, PhD, Professor of Religion and Assistant Professor of Medicine, Loma Linda University.

**Ralph D. Winter**, PhD, Founder of the US Center for World Mission, William Carey International University, and the Roberta Winter Institute; former Professor of Missions, Fuller Theological Seminary; former editor, *Mission Frontiers Bulletin* and *International Journal of Frontier Missiology*.

# Foreword

—Michael J. Soderling

A MORE OPPORTUNE TIME for this book to be published could not have occurred than the one in which the world finds itself presently. With the COVID-19 pandemic causing over a million deaths as of this writing, and a significant downturn in the global economy, the need for this carefully crafted work is more urgent than ever.

We humans are once again at a significant crossroads in our existence. It is a time not unlike what humans were experiencing one hundred years ago. At the turn of the twentieth century, there was much optimism about human existence. Darwin had provided a framework for understanding human existence that left no room for an all-powerful transcendent creator-God, and scientific discoveries were propelling humans at an ever-increasing pace into a mindset that left no room for myths and miracles. We humans were going to sort things out now that we could really discover truth through scientific inquiry. At the same time the communist ideology of Karl Marx was beginning to be applied to a large segment of the world. If it could not be proven with human reason on a materialist basis, then it wasn't truth! Add to this, German higher criticism that was doing its best to deconstruct how humans viewed the Bible's storyline and its portrayal of the historical Jesus, and it seemed to many humanists that we were soon to enter a time of unparalleled knowledge and understanding of our world. Autonomy was nearly complete. Utopia was just a breath away.

This all came crashing down with the first volleys of cannon that would lead the world into a darkness she had never known before. The scale of this cataclysmic world disaster was unforeseen by even the most well-informed futurists. By the end of "The War to End all Wars," twenty million people had lost their lives. What helped facilitate the end of this global disaster? The death of up to fifty million more as the Spanish flu (H1N1) pandemic ravaged the world further during its two-year reign of terror between 1918 and 1920.

Humanist optimism did not die out completely, but received additional setbacks with the onset of the worldwide economic depression that was set off by the stock market crash of 1929 in the United States. Then another challenge to the humanistic/naturalism marketing campaign occurred with the onset of the second global scale conflagration in 1939 leading to six years of war and the loss of an additional seventy million lives, including the systematic genocide of six million Jews. However, mankind emerged from these horrific global disasters and entered a new phase of optimism. Economies boomed around the world, though many billions were left behind, still suffering in countries and cultures that offered little hope of prosperity. Between 1917 and 2017, one hundred million people were executed or died of war, famine, or disease at the hands of communist regimes.[1]

Other pandemics have occurred since the Spanish flu but none to that degree of devastation. In the 1980s, while I was in my residency in Baltimore, Maryland, we began hearing of a new and deadly disease called Human Immune Deficiency Syndrome for which no treatment was available. While there is now treatment available to some, there is still no cure. It is estimated that thirty-two million have died from this human scourge, some seven hundred seventy thousand in the year 2018 alone.[2]

Ebola, first discovered in 1976, killed more than eleven thousand men, women, and children in West Africa between 2014 and 2016.[3] Daniel Fountain, my long-time mentor, used to tell the story of how he was blamed for an outbreak of Ebola in the Democratic Republic of the Congo (DRC). Some posited that he transformed himself into a hippo after giving a lecture on AIDS in Kikwit, DRC, and then infected doctors and medical staff in the location where he had lectured! This illustrates how humans are driven to seek causes of disease or place blame on others based on their worldview paradigms. People then craft solutions based on their understandings.

More recent outbreaks of SARS (in 2003 with 813 deaths)[4] and MERS (beginning in 2012, causing 858 deaths as of November 2019)[5] outbreaks have dealt out their own level of disease and high mortality rates. But this

1. Satter, "One Hundred Years of Communism."
2. "Number of Deaths Due to HIV/AIDS."
3. "History of Ebola Virus Disease."
4. "Cumulative Number of Reported Probable Cases."
5. "Middle East Respiratory Syndrome Coronavirus (MERS-CoV)."

is to say nothing about the massive toll in human life from mosquito borne pathogens. West Nile Virus, various kinds of Encephalitis, Dengue Fever, Yellow Fever, and Zika Virus, are well-known examples. But all combined, these pale in comparison to the death toll from malaria—a parasitic disease that is treatable and preventable, but has not yet been eliminated from the Earth as was smallpox.

Other ancient diseases which still present a hazard to humankind include bubonic plague (still around since killing nearly one third of Europe's population in the fourteenth century),[6] leprosy, and the last remaining strain of polio. These are, theoretically, diseases that could be eliminated as a threat to human health, reduced to a vial in a secure laboratory, if only there were the right amount of resources and collective will.

Similar to the optimism prior to the turn of the twentieth century, there has been, since the turn of the twenty-first century, a growing optimism among many, as the internet and smartphones have brought the world to our fingertips. Access to this knowledge can be seen as the great leveler between the haves and have-nots. Information is power to all who can access it, yet human capital is still recognized as the most important type of capital in our modern times. In the Information Age we were once again on the verge of something great. A world system interconnected by the world wide web, and social media outlets promising to provide the type of relationships everyone was yearning for.

Yet despite this burgeoning information and electronic connectivity, rates of depression, addictions, and suicide are soaring, even in what are considered the "happiest" countries on the planet.[7] Non-communicable diseases are becoming leading causes of death in most countries of the world, often fueled by the electronic marketing of harmful products and subversive ideologies. The globally interconnected world is not proving to be the answer to what ails us humans. The COVID-19 global pandemic has brought the world to a keen awareness of our common humanity, our vulnerabilities, our social disparities, and our need to work together for the common good. Disrupted globalized economies, social disintegration, fear, and despair have been magnified. We are still in need of rescue.

Amid such global disruptions, we in the church must carefully examine our response as to why such things are happening, and what may be done about them. Many are the voices that would blame God for this pandemic—as if God in his retributive anger and sovereignty decided to *cause* a mutation in an otherwise fairly harmless coronavirus residing in

6. "Black Death."

7. Savage, "Being Depressed."

a horseshoe bat in China. This then, these voices believe, providentially infected an intermediary host which, because of wet market novelty meat consumption, skipped hosts to infect a few humans, causing a mass exodus from Wuhan, out to surrounding towns and villages. This fleeing mass of humanity caused others to become infect others and they went on to infect others who freely traveled abroad. This set the stage for what we are experiencing now in 2021. And this is the God we hope others, who are truly seeking truth, will wish to follow?!

Dr. Dan Fountain became one of my chief mentors for understanding a Christian view for global health and mission. He addressed these issues in his groundbreaking BGC monograph, *Health, the Bible, and the Church.*[8] He clearly understood that the world was corrupted by evil when a third of the angels rebelled, and, enticed to follow suit, Adam and Eve decided they wanted to be like God, autonomous masters of their own destinies. This corruption of God's creation and rebellion against God's intended order has led to all manner of destruction, disease, and death. But the blame for such corruption must be placed where it belongs—primarily at the feet of Satan and at the feet of humans who too often choose paths that lead to their own destruction. We acknowledge that God is ultimately in control of history and that it is only with God's permission that such devastating things happen. But at a time when so many Nones (no religious affiliation), SBNRs (Spiritual but Not Religious), and the remaining unreached people groups who have not yet experienced the healing power of the gospel of Jesus Christ are seeking answers to these most difficult questions, are we justified in telling them that it is the will and actions of an angry God that such things happen? May it not be so!

I believe Dan Fountain and Ralph Winter would have found much to like in each others' thinking and teaching on this topic. Dr. Winter had a keen mind focused on the question of why the church had not been planted in all people groups, and why she wasn't more engaged in eliminating disease on Earth, if at all possible. Dr. Fountain didn't have this so much in mind as he did the complexity of the origin of disease and how to address it at the community level. In the chapter I identified above he wrote;

> One further confusing issue remains. The Bible on occasion refers to certain physical or emotional ills as coming "from the Lord." Elsewhere it speaks of disease, disaster, or death as the "curse of God." We must be very careful here in our application of these passages. All that destroys is evil and we must not ascribe evil to God. God has created all things according

---

8. See especially chapter 9 in that book, "Coping with Suffering."

to his orderly laws and patterns, which permit the harmonious productive functioning of the world, including us. If we rebel against these laws, which govern the physical, social, and spiritual environment, we incur the consequences of our rebellion. If we label these consequences as God's punishment or "curse" because they come from the rejection of God's laws made for our benefit, we must remember that the responsibility for bringing these consequences upon us is ours, not God's.[9]

Daniel O'Neill, co-editor of this book, is a physician-theologian and colleague of mine in the Health for All Nations organization in which we both have leadership responsibilities. He has participated in multiple health and development projects among impoverished and displaced populations in Central and South America, West Africa, North India, Indonesia, and the Middle East. He is the founder and managing editor of the *Christian Journal for Global Health*[10] and is co-facilitator of the Evidence Working Group of the World Bank's Faith Initiative (Moral and Spiritual Imperative). With his strong background in medicine, missiology, theology, development, and journalism, he is well qualified to write and edit this important book.

Co-editor Beth Snodderly is a past president of William Carey International University. She was instrumental in my decision to join Frontier Ventures, formerly the US Center for World Mission, founded by Ralph Winter. She has written and edited several insightful books and now serves as editor for the university's online journal and its Ralph D. Winter Research Center and the Roberta Winter Institute. Along with her co-editor, she has recruited a tremendous list of diverse contributors and her ability to synthesize and edit the prior literary works of both Winter and Fountain for a new generation is unmatched. I am sure Daniel Fountain would have agreed wholeheartedly with the result.

At a time when so many people are seeking answers to these most difficult questions, and longing for release and protection as well as meaning in suffering, a clear theology of disease is now more needed than ever. Vital also is a compelling call to engage in the mission of God toward global health and human flourishing with renewed hope and well-informed humility.

9. Fountain, "Coping with Suffering," 115.

10. See http://www.cjgh.org

## Bibliography

"Black Death." *History.com*, September 17, 2010. Revised July 6, 2020. Online. https://www.history.com/topics/middle-ages/black-death.

"Cumulative Number of Reported Probable Cases of SARS." *World Health Organization*, May 28, 2003. Online. https://www.who.int/csr/sars/country/2003_05_28/en.

Fountain, Daniel E. "Coping with Suffering." In *Health, the Bible and the Church*, by Daniel E. Fountain, 103–23. BGC Monograph. Wheaton, IL: Wheaton College, 1989. Online. https://www.healthforallnations.com/coping-with-suffering-dr-daniel-fountain.

"History of Ebola Virus Disease." *Centers for Disease Control and Prevention*, n.d. Revised January 22, 2021. Online. https://www.cdc.gov/vhf/ebola/history/summaries.html.

"Middle East Respiratory Syndrome Coronavirus (MERS-CoV)." *World Health Organization*, n.d. Online. https://www.who.int/emergencies/mers-cov/en.

"Number of Deaths Due to HIV/AIDS. Estimates by WHO Region." *World Health Organization*, July 7, 2020. Online. https://apps.who.int/gho/data/node.main.623?lang=en.

Satter, David. "One Hundred Years of Communism—and One Hundred Million Dead." *Wall Street Journal*, November 6, 2017. Online. https://www.wsj.com/articles/100-years-of-communismand-100-million-dead-1510011810.

Savage, Maddy. "Being Depressed in the 'World's Happiest Country.'" *BBC*, September 25, 2019. Online. https://www.bbc.com/worklife/article/20190924-being-depressed-in-the-worlds-happiest-country.

# Foreword

—Rebecca Winter Lewis

WHY INITIATE A CONTEMPORARY theological dialog about disease, and the missiological implications of that theology? Our understanding of disease and disease mechanisms have deepened greatly in the last century. My father, the late missiologist Ralph D. Winter, used to plead for an updated public theology about disease, saying, "Our theologies, that is, our formalized ways of attempting to think biblically, were hammered out during centuries that were totally blind to the microscopic world."[1]

We stand at a significant turning point in history. Our scientific knowledge about creation and disease is rapidly expanding, including how the body functions at the cellular and chemical level, and how it interacts with various treatments. With this knowledge comes responsibility before God to use this knowledge for compassion to bring blessing and health.

Therefore, we must seek to re-understand theologically the role God wants believers to play in the twenty-first century with respect to both communicable diseases as well as the explosion of new types of non-communicable diseases and physical disorders.

For example, we now know we are introducing gender-bending endocrine-disrupting chemicals and even death-causing chemicals into our environment.[2] Plastics, herbicides, pesticides, chemical fertilizers, excitotoxins, and carcinogens are polluting our environment with harmful consequences to many life forms and ecosystems, including the complex ecosystem of the human gut. Most of these consequences were unexpected and scientists are only beginning to figure them out. Others still remain a mystery.

1. Winter, "Theologizing the Microbial World," 203.
2. Cadbury, *Altering Eden*.

Autoimmune diseases are turning our incredibly complex and intelligent immune system into a self-destruction machine. There are also morally questionable "death industries"[3] marketing with impunity ever more powerful, addictive chemicals which enslave and even kill humanity.

All of this has come about in the last one hundred to one hundred fifty years. In his last years, my father, Ralph Winter, was advocating for a theology of disease that is up to date. He felt strongly that with the new understanding of DNA and other scientific advances we now have a "vast new opportunity and unacknowledged new responsibility."[4]

All of the life forms on our planet appear to have amazing built-in mechanisms both for ongoing growth and for the replenishing of damaged or old cells. They also have mechanisms for correcting things that have gone wrong and for fighting off the invasion of destructive microorganisms.

Significant progress has been made in the last decade in actually identifying the genes and enzymes (telomeres and telomerase) that keep a body's cells rejuvenating or cause them to age. In other words, it is no longer inconceivable scientifically that the body could indefinitely replenish and restore itself apart from being overcome by foreign invaders or toxic substances that disrupt this self-healing process. Some life forms even show the amazing ability to regrow entire limbs if injured, so we know that DNA potentially also has this amazing capability.

Scriptures relate some unusual things that show the writers believed God had not originally designed life to lead inexorably to disease and death. For example, Genesis and Romans explain that death entered the world through satanic intrusion and human disobedience. Indeed, all of nature is groaning and awaiting a day when it will be restored to a different disease-free and death-free reality, redeemed from the law of sin and death (Rom 8:22). So, creation is longing to be set free from its slavery to corruption, and we likewise are awaiting not just spiritual but also physical redemption.

Therefore, it appears to some that disease and death were not a part of God's original creation nor his ultimate will. Rather, these entered the world at the point when Satan successfully tempted Adam and Eve to disobey God. In other words, disease and death are a consequence of sin and deviation from God's design—a twisting and distortion of that design. If so, what is our role as God's people? The teachings of the Bible, even the specific laws of Leviticus, would suggest that we are to live in a way to promote the healthy functioning of our bodies and to destroy pathogens, for example mold, whenever they are discovered in inappropriate places. We are to proactively

---

3. See Lewis, "Challenging the Death Industries."

4. Winter, "Other Terrorists."

war against these rogue and destructive forces. Today we know much more about biological pathogens, as well as chemical and environmental toxins or nutritional deficiencies that can cause disease, and we have the capacity to discover even more.

What should be our role as God's people in fighting for health today? E. Stanley Jones, in his book, *Christ and Human Suffering*, points out that all of humankind is struggling with the horror of suffering and death. Our spirits rebel against these things, and therefore religious systems have come up with explanations that enable people to cope. In India, more than a billion people with a Hindu worldview[5] have come to the conclusion that their *karma* will determine when they will die, and nothing can be done to prevent that.[6] Most Hindus believe that much of the suffering they endure is a result of their own actions either in this or a previous life. This makes them passive in the face of disease and suffering.

Similarly, I have found through personal experience that Muslims usually believe "whatever is, is God's will," namely that God must have good reasons for allowing or even sending these sufferings into our lives, reasons we may never understand but that are just. This perspective also equates suffering with punishment, whether for personal or corporate sin, and thus likewise produces passivity in response to human suffering.

Job's friends fell into this perspective, as have many Jews and Christians throughout history. When ignorance of causes of disease or suffering frustrates our attempts to restore health or prevent injury, Christians can easily fall back into a more fatalistic outlook, cease to look for causes and solutions, and accept even things like cancer, blindness, autism, or Alzheimer's as the will of God.

However, this is not the position of the Bible nor what we see in the life of Christ. The Bible shows us to be in a war against evil—moral, spiritual, and physical—and that God is not the author of evil but overcomes evil with good.

Jesus explained that the men who were killed by the falling tower were not being punished for their evil deeds, otherwise we would all deserve such a fate (Luke 13:4–5). Similarly, the man born blind was not blind due either to his own sin or that of his parents (John 9:3). Instead God was glorified when Jesus healed the man's eyes. The picture painted is that the world is in the grip of a strangulating evil, and that suffering can be as indiscriminate as the rain that falls on the just and unjust.

5. "Hindu Countries."
6. Pargament et al., "Methods of Coping," 272.

Jesus' own life demonstrated a determination to overcome the evil of sin, suffering, and death. He did this not merely by healing many, but through his own suffering and death, Jesus broke the power of Satan's rule on Earth. Through Jesus' obedience, he reversed the disobedience of Adam and overcame evil with good.

Throughout history, the most dedicated followers of Jesus have followed his example. In the book, *The Rise of Christianity*, Rodney Stark demonstrates how faith in Jesus spread in part because the Christians were alleviating the suffering not only of their own sick but also caring for pagans during times of plague and famine.[7] These early believers were pacifists, refusing to defend their own lives through violence, yet they were not at all passive toward disease and suffering, fighting against them with whatever means and knowledge they had. They understood through faith that we are in a battle against sin, disease, and death, not merely waiting for some grand deliverance at the end of the age.

Likewise, the vast majority of hospitals and curative medical innovations throughout history have been initiated by men and women impacted by the Bible.[8] Florence Nightingale fought a long war against the ignorance that led to untold numbers of deaths in times of war. Once it was clear that germs were causing the infections killing thousands of wounded, why did it take a twenty-year campaign by a committed Christian to make sterile nursing the standard, first in war zones and later in hospitals? And why were the doctors, Christian and otherwise, so reluctant to accept her challenge until she marshaled shocking statistics? I believe the reluctance came from a failed medical tradition that was slow to give way to new data and the need for new practice. My father would have said it was due to a "diabolical complex of misunderstandings."[9]

Throughout history, whenever causes of suffering have been clearly identified, believers have sought to come up with solutions that will proactively prevent or cure that suffering. Foundational to these sustained efforts is not only the theology that God expects us to fight against disease and suffering, but also that God cares about each human life specifically and individually.

My father knew what a powerful force in history followers in Christ can be when they are determined to be proactive about disease and suffering, and what a powerful witness that is to the love of God for the families of the Earth. He wanted to see believers working on discovering the origins of diseases, and finding ways to eliminate or eradicate them, as a means of intentionally demonstrating God's love. He knew that believers could in this

7. Stark, *Rise of Christianity*, 1996.

8. See Armstrong, *Healthcare and Hospitals*.

9. Winter, "Story of Our Planet," 216.

way bring the knowledge of God's love to the peoples of the Earth—overcoming evil with good.

Some people have ceased to view disease as a destruction of God's good design and plan. Instead of recognizing the role of the evil one in deceiving humans and influencing biological processes, people may tend to blame God for everything from autism and Alzheimer's to cancer or obesity. We need a contemporary biblical theology of disease in order to understand what God would have us as believers do in the twenty-first century to partner with him in the cosmic battle between good and evil, between health and disease, between life and death. May this book lead us in that direction, that God may be glorified and God's love for each human life be made manifest.

## Bibliography

Armstrong, Chris R., ed. *Healthcare and Hospitals in the Mission of the Church. Christian History* 101 (2011). Online. https://christianhistoryinstitute.org/uploaded/5ocf8e 35c4ae27.43897050.pdf.

Cadbury, Deborah. *Altering Eden: The Feminization of Nature.* New York: St. Martin's, 1997.

"Hindu Countries Population." *World Population Review,* 2021. Online. http://worldpopulationreview.com/countries/hindu-countries.

Jones, E. Stanley. *Christ and Human Suffering.* Nashville: Abingdon, 1933.

Lewis, Rebecca W. "Challenging the Death Industries: Duty or Distraction?" *Mission Frontiers,* September 1, 2019. Online. https://www.missionfrontiers.org/issue/article/challenging-the-death-industries-duty-or-distraction.

Pargament, Kenneth I., et al. "Methods of Coping from the Religions of the World: The Bar Mitzvah, Karma, and Spiritual Healing." In *Coping with Stress: Effective People and Processes,* edited by C. R. Snyder, 259–84. New York: Oxford University Press, 2001.

Stark, Rodney. *The Rise of Christianity: How the Obscure, Marginal Jesus Movement Became the Dominant Religious Force in the Western World in a Few Centuries.* Princeton: Princeton University Press, 1996.

Winter, Ralph D. "The Other Terrorists." *Mission Frontiers,* November 1, 2001. Online. http://www.missionfrontiers.org/issue/article/the-other-terrorists.

———. "The Story of Our Planet: Origins, Evil, and Mission." In *Frontiers in Mission: Discovering and Surmounting Barriers to the Missio Dei,* edited by Ralph D. Winter, 216. 4th ed. Pasadena, CA: William Carey International University Press, 2008.

———. "Theologizing the Microbiological World: Implications for Mission." In *Frontiers in Mission: Discovering and Surmounting Barriers to the Missio Dei,* edited by Ralph D. Winter, 203–5. 4th ed. Pasadena, CA: William Carey International University Press, 2008.

# Acknowledgments

THE CO-EDITORS WOULD LIKE to thank the co-authors, who were willing and eager to engage in very thoughtful and innovative writing on the subject presented in this book. They have done so with clarity, unity, and wisdom. As is true of every human intellectual endeavor, we stand on the shoulders of those who have offered their own unique perspectives, many of which are well-represented in the text and references. We also appreciate the patience, support, feedback, and challenges given by our respective families and colleagues as we took time in writing, editing, and promoting this project. We are especially grateful to our Living God whose living Word, incarnate Healer, and global Spirit, speak a deeper praxis of hope and healing than the blood of Abel for the families of the earth.

# Introduction

—Daniel W. O'Neill and Beth Snodderly

At such a time as this, when the entire world is reeling with the devastation of the novel coronavirus disease (COVID-19) pandemic, Christians are more acutely aware than ever of the ubiquitous effect disease has on humanity. All over the Earth people are suffering and dying due, in part, to an onslaught from the microbiological world that scientists are still trying to fully understand, and that has not been widely understood theologically. Why should theologians and churches now be considering theological approaches toward community and global health? Or, as Ralph Winter asked, "What would Jesus have said about fighting germs had the people of his time known about germs? How would that amplify and refocus our global mission?"[1]

There has been an increasingly recognized disconnect between healthcare endeavors, public health initiatives, and spiritual pursuits in the church, and this book presents a call to recapture an important theological correction to the exclusively soul-focused endeavors of evangelicals in the late twentieth century. There is an increasing call in the Christian community to promote global health, as an indispensable part of glorifying God, by thoughtful application of evidence-based and biblically-based approaches for new levels of innovation and service, which is the mission of Health for All Nations.[2]

The globalized church is challenging the exclusively-materialist assumptions of Western biomedicine, the overly-secularized field of international development, the extremes of some overly-spiritualized miracle-seeking pentecostal movements, and the de-mythologized and exclusively

1. Winter, "What Is a Christ-Centered Church?" 168.
2. See https://www.healthforallnations.com.

social tendencies of liberal theology. This book attempts to begin filling these gaps by addressing theological questions such as the following, from a variety of biblical, philosophical, historical, global, ecological, scientific, contemporary, and practical perspectives:

- Does the church's mandate to care for creation include fighting the causes of disease as part of taking creation back for God's purposes?

- By tracing the origins of disease—physical, social, and spiritual—can more effective approaches to disease be embraced when faced with major global health challenges?

- How do we embrace a wholistic approach to life and death given the reality of evil, the powers, corruption, and disordered relationships?

- In what ways are we to understand the atonement as the continuum of the healing and liberating action of Christ and that of Christ's followers throughout the world?

This book is, in an informal sense, a posthumous *festschrift* for missiologist Ralph Winter and medical missionary Daniel Fountain. We are committed to building on the legacies of these two men, and enhancing a long-overdue theological and missiological conversation that highlights the often-forgotten responsibility of the body of Christ for health and wholeness wherever God's people begin to live, move, and have their being. This will have particular value in framing a theology of disease and healing for church leaders, theological students, missionaries, health workers, and those engaged in global health in the private and public sector.

Winter expressed a passionate desire, in the last years of his life, to prompt the theological world to begin working on a theology of disease. Admittedly this came to his mind as a crucial need due to his first wife Roberta's fatal bout with cancer. Throughout the last years of his life he reflected on the types of inadequate responses to disease that are prevalent in the Christian world and concluded that this was an obstacle to the spread of the gospel among major unreached blocs of the world's peoples. After his first wife's death he founded the Roberta Winter Institute (RWI) with the mission, "to ignite in the body of Christ a theological shift regarding disease and its eradication."[3]

Winter challenged believers to realize that "*thinking theologically* also means using the Bible to face situations that are wholly new to the Bible."[4]

---

3. See http://www.robertawinterinstitute.org.

4. Winter, "Seminary," 69.

He felt the Christian world lagged in applying the Bible to new circumstances, asking,

> If there is not a defective understanding of the Bible at work in [the] long-standing Christian paralysis in the face of evil, then why is it a Sunday School teacher *who has not gone to seminary*, namely former US President Jimmy Carter, who is the only one Christian leader I know who has set out to "eradicate" major diseases? And why is he getting his vast funds not from the denominations and mission agencies but from secular corporations? Yes, *thinking theologically* means using the Bible to review and refine our existing theology. The Bible, not our theological tradition, is the *given*.[5]

"The least we can do," Winter said, "is set something in motion that may rectify our understanding of a God who is not the author of the destructive violence in nature and who has long sought our help in bringing His kingdom and His will on Earth."[6]

This book attempts to address Winter's concerns by showing that preliminary work has been done, much of it since his death in 2009, toward a theology of disease. In fact, as a result of the COVID-19 pandemic, N. T. Wright has aligned himself with Winter's major desire to "rectify our understanding" of God, though he remains relatively agnostic to the "dark power that from the start has tried to destroy God's handiwork."[7] Wright notes Jesus' approach was not to "look back to a hypothetical cause which would enable onlookers to feel smug that they had understood some inner cosmic moral mechanism, some sin that God had to punish. He looks forward to see what God is going to do about it."[8] God does this through human agency: "The Creator God called a people to be his partner in rescuing the human race and restoring creation . . . creating a context for the multiple works of healing and hope."[9]

Ralph Winter often referred to disease as an example of the "works of the devil" mentioned in 1 John 3:8. But the editors caution against an approach which absolves humans of responsibility in disease causation. Rather, the awareness of evil powers lying behind some disease provides all the more motivation for humans to be part of the solution instead of being passive in the face of suffering, or complicit in the cause or propagation of disease. This

---

5. Winter, "Seminary," 69.

6. Winter, "Blindspot in Western Christianity?" 202.

7. Wright, *God and the Pandemic*, 14.

8. Wright, *God and the Pandemic*, 17.

9. Wright, *God and the Pandemic*, 13, 51.

challenge is reflected throughout the book and in the final chapters in which Gregory Boyd presents a persuasive theology of disease as a corruption of nature, and the responsibility of humans in fighting back against disease as an act of glorifying God and serving their neighbors.

N. T. Wright explains the importance of believers' involvement in correcting evils in this world in his book, *Evil and the Justice of God*:

> The New Testament points to the ultimate future, to the promise of a world set free from evil altogether, and invites us to hold that in our minds and hearts so that we know where we're going. We are to implement the achievement of Jesus and so to anticipate God's eventual world.[10] The Christian imagination . . . needs to be awakened, enlivened, and pointed in the right direction. . . . Christians need to sense permission, from God and from one another, to exercise their imaginations in thinking ahead into God's new world and into such fresh forms of worship and service as will model and embody aspects of it. We need to have this imagination energized, fed, and nourished, so that it is lively and inventive, not sluggishly going around the small circles of a few ideas learned long ago.[11]

It seems that what Wright is calling for is precisely the purpose for which the Roberta Winter Institute was founded: to awaken, energize, and nourish the Christian imagination to include a new form of service to bring glory to God by exploring and conquering the roots of diseases. Once we acknowledge disease in the category of "evil," we can see the need to mobilize the body of Christ to seek to fight disease at its origins as a means of anticipating "God's eventual world." A scientist or health worker who is consciously, in faith, seeking to prevent, minimize, contain, or eradicate disease can be assured that he/she is aligning with God's will and looking toward the renewal of all of creation in the *eschaton*. A church leader who mobilizes his/her congregation to engage in promoting human and ecological health is doing the same. "We have to regard ourselves as sealed, even branded, by this mission of bringing light, blessing, enlivening, raising up, healing, and freeing."[12]

This perspective is reflected throughout this book. Several chapters offer ways Christ-followers can glorify God by fighting disease:

---

10. Wright, *Evil and the Justice of God*, 104.

11. Wright, *Evil and the Justice of God*, 126.

12. Francis, "Evangelii Gaudium" 273.

- In public health service (chapter 12: "Public Health Approaches to Disease from Antiquity to the Current Day")

- In social justice activism (chapter 9: "Health and Disease: Why Mercy and Compassion Matter")

- In scientific research (chapter 15: "A Scientist's Perspective on Disease and Death")

- In serving as medical personnel across other cultures (chapter 6: "A Theology of Health for the Nations"; chapter 13: "A West African Perspective on God and Disease"; chapter 14: "An East African Perspective on God and Disease"; chapter 16: "A Practical Missiology Regarding Disease and Healing"; chapter 17: "A Missiology that Includes Fighting Disease")

- In leadership for congregations and as healing agents in community (chapter 8: "A Theology of Love in the First Epistle of John"; chapter 10: "The Concept of Disease in the Pentecostal Tradition"; chapter 11: "Life from Death: Illness, Anthropology, and the Christian Faith").

Each contributor offers their unique perspective toward the unified theme of believers' responsibility toward the groaning creation, specifically in the realm of disease. In chapter 1, "Historical, Contemporary, and Globalized Theologies of Disease," physician-theologian Daniel O'Neill gives an assessment of his personal interactions with Winter and Daniel Fountain. He then provides an overview of historical theologies of disease from the patristic era to the current day, including thinking emerging from an increasingly globalized church. This provides some basic context by which to evoke a stream of meaningful contextualized approaches to the problem of evil powers and corruption involved in disease causation globally.

Ralph Winter gives further context in chapter 2, compiled from his writings, "The Biblical Context for a Theology of Disease." He overviews the biblical story from Genesis to Revelation from the standpoint of the "blessing" God desires to give all peoples. In this story, Winter includes the call to release all nations from the effects of disease as part of the Abrahamic blessing.

That which opposes God's blessing is described in chapter 3, "A Theology of Creation," as Beth Snodderly elaborates on the Hebrew term, "*tohu wabohu*" (Gen 1:2). She gives exegetical analysis showing that this term describes conditions that are the opposite of God's creational intent, including chaos and disease. Humans were created to join God in subduing the disorder of a world that had fallen under the "power of the evil one" (1 John 5:19 ESV). This pervasive influence of the evil one leads to sin, which in turn leads to death, which is a universal aspect of embodied life, often mediated through disease processes. Once freed from sin, humans can resume their original mandate (Gen 1:28) to "subdue" what has gone wrong in creation.

Winter used to say, "To me the most profound issue facing missions today is the absence of a concept of an Adversary in our theology of church life and mission."[13] The early church understood very well that the Earth was the stage of a cosmic conflict that involved God, human beings, and angelic beings including Satan, as theologian-physician Sigve Tonstad describes by analyzing the teachings of Origen in chapter 4, "Early Church Perspectives on the Cosmic Conflict." Maintaining this larger narrative applied in the current day leads to a more complete approach to healing.

Daniel O'Neill then emphasizes in chapter 5, "Sin and the Etiology of Disease," the multi-faceted causes of disease and the upstream effects of sin and evil (both angelic and human) on human and planetary health, and the efficacious remedy that Jesus brings as global Redeemer, as he continues to work through his redeemed people as healing agents.

As Professor Christoffer Grundmann recounts, Christians of the late nineteenth and early twentieth centuries fought against disease in God's name and produced a great mobilization of medical missionaries throughout the twentieth century who attended the body as well as the soul for community transformation as a sign of the corporeality of salvation.[14] One of those mobilized was Dr. Daniel Fountain, the late medical missionary to the Democratic Republic of the Congo. Excerpts from his classic monograph, *Health, the Bible, and the Church*, comprise chapter 6, "A Theology of Health for the Nations." He described what God's kingdom looks like through the lens of health and wholeness:

> Put quite simply, God's plan for the world is this: that all persons everywhere, in every nation, know God's saving health and be delivered from disobedience, disruption, despair, disease, and all that would destroy our wholeness.[15]

This leads us back to the problem of evil: what is causing disease, instead of health, to be prevalent in our world? Theodicies challenge belief in a God of sovereignty, love, and compassion. Those theologians with a high view of the sovereignty of God might conclude that disease is God-ordained, although this does not preclude the fight against disease as an act of God's grace, and an exercise of human dominion on Earth. John

---

13. Winter, "Editorial," 4.

14. Grundmann, "Sent to Heal!," 6–15.

15. Fountain, *Health, the Bible, and the Church*, 48.

Piper notes that God "permits things for a reason," but we should not be "join[ing] the ranks of the indifferent . . . but mobilizing them with compassion," in acts of "futility-lifting."[16]

All creation is groaning in the throes of futility in many ways and is in need of the engagement of God's intended stewards of the Earth. In chapter 7, "A Theology of Ecology: Earth Care and Health," Sigve Tonstad presents a contemporary challenge to Christ-followers to recognize that health is a precious thing, as we have been reminded in these COVID-19 times. The spillover of coronavirus SARS-CoV-2 animal infection into the human host, leading to a devastating global pandemic, has given a wake-up call that human health cannot be seen or achieved in isolation from animal health and compassionate care of the whole of creation.

Acts of compassion are implied in a theology of love. Hospital chaplain Lizette Acosta describes in chapter 8 how the First Epistle of John contributes toward a theology of disease through a description of the state of world systems contrasted with God's desire for the world and God's character as light and love. This has implications for God's children whose lives must be grounded in imitation of God's character, sustaining the outpouring of love by abiding in God and walking in the light. She concludes with a moving example of love promoting life amidst COVID-19.

In chapter 9, Dr. Keith So provides another example of the need for love promoting life. He argues that justice, mercy, and advocacy for those who are marginalized and captive to culture and disordered power structures, which are antithetical to freedom and abundant life, should be an essential attitude displayed by a globally-conscious church. As an example, he draws from his experience of addressing infectious and non-communicable diseases in the restricted-access impoverished country of the DPRK (North Korea).

In chapter 10, "The Concept of Disease in the Pentecostal Tradition," Daniel Isgrigg gives historical background on the healing ministry of the burgeoning pentecostal stream of Christianity, with particular scholarly emphasis on the controversial but misunderstood American faith-healer Oral Roberts who founded a medical school, seeing a seamless continuity between Christian theology, charismatic healing, and biomedical research and healthcare.

While healing is always desirable, Fr. Giuseppe Cinà of the Order of St. Camillas (Ministers to the Sick), offers a Catholic perspective in chapter 11 on "Life from Death: Illness, Anthropology, and the Christian Faith." He explains the embodied question mark elicited by the evil experienced by illness

---

16. Piper, "If God Wills Disease."

and how this can be addressed by the biological and pastoral sciences—redeemed by the incarnate, suffering Servant. Through his passion and by his stripes we are healed to become healing agents.

Jesus expressed pastoral and healing care toward both individuals (sparrows) and the public (crowds). In chapter 12, Professor Stephen Ko, physician-pastor of New York Chinese Alliance Church, presents a public health perspective, explaining the overlap between the individual experience of disease and the sacrifices needed for communities to flourish. Tracing the biblical origins of public health, he develops the modern public health approach to pandemics like COVID-19. Global pandemics like this awaken humanity to our vulnerability and give Christians the opportunity to follow Jesus by sacrificially engaging in the promotion of health for communities.

Mwambazambi Kalemba presents a West African perspective in chapter 13, on disease and the interface of the unseen spiritual world with the tangible physical world. In the context of the primal worldview of spirits, ancestors, and disease, he addresses the HIV pandemic and the progress the church has made in removing stigma, preventing transmission, and enabling life-sustaining treatment. HIV/AIDS is an example of many diseases that theologian Christopher Wright recognized as the "distorted, devouring, and diabolical face of an evil that tears at the very heart of human life."[17]

The next two chapters present very different perspectives on death and disease by long-term missionary to East Africa, Jim Harries (chapter 14), and biochemical geneticist, Richard Gunasekera (chapter 15). In spite of their differing approaches to understanding disease and its source, both authors acknowledge the contributing role of the evil one. Their differences are encapsulated in Winter's comment and question: "Jesus extensively demonstrated God's concern for the sick. Are we today under any obligation to demonstrate even more cogent ways of fighting off illness, due to the additional insight God has allowed us to gain?"[18] This resonates with Gunasekera's insights into genetics and the application of nanotechnology to eradicate pathogens, including emerging research on treatments for COVID-19. But Harries, on behalf of East Africans, takes exception to the allurement of a Western technological approach. Instead, he emphasizes the importance of the gospel in character development, and for Westerners to retain their vulnerabilities. This, he believes, will empower African people to trust one another and to trust God, and so to creatively develop their own approaches to dealing with diseases.

17. Wright, *Mission of God*, 435–37.

18. Winter, "Beyond Unreached Peoples," 186.

Sensitivity to other cultures is an essential aspect of missiology and for the promotion of global health. The next two chapters deal with the relationship between missions and addressing disease. In chapter 16, "A Practical Missiology Regarding Disease and Healing," Daniel O'Neill offers a comprehensive theological framework to approach disease with a view toward sustainable healing in both local and global contexts. In chapter 17, "A Missiology Which Includes Fighting Disease," Ralph Winter's writings on this subject are brought together by Beth Snodderly and conclude, "Attacking the roots of disease is part and parcel of our basic mandate to glorify God in all the Earth."[19]

The final two chapters, by theologian-pastor Gregory Boyd, make a compelling biblical and philosophical case for the corruption of nature by fallen spirit-agents. In chapter 18, "An Enemy Did This: A Cosmic Conflict Understanding of 'Natural' Evil," Boyd addresses the question, "How can we believe that God is love when nature is 'red in tooth and claw'?" He concludes that when we come upon "tares"—things in creation that do not reflect the loving character of God, such as diseases, parasites, viruses, corrupt systems, etc.—we must acknowledge that "an enemy did this." In response, we are called to do whatever we can to uproot these enemy-sown weeds, to alleviate suffering, and to thereby bring creation more in line with God's original ideal for creation and consummation.

In chapter 19, "Why Creation Groans: Responding to Objections to the Corruption of Nature (CON) Hypothesis," Boyd describes and refutes five major objections to the premise that nature has been corrupted at a fundamental level. He presents the need to recapture the purpose of the incarnate Son of God and his followers to destroy works of the devil and honor God by aligning with his healing intentions in the world. Boyd affirms the vocation of the church in fighting diseases and rebuking the curse that keeps the whole creation groaning as it "waits in eager expectation for the children of God to be revealed" and to be "liberated from its bondage to decay and brought into the freedom and glory of the children of God" (Rom 8:19, 21).

An Epilogue by Daniel O'Neill brings together the unifying themes of the authors, with an appreciation for the diversity of views in our mutual journey of engaging with a world tainted by evil and filled with disease, yet that is not beyond hope. The current COVID-19 pandemic has already stimulated significant theological reflection within the church. This book, it is prayed, will contribute to a renewed commitment to fulfil the desires of God with renewed purpose and profound efficacy.

19. Winter, "Theologizing the Microbiological World," 205.

As a part of Ralph Winter's and Daniel Fountain's legacies, and as a joint project of the Roberta Winter Institute and Health for All Nations, this book is offered as a motivational tool for the global church, the global health community, scientific researchers, and cross-cultural workers on the frontiers of mission. These chapters urge the body of Christ to consider an expanded *missio Dei*, bringing the exegetes of scripture, the exegetes of nature, and the exegetes of humans together in a full-orbed response to disease in a long-overdue convergence. This includes well-informed, intentional efforts by Christ-followers to represent God well in how they deal effectively with disease and its origins, to glorify God as Healer, and to promote widespread global health among all nations until Jesus returns to complete his ongoing work of making all things new.

## Bibliography

Boyd, Gregory A. "A War-Torn Creation." In *Evangelical and Frontier Mission Perspectives on the Global Progress of the Gospel*, edited by Beth Snodderly and A. Scott Moreau, 286–93. Edinburgh: Regnum, 2010. Online. https://digitalshowcase.oru.edu/cgi/viewcontent.cgi?article=1008&context=re2010series.

Fountain, Daniel E. *Health, the Bible, and the Church*. BGC Monograph. Wheaton, IL: Wheaton College, 1989.

Francis. "Evangelii Gaudium." Apostolic Exhortation given November 24, 2013. Online. http://www.vatican.va/content/francesco/it/apost_exhortations/documents/papa-francesco_esortazione-ap_20131124_evangelii-gaudium.html.

Grundmann, Christoffer H. "Sent to Heal! About the Biblical Roots, the History, and the Legacy of Medical Missions." *Christian Journal for Global Health* 1.1 (2014) 6–15. Online. https://journal.cjgh.org/index.php/cjgh/article/view/16.

Piper, John. "If God Wills Disease, Why Should We Try to Eradicate It?" *desiringGod.org*, March 8, 2006. Online. https://www.desiringgod.org/articles/if-god-wills-disease-why-should-we-try-to-eradicate-it.

Winter, Ralph D. "Beyond Unreached Peoples." In *Frontiers in Mission: Discovering and Surmounting Barriers to the Missio Dei*, edited by Ralph D. Winter, 186–90. 4th ed. Pasadena, CA: William Carey International University Press, 2008.

———. "A Blindspot in Western Christianity?" In *Foundations Reader*, edited by Ralph D. Winter and Beth Snodderly, 319–23. Pasadena, CA: Institute of International Studies, 2009.

———. "Editorial." *International Journal of Frontier Missiology* 19.2 (2002) 4. Online. http://www.ijfm.org/PDFs_IJFM/19_2_PDFs/02%2004%20Editorial_19_2.pdf.

———. "Getting to Know the Bible." In *Frontiers in Mission: Discovering and Surmounting Barriers to the Missio Dei*, edited by Ralph D. Winter, 248. 4th ed. Pasadena, CA: William Carey International University Press, 2008.

———. "Roberta Winter Institute." In *Frontiers in Mission: Discovering and Surmounting Barriers to the Missio Dei*, edited by Ralph D. Winter, 177–80. 4th ed. Pasadena, CA: William Carey International University Press, 2008.

———. "The Seminary, Whence and Whither?" In *Frontiers in Mission: Discovering and Surmounting Barriers to the Missio Dei*, edited by Ralph D. Winter, 68–70. 4th ed. Pasadena, CA: William Carey International University Press, 2008.

———. "Theologizing the Microbiological World: Implications for Mission." In *Frontiers in Mission: Discovering and Surmounting Barriers to the Missio Dei*, edited by Ralph D. Winter, 203–5. 4th ed. Pasadena, CA: William Carey International University Press, 2008.

———. "What Is a Christ-Centered Church?" In *Frontiers in Mission: Discovering and Surmounting Barriers to the Missio Dei*, edited by Ralph D. Winter, 168. 4th ed. Pasadena, CA: William Carey International University Press, 2008.

———. "When Mission Can Be Business." In *Frontiers in Mission: Discovering and Surmounting Barriers to the Missio Dei*, edited by Ralph D. Winter, 41–47. 4th ed. Pasadena, CA: William Carey International University Press, 2008.

———. "Where Darwin Scores Higher than Intelligent Design." *International Journal of Frontier Missiology* 20.4 (2003) 113–16. Online. https://www.ijfm.org/PDFs_IJFM/20_4_PDFs/113_Darwin.pdf.

Wright, Christopher. *The Mission of God*. Downers Grove, IL: InterVarsity, 2006.

Wright, N. T. *Evil and the Justice of God*. Downers Grove, IL: InterVarsity, 2006.

———. *God and the Pandemic*. Grand Rapids: Zondervan Reflective, 2020.

# Historical, Contemporary, and Globalized Theologies of Disease

## —Daniel W. O'Neill

An understanding of the interface between the spiritual realms and the physical causes of disease has not been well developed. I live in the Western world of biomedicine for which I have trained and practiced my whole adult life—a complex discipline of identifying the origin of disease and seeking to prevent, displace, or destroy the causative agent, and to restore normal structure and function. I also dwell in the world of Christian theology and mission in various contexts, seeking to wisely engage the world of brokenness with purpose, informed by the ancient texts, and driven to expand the reign of God. So it seems vital to articulate spiritual, metaphysical, social, and moral elements of disease and health for the development of a sound practical theology, a relevant missiology, an effective global health engagement, and a more informed practice of medicine.

## Winter's and Fountain's Contributions

In my readings and personal conversations with missiologist Ralph Winter and medical missionary Daniel Fountain, I was challenged to integrate my understanding of biblical realities, missional priorities, and my daily work on the human person—what Albert Schweitzer called "the fellowship of those who bear the mark of pain."[1] Fountain called for active resistance in the fight against personified evil and the multitude of etiologies of disease, with "the hope of *ultimate liberation* from evil and the *strength to cope*

1. Martin, *Schweitzer*, 57.

with the present experience of suffering."[2] His was a comprehensive approach, which accounted for both the promises and limitations of medical care, counseling, and social movements for justice. It was tempered by his decades of service in Central Africa where he applied Scripture to the front lines of life and death. Fountain found that a gospel-focused approach to illness liberated others from disease, addictions, and sin, even as the inevitability of death is approached. I agree with him that this engagement is the most exciting adventure of life.[3]

Winter emphasized the value of engaging with the proximate causes of disease and exploring the connections between the physical and metaphysical in a broader scope of Christian mission. Though I embraced this integrated view which affirmed my profession and pastoral calling, his modernist approach seemed a bit narrow in that he reduced human affliction to "germs" and seemed, to many, as overly prescriptive in suggesting that Christians should turn their attention to "eradication." He may have used a bit too much hyperbole in downplaying the care given to the already-afflicted, the spiritual value of lament, or the patient endurance called for in the context of suffering.

But Winter wisely suggested turning our attention to the diabolical upstream etiologies of "physical distortions and intellectual delusions" which affect human health on a global level.[4] This represented an important theological correction to the soul-focused, proclamation-based (or even prioritized) endeavors of evangelicals in the late twentieth century. It also challenged the materialist assumptions of Western biomedicine, and the de-mythologized tendencies of liberal theology. God is indeed able to work through people to practice what Winter called a "public theology."[5] In tangible ways, God's people can bring about transformation and reflect the healing presence of the God who saves and rescues from the distortions and delusions that undermine human flourishing. This is similar to what Francis Schaeffer called "substantial healing,"[6] and what Samuel Escobar called "transforming service,"[7] which validates and confirms the truth and fullness of the gospel message. But how can this be worked out in practice?

2. Fountain, *Health, the Bible, and the Church*, 110–11.

3. Fountain, *God, Medicine, and Miracles*, 70, 255.

4. Winter, "Missions' Greatest Enemy," 175–93.

5. Winter, "Beyond Transformation," 279–85.

6. Schaeffer, *True Spirituality*, 158.

7. Escobar, *New Global Mission*, 143–54.

It might be construed as a utopian ideal to "scout the very origins of disease," in order to "destroy the works of the devil" (1 John 3:8 ESV).[8] But passive waiting for the *parousia* or practicing idleness (*ataktos*, disorder) was rebuked in the first century (1 Thess 5:14) as against the creation mandate of Genesis 1:28. God commissioned the first humans to procreate, replenish, care for, and rule over the Earth. The clarion call of the new covenant was to expand the boundaries of the reign of God, including the domains of the human mind and body as well as the spirit. This was to be extended to the whole Earth. Indeed, the whole of creation is groaning and longing for revelation and redemption (Rom 8:18–25), and God's vice-regents are to engage in this redeeming work.

Global eradication of sin, sickness, disorder, and death is the promised work of God in the *eschaton*, but there is no reason, given the "already and not yet" nature of the kingdom of God, not to pursue feasible eradication as an exercise of good dominion until then. However, it is first important to note that the concept of eradication should be more broadly applied to three spatial domains:

1. Individuals, e.g., physicians and nurses clearing an infection or destroying mutated cells in an individual patient.

2. Communities and regions, e.g., through public health measures leading to clearing or containing an epidemic like Ebola, COVID-19, or HIV/AIDS.

3. The planet, e.g., completely removing the plight of small pox or polio globally through vaccination programs.

Those working within each category can be considered as laboring to push back the effects of disease in a particular time and space. There are some parallels with purification and quarantine laws of the *Torah* and the call to moral and physical purity in the new covenant (1 Pet 1:22). It can be thought of as reclaiming ground lost to the devastating effects of the taint of creation's rebellion to implement strategies in public health systems. For example, after a coordinated vaccination effort by WHO, CDC, UNICEF, Rotary, and the Gates Foundation, it was announced on October 17, 2019, that indigenous wild poliovirus Type 3 was eradicated worldwide, leaving only two countries (Afghanistan and Pakistan) with pockets of poliovirus Type 1, for which global leaders pledged US $2.6 billion to reach the last mile.[9] Participating in these collaborative engagements can

---

8. Winter, "Blindspot," 200–202.

9. "Two Out of Three Wild Poliovirus Strains."

be an alignment with God's healing intentions, and does not necessarily indicate "mission drift."

Fountain challenged people to embrace hope in the God who speaks to us in the midst of our diseases, and to become whole, not turning away from him in anger or rebellion.[10] Winter challenged believers to demonstrate by their actions against diseases that God is grieved with the existence of those diseases, taking no pleasure in the death of anyone (Ezek 18:32). Winter and Fountain both longed to see the people of God supporting efforts to control, contain, or eradicate disease, and to do so intelligently at its up-stream origins. This would then be one of a multitude of other demonstrations of the incalculable worth of the people Christ died for, in the midst of a world under the power of an oppressive, occupying force (1 John 5:19). Characterizing this force, and identifying approaches to undermine its destructive effects, helps sharpen the interface for promoting human flourishing as a kingdom activity.

Reviewing briefly some historical, contemporary, and globalized theologies of disease will help move us further toward a more concise and nuanced understanding by which to inform approaches to this problem.

## Historical Theologies of Disease

### Patristics

Though the patristic literature identifies demons as one of many other causes of illness, they also extol the spiritual benefits of illness, seeing God not as the author, but as one who permits illness. "Do not admire every form of health, and do not condemn every illness" wrote St. Gregory of Nazianzus.[11] Illness awakens in the sufferer a palpable need for rescue and deliverance, but one who retains perfect health and wealth can become indifferent to the need for God or indifferent toward the needs of others. Experiencing disease can be the furnace in which we are purified of our sin, weakening our disordered attachments to the promises of this world, and strengthening our resolve to trust God.[12] Alternatively, it can become a place of torment, which de-animates, distracts, weakens, and ultimately leads to cursing God and death. Managing disease with the former approach and rescuing from the latter response is part of a more comprehensive global *Missio Dei*.

---

10. Fountain, *Health, the Bible, and the Church*, 122.

11. Larchet, *Theology of Illness*, 47–60.

12. Larchet, *Theology of Illness*, 64.

Lord, by such things people live;
  and my spirit finds life in them too.
You restored me to health
  and let me live.
Surely it was for my benefit
  that I suffered such anguish.
In your love you kept me
  from the pit of destruction (Isa 38:16–17).

## Aquinas

Thomas Aquinas viewed evil as a failure or privation in the realization of an entity's proper ends, which is mediated through the practice of virtues and acquired by the gift and grace of God. For Aquinas, the end of human life is not health (*sanitas*) but human flourishing (*beatitudo*). He drew from Aristotelian concepts of form as final cause, and identified the end of human life being *eudaimonia*: "an integrated life in which the enlivened body, habituated through teaching and practice to desire what is life-giving and to shun what is harmful . . . and that contributes to the flourishing of the community of which it is a part."[13] The Catholic teachings of the cardinal virtues (prudence, courage, temperance, and justice) and the corporal and spiritual acts of mercy create an excellent framework for engaging both elements of life simultaneously. "No disposition of the body is ultimately life-giving if it does not aid the journey to God."[14]

## Luther

Martin Luther clearly recognized the great strength and power of pervasive demons and Satan, the "ancient foe [who] doth seek to work us woe." He promoted the power of Christ over evil, and advocated personal engagement toward liberation, yet he saw the value of illness in refinement. "Afflictions when sanctified, make us grateful for mercies which before we treated with indifference."[15] There was a degree of ambivalence about disease, fighting it on the one hand as a work of the devil, but embracing it as a sovereign gift on the other hand. "We would like to be rid of all our infirmity which, to our superficial conception, appear to be a great hindrance

13. Kinghorn, "St. Thomas," 132.
14. Kinghorn, "St. Thomas," 134.
15. Luther, *Table Talk*, 296.

to doing useful things, and yet it is most questionable if we should bring forth any fruit unto God without them."[16] Thus, he thought of disease not being God-caused or God-designed, but God-permitted for purposes that are greater than the penultimate *teleios* of human health.

## Calvin

John Calvin de-emphasized demonic influence in disease causation, and like Luther, emphasized the divine will and the spiritual value of enduring suffering. Yet his influential teaching on the providence of God and polemics against the superstition of relics and saint petition led to the development of medical science. This, in turn, led to inquiry into material causation in sixteenth- and seventeenth-century Europe, thought to be a means to accomplish God's divine decrees.[17] A high view of the sovereignty of God does not preclude, and indeed could enhance, efforts toward fighting the effects of the curse, such as illness, as a calling for the redeemed. Calvinist theology does not necessarily lead to passive resignation that all is the will of God.

## Sweet

Leonard Sweet, articulating a broad evangelical perspective, sees sickness as "a power hostile to God that destroys life."[18] Though he notes that moral defects and diseases are not unrelated, he writes that suffering can have a purifying effect. It can also awaken our own compassion toward others, but he cautions on the presumption of singular etiologies. "To attribute the wreck of well-being to a single cause—divine command or satanic powers or punishment for sin—simply allows people to avoid what nature, science, medicine, and religion offer for restoration."[19] This ultimate restoration may not be perfect physical health, but it includes people fitting themselves into the Creator's context for them, including as healing agents.

16. Luther, *Table Talk*, 306.
17. Payne, "Medicine," 254–76.
18. Sweet, *Health and Medicine*, 42.
19. Sweet, *Health and Medicine*, 46.

## Trudeau

The aphorism, "To cure sometimes, to relieve often, to comfort always," originated in the 1800s with Dr. Edward Trudeau,[20] founder of the Adirondack tuberculosis sanatorium and pioneer of the value of fresh air, exercise, and a healthy diet to fortify the immune system before the era of antimicrobial drugs. A man of deep Christian conviction, he was afflicted with the chronic disease of tuberculosis, and could barely stand or speak when he delivered his final address to the Congress of Physicians and Surgeons at Washington, DC, in 1911 on "The Value of Optimism in Medicine."

> Let us not, therefore, quench the faith nor turn from the vision which, whether we own it or not, we carry; and, thus inspired, many will reach the goal; and if for most of us our achievements must fall short of our ideals, if when age and infirmity overtake us we come not within sight of the castle of our dreams, nevertheless, all will be well with us; for . . . to travel hopefully is better than to arrive, and the true success is in labor.[21]

Fittingly, Trudeau's favorite hymns were sung at his funeral service: "Lead Kindly Light," "Work for the Night Is Coming," and "Peace, Perfect Peace."[22]

## Emerging Integrative Theologies

Trudeau did not envision an age of multi-drug resistant tuberculosis fought by champions like Dr. Paul Farmer a century later, whose work was inspired by liberation theologians like Fr. Gustavo Gutierrez. They championed action, based on more than the science of microbial resistance, but also a deeper knowledge of the evils of social and economic structures—pursuing etiologies in the fight to release the poor from oppression and bodily afflictions.[23] Contemporary and globalized theologies have emerged since Winter's death in 2009 and Fountain's death in 2013, which further develop an integrated view of disease and a healing metanarrative. Some examples of these are included here, in an effort to move further toward a practical and nuanced globalized theology of disease. This will hopefully inspire further development and application toward more effectively joining in God's healing work.

20. Siegel, "To Comfort Always."
21. Chalmers, *Beloved Physician*.
22. "Edwin Livingston Trudeau."
23. Farmer, *Pathologies of Power*, 144–45.

## Contemporary Theologies from the West

### WILLARD SWARTLEY

Willard Swartley, the late professor at Mennonite Seminary in the US, presented a trinitarian view of God as healer, and the first of seven theses is that, "God intends *shalom* and community for humans and all creation, but sin and Satan play adversarial roles against us and against God's intentions for us."[24] Yet he is clear that *shalom* is not to be equated with human health (which can itself become an idol), and that an authentic Christian life may be marked by illness suffered in the service to others.[25] Though suggesting disease and disasters are *not* directly of the devil, he recently presented a contemporary biblical-historical approach to deliverance ministries for persons possessed with demons (which have health consequences). His approach also included witnessing to powers (*exousiai*) responsible for systemic structural evils, which have widespread effects on human flourishing, in economies, nations, and religions.[26]

### NEIL MESSER

Neil Messer, from University of Winchester in the UK, drawing from Karl Barth's understanding of health as "strength for human life," and the divine command to "will to be healthy," gives a cogent argument for the church's role in health promotion and fighting disease. Messer advocates health promotion both for individuals in community as well as public health pursuits for the common good globally. Yet, he cautions that embodied life is finite, and the call to continued *care*, even without hope for cure (or eradication), is the highest mandate. Using Bonhoeffer's terminology, human health is a genuine good, but a *penultimate* or limited good—the ultimate good being eternal life in union with Christ.[27] Messer notes that the biblical healing narratives witness that God is "declaring war on the chaotic and destructive forces that threaten creation's well-being," but he

---

24. Swartley, *Health, Healing*, 27.

25. Swartley, *Health, Healing*, 228.

26. Swartley, *Jesus, Deliver Us*, loc. 238. Editors' Note: For more on the "powers" behind the evils in this world, see chapter 4, "Early Church Perspectives on the Cosmic Conflict"; chapter 18, "An Enemy Did This: A Cosmic Conflict Understanding of 'Natural' Evil"; and chapter 19, "Why Creation Groans: Responding to Objections to the Corruption of Nature (CON) Hypothesis."

27. Messer, *Flourishing*, 201–10.

does not identify these forces. He just calls for a compassionate response in patient hope for the consummation.[28]

## JAMES BRUCKNER

James Bruckner, from North Park Seminary in the US, gives a biblical witness to healthy human life which comes from the Lord, often through human agency. But, like Messer, he gives no attention to the diabolical elements which oppose it. In a list of causes of suffering, he lists "an enemy has done it," but only in the context of diseases caused by the sin of other human beings.[29] He calls for, "subduing any chaos that would disturb or destroy human life," through the exercise of "good dominion" without explaining what "bad dominion" might look like in the overarching biblical narrative.[30]

## FREDERICK GEISER

The reluctance of Western theologians to acknowledge the etiology of resident evil is common but not universal. If healing is a *penultimate* good, then disease-promoting demons are a *penultimate* reality. Contemporary Lutheran professor Frederick Geiser notes that, "demons are a reality, but a penultimate reality. . . . To spend too much time speculating about them . . . is to give them in practice more power than they have in reality."[31] Demons are for driving out, Geiser says. They flee in the presence of the living, healing God when communities recognize (and proclaim) God's supreme power and providence. But he claims they are not "primarily to explain the etiology of disease."[32]

Without being incredulous or ignorant about evil as a source of disease, we can promote spreading the presence of the healing God as a solution to the problem of evil. C. S. Lewis's conception is instructive at this point.

> There are two equal and opposite errors into which our race can
> fall about the devils. One is to disbelieve in their existence. The
> other is to believe, and to feel an excessive and unhealthy interest

---

28. Messer, *Flourishing*, 129.
29. Bruckner, *Healthy Human Life*, 160.
30. Bruckner, *Healthy Human Life*, 14.
31. Gaiser, *Healing in the Bible*, 149.
32. Gaiser, *Healing in the Bible*, 248.

in them. They themselves are equally pleased by both errors and hail a materialist or a magician with the same delight.[33]

## BRYANT MYERS

Bryant Myers, from Fuller Theological Seminary, advanced a collective concept of *shalom* being the central biblical metaphor for health, healing, and wholeness. Working toward health and wholeness is working with God's intentions to redeem and restore the fractured creation.[34] Salvation (*soteria*) takes on a broader meaning, inclusive, and marked by healing and deliverance from the powers of sin, death, and Satan.[35] The whole gospel is represented in practice by life, deed, word, and sign—being with, healing, preaching, and casting out, in order to begin to restore the marred image of God in humans and the chaos resident in the created but broken world.[36]

## Globalized Theologies

As I have written about elsewhere, the globalization of Christianity has produced important theological reflections that give a fuller understanding on the problem of sin, evil, disease, and death, and a renewed *praxis* for the church's life-giving response to it.[37] Likewise, the secular global health community is learning from Christians in Africa, Asia, and Latin America that spirituality is critical for health and well-being. Believers outside the US, who are a large percentage of those engaging in the promotion of health, are showing the world that religion matters as a key social determinant of health. Religious beliefs affect behavioral risk factors as well as responses to infectious diseases.[38]

Vishal Mangalwadi sees the church in India as a power structure that provides an antidote to structural evil in its many forms. In his view, church planting is a means of fighting evil and promoting well-being globally. He sees Christ's victory over sin, Satan, and death as the source of Christian hope, and Christ's saving action as meant to restore human dominion on Earth,

33. Lewis, *Screwtape Letters*, ix.
34. Myers et al., *Health, Healing, and Shalom*, 22.
35. Myers et al., *Health, Healing, and Shalom*, 26.
36. Myers et al., *Health, Healing, and Shalom*, 44.
37. O'Neill, "Toward a Fuller View," 204–14.
38. Oman, *Why Religion*, 153–54.

especially in the area of fighting corruption in its many forms.[39] Contemporary practitioners of health-related mission in India also see their work in continuity with Jesus' healing work of compassion, confirmation, sign, deliverance from sin, and liberation from the power of the evil one.[40]

Asamoah-Gyadu notes the resilience in the pneumatic churches in Africa to the reality of the destructive powers of witchcraft and the primal worldview, and the weakness of the Western Christian mission approach to these realities.[41]

Simon Chan observes that in contrast to (or in addition to) Latin American theologies of liberation from poverty and political oppression, Asian grass-roots theologies have emerged which see healing as an inclusive paradigm of liberation, "physical and psycho-spiritual: healing of bodies and freedom from the fear of evil spirits and fatalism."[42]

## Conclusion

By presenting this brief survey of some early, contemporary, and globalized theological approaches to the interface of disease and evil with sin and suffering, we have begun to expand the context in which to evoke a stream of meaningful approaches toward global health. Considering the integration of fallen created moral agents into the material panoply of disease causation, and framing healing as a liberation from evil as an exercise of dominion in the material and spiritual realms, is neither novel nor archaic. But it is a song widely unsung. A variety of voices from the diverse choir must be heard in order to capture a sound orthodoxy and effective orthopraxis to address the problem of disease globally.

## Bibliography

Asamoah-Gyadu, J. Kwabena. "Witchcraft Accusations and Christianity in Africa." *International Bulletin of Missionary Research* 39.1 (2015) 23–27.

Bruckner, James K. *Healthy Human Life: A Biblical Witness.* Eugene, OR: Cascade, 2012.

Chalmers, Stephen. *The Beloved Physician.* New York: Houghton Mifflin, 1916. Online. https://archive.org/stream/belovedphysicianoochal/belovedphysicianoochal_djvu.txt.

39. Mangalwadi, *Truth and Transformation,* 226.

40. Philip, "Essence," 24–25.

41. Asamoah-Gyadu, "Witchcraft Accusations," 23–27. Editors' Note: For further details, see chapter 13, "A West African Perspective on God and Disease."

42. Chan, *Grassroots Asian Theology,* 126.

Chan, Simon. *Grassroots Asian Theology: Thinking the Faith from the Ground Up.* Downers Grove, IL: InterVarsity Academic, 2014.

"Edwin Livingston Trudeau." *Historic Saranac Lake, LocalWiki,* n.d. Online. https:// localwiki.org/hsl/Edward_Livingston_Trudeau.

Escobar, Samuel. *The New Global Mission: The Gospel from Everywhere to Everyone.* Downers Grove, IL: InterVarsity, 2003.

Farmer, Paul. *Pathologies of Power: Health, Human Rights, and the New War on the Poor.* Berkeley: University of California Press, 2005.

Fountain, Daniel E. *God, Medicine, and Miracles: The Spiritual Factor in Healing.* Colorado Springs: WaterBrook, 1999.

———. *Health, the Bible, and the Church.* Wheaton: BGC Monograph, n.d.

Gaiser, Frederick J. *Healing in the Bible: Theological Insight for Christian Ministry.* Grand Rapids: Baker Academic, 2010.

Kinghorn, Warren. "St. Thomas Aquinas and the End(s) of Religion, Spirituality, and Health." In *Healing to All Their Flesh: Jewish and Christian Perspectives on Spirituality, Theology, and Health,* edited by Jeff Levin and Keith G. Meador, 123–49. West Conshohoken, PA: Templeton, 2012.

Larchet, Jean-Claude. *The Theology of Illness.* Crestwood, NY: St Vladimir's Seminary Press, 2002.

Lewis, C. S. *The Screwtape Letters.* New York: HarperCollins, 1942.

Luther, Martin. *Table Talk.* Grand Rapids: Christian Classics Ethereal, 1990s.

Mangalwadi, Vishal. *Truth and Transformation: A Manifesto for Ailing Nations.* Seattle: YWAM, 2009.

Martin, Mike W. *Albert Schweitzer's Reverence for Life: Ethical Idealism and Self-Realization.* New York: Routledge, 2016.

Messer, Neil. *Flourishing: Health, Disease, and Bioethics in Theological Perspective.* Cambridge: Eerdmans, 2013.

"More Americans Believe in the Devil than Darwin." *Reuters,* November 29, 2007. Online. https://www.reuters.com/article/us-usa-religion-beliefs/poll-finds-more-americans-believe-in-devil-than-darwin-idUSN2922875820071129.

Myers, Bryant L., et al. *Health, Healing, and Shalom: Frontiers and Challenges for Christian Health Missions.* Pasadena, CA: William Carey Library, 2015.

Newport, Frank. "Most Americans Still Believe in God." *Gallup,* June 29, 2016. Online. https://news.gallup.com/poll/193271/americans-believe-god.aspx.

Oman, Doug, ed. *Why Religion and Spirituality Matter for Public Health: Evidence, Implications, and Resources.* New York: Springer, 2018.

O'Neill, Daniel W. "Toward a Fuller View: The Effect of Globalized Theology on an Understanding of Health and Healing." *Missiology* 45.2 (2017) 204–14. Online. https://doi.org/10.1177/0091829616684863.

Payne, Franklin E. "Medicine: In the Biblical Tradition of John Calvin with Modern Application." In *Calvin and Culture: Exploring a Worldview,* edited by David W. Hall and Marvin Padgett, 254–76. Phillipsburg, NJ: P&R, 2010.

Philip, Sunny. "The Essence of Medical Mission in Today's Context: Some Theological and Kingdom Perspectives." In *On the Wings of the Dawn: Medical Mission in India Today,* edited by Varghese Philip, 22–30. Chennai, India: EMFI, 2015.

Schaeffer, Francis. *True Spirituality.* Wheaton: Tyndale, 2001.

Siegel, Mark David. "To Comfort Always." *Yale School of Medicine,* June 24, 2018. Online. https://medicine.yale.edu/news-article/17719.

Swartley, Willard M. *Health, Healing, and the Church's Mission: Biblical Perspectives and Moral Priorities.* Downers Grove, IL: InterVarsity, 2012.

———. *Jesus, Deliver Us: Evil, Exorcism, and Exousiai.* Eugene, OR: Cascade, 2019.

Sweet, Leonard I. *Health and Medicine in the Evangelical Tradition.* Valley Forge, PA: Trinity, 1994.

"Two Out of Three Wild Poliovirus Strains Eradicated." *World Health Organization,* October 24, 2019. Online. https://www.who.int/news-room/feature-stories/detail/two-out-of-three-wild-poliovirus-strains-eradicated.

Winter, Ralph D. "Beyond Transformation: An Ancient Syncretism as a Handicap to 'Public Theology.'" In *Frontiers in Mission: Discovering and Surmounting Barriers to the Missio Dei,* edited by Ralph D. Winter, 279–85. 4th ed. Pasadena, CA: William Carey International University Press, 2008.

———. "A Blindspot in Western Christianity?" In *Foundations of the World Christian Movement: A Larger Perspective,* edited by Beth Snodderly and Ralph D. Winter, 319–22. Pasadena, CA: Institute of International Studies, 2009.

———. "Missions' Greatest Enemy, Greatest Violence." In *Missions in the Context of Violence,* edited by Keith E. Eitel, 175–94. EMS 15. Pasadena, CA: William Carey Library, 2007.

2 _____

# The Biblical Context for a
# Theology of Disease[1]

—RALPH D. WINTER WITH BETH SNODDERLY

THE OPENING CHAPTERS OF Genesis confront the reader with an almost insoluble problem—a problem so serious that the whole Bible is centered around it. Genesis chapters 1–11 constitute a scary "introduction" to the plot of the entire Bible that describes three things:

1. A glorious and "good" original creation and Creator

2. The entrance of a rebellious, God-defying, evil person who is still alive and menacing today resulting in

3. A humanity caught up in that rebellion and brought under the power of that evil person. In these chapters we see the hopelessness of humans whose thoughts were "only evil continually" (Gen 6:5 ESV).[2]

## The Biblical Mystery: What Is God Going to Do about the Vast Distortion of God's Purposes?

This mystery is the major theme of the Bible itself. The divine response is a plan to counteract evil—a continuous story running from Abraham to Christ, of God's re-conquering of a planet which has been distorted from God's intent and seduced out of his fellowship. In order to defeat the evil one

1. This article consists of excerpts from the Winter writings listed in the Bibliography. Used by permission.

2. Winter, "Kingdom Strikes Back," 209.

and restore creation to its original "good" purposes, the divine response is a plan whereby all of the peoples of the Earth will be reclaimed and reconciled through a chosen nation. The principal means for this is the redemption of humans on the basis of "the Lamb slain from the foundations of the world" (Rev 13:8 KJV). An understanding of this mystery begins to bring meaning into all else. What unifies the Bible is not simply the redemption of humans but their redemption in order to fight a war against evil.

## The Unfolding Drama of the Bible

From Genesis 12 to the end of the Bible, and indeed until the end of time, there unfolds one, long, sustained, dramatic account of the gradual redemption of this planet—the story of "the kingdom strikes back." In this unfolding drama we see the gradual but irresistible power of God reconquering and redeeming the fallen creation through the giving of God's own Son. This is tersely summed up: "The reason the Son of God appeared was to destroy the works of the devil" (1 John 3:8 ESV).[3]

If the blessing of God through Abraham, described in Genesis 12, actually inducts those who respond into a kingdom already at war, then we can easily note that the first defeat came when Satan seduced Adam and Eve. God struck back with the choice of Noah and the elimination of an evil generation. Then God's choice of Abraham is seen as another "selectivity" which enabled another new beginning to be played out in the text of the rest of the Bible. The special revelation to and through Abraham is God's gift to all peoples, and what is later termed the kingdom of God begins to expand into all the Earth.

The time of Abraham, Isaac, Jacob, and Joseph (often called the Period of the Patriarchs) displays some small breakthroughs of witness to the surrounding nations. Joseph observed to his brothers that they sold him, but God sent him (Gen 45:4–5). Joseph was obviously a great blessing to the nation of Egypt. Even Pharaoh recognized that Joseph was filled with "the spirit of God" (Gen 41:38). But this was not the intentional missionary obedience God wanted. Joseph's brothers, for example, had not taken up an offering and sent him to Egypt as a missionary! God was in the missions business whether they were or not. Even though the central mandate to restore God's authority and blessing over all nations (Gen 12:1–3) is repeated twice again to Abraham (Gen 18:18; 22:18), and once to both

---

3. Winter, "Kingdom Strikes Back," 209.

Isaac (Gen 26:4) and Jacob (Gen 28:14–15), we see relatively small break-throughs in the patriarchal period.

The next four periods, roughly four hundred years each, are (2) the Captivity in Egypt, (3) the Judges, (4) the Kings, and (5) the Babylonian Exile and dispersion (diaspora). During this rough and tumble, the promised blessing and the expected mission (to extend God's rule to all the nations of the world) all but disappeared from sight. As a result, where necessary, God worked through involuntary means. Joseph, Jonah, the nation as a whole when taken captive, each represent the category of involuntary missionary outreach intended by God to force the extension of the blessing. The little girl carried away captive to the house of Naaman the Syrian was able to share her faith. Naomi, who "went" a distance away, shared her faith with her sons' non-Jewish wives. On the other hand, Ruth, her daughter-in-law, Naaman the Syrian, and the Queen of Sheba all "came" voluntarily, attracted by God's blessing-relationship with Israel.

During the Babylonian captivity it is possible that the Jewish theologians had their awareness sharpened regarding Satan, due to their many years of living in the domain of the dualistic Zoroastrians who acknowledged two equal gods, one good and one bad. The Jews rejected the dualism but may have recognized more clearly than before the existence of a personal opponent and destroyer of God's work. The result is a striking difference between the Old and New Testament perspectives on evil.

As the drama of the Bible unfolds, the cast suddenly reveals a new Person as we open to the New Testament—the long-promised Seed, the Messiah, the One who would restore fellowship between God and humans forever. We earthlings needed Jesus to come precisely because all through the Old Testament an evil darkness had in fact many times overcome the light. Global history has seen no greater impact from any other person. Virtually everything that is happening today in the entire world is either different because of Jesus or is best understood through his eyes.

The four Gospels lay out the story of the disturbing discrepancy between the meaning of the Bible and religious configurations of Jesus' day. The rest of the New Testament describes in some detail just how biblical faith flowed beyond Jewish ethnic boundaries. Surely after the resurrection, the disciples should have understood what Christ's coming was all about. Yet one of the very first episodes portrays their continued grasping for power, stated now in terms of "Lord, are you at this time going to restore the kingdom to Israel?" (Acts 1:6). How often we have naively read Acts 1:8 as just one more pleasant reiteration of the Great Commission, but now we see that instead of being an unconditioned promise of power, the promise was that the power from the Holy Spirit would be given them because they would need it in the job they were to do. In other words, the power of the Holy Spirit was not for their enjoyment, nor even primarily for their own spiritual growth—as important as that was—but so that they could "be my witnesses . . . to the ends of the earth" (Acts 1:8). See how similar this is to Genesis 12:1–3, where the promise to be blessed carried with it the responsibility to be a blessing to all the families of the Earth? In Romans Paul speaks to both Jews and Greeks and makes it very clear that the children of Abraham who were to receive the blessing were not just those who had his seed (after all Esau and Ishmael had been rejected!) but rather those who had Abraham's faith, and that would include peoples from every nation, every ethnic unit (Rom 4:17).

## Passing on the "Blessing"

Therefore this "blessing" is a key concept. The English word "blessing" is not an ideal translation. We see the word in use where Isaac confers his "blessing" on Jacob and not on Esau. It was not "blessings" but "a blessing," the conferral of a family name, responsibility, obligation, as well as privilege. It is not something you can receive or get like a box of chocolates you can run off with and eat by yourself, or a new personal power you can show off like rippling muscles. It is something you become in a permanent relationship and fellowship with your Father in heaven.

As we have seen earlier, this "blessing," this new birth, inducts us into a kingdom at war, not just to a safe holding tank awaiting heaven. The "blessing" is for the purpose of returning "families," that is, nations, to God's household, to the kingdom of God, so that the nations will declare his glory. But the nations are being prevented from declaring God's glory by the scarcity of evidence of God's ability to cope with evil. The Bible makes it clear that our mission is to glorify God among all peoples and that this is essentially a battle against "the works of darkness" (Eph 5:11 ESV).

If the Son of God appeared to destroy the works of the devil, then what are the followers and "joint heirs" of the Son of God supposed to do to bring honor to God's name? In the New Testament "the works of the devil" to which Jesus and the biblical writers could refer were drastically limited by the hearers' limited understanding of creation and of the fallen condition of creation. For example, they knew no more about germs than John Calvin did. The challenge for us today is to discover what Jesus would have said to them had they known what we know about germs, in other words, would Jesus have said that germs are one of the works of the devil, which he and his followers are to set out to destroy?

## Conclusion

It is common today among many evangelicals to be content with the first-century understanding of nature, but a major challenge faces anyone who lives in the age where we can actually see tiny parasites, like the one that causes malaria, in microscopes, and we can trace the four very clever stages of their attack on the human body. We have even noticed the insidious change in their human hosts to make the bodies of those infected attract more mosquitoes so their infected blood can be transmitted to still more victims.

I point this out simply to illustrate the extensive difficulties in understanding for our day what Jesus wants to say to us if we merely focus on what he said in the first century. With increased insight into the works of the devil we have an increased span of responsibility. Our Christian mission becomes different and larger.

Once restored in repentance and faith, in the blessing of God, redeemed people are now expected to resume humankind's original purpose, to work with God for the restoration of all creation, and in the process make crystal clear that Satan, and not God, is the initiator of evil and depravity. It may well be that neither a full restoration of creation nor even the full restoration of humans will take place before the end of time. Meanwhile, humans must continue not just to resist, but to fight Satan, joining with the Son of God in the destruction of Satan's works.

The theme that links the biblical drama is the grace of God intervening in a world which "lies in the power of the evil one" (1 John 5:19 ESV), contesting an enemy who temporarily is "the god of this world" (2 Cor 4:4 ESV) so that the nations will praise God's name. By contrast, the evil one's plan is to bring reproach on the name of God. The evil one stirs up hate, distorts even DNA sequences,[4] perhaps authors suffering and all destruction of God's good creation. Satan's devices may very well include devising virulent germs in order to tear down confidence in God's loving character.

The Gospels focus on God's will, God's kingdom, becoming a reality in this life. I am still enough of a fundamentalist not to think that the world is going to get better and better until Jesus comes to congratulate us on our accomplishments. But I do think God expects us to work toward that end whether it is attainable or not. This is a means of glorifying God's name, and empowering our evangelism. What rings in my ears is the phrase in the parable, "Occupy till I come" (Luke 19:13 KJV). At the end of history, all of creation will be restored. Lions will lie down with lambs. Disease will have disappeared. God will reign in heaven and Earth.

4. Editors' Note: See chapter 15, "A Scientist's Perspective on Disease and Death."

# Bibliography

Winter, Ralph D. "The First Chapter of the Bible: Genesis 12–50." In *Foundations of the World Christian Movement: A Larger Perspective*, edited by Beth Snodderly and Ralph D. Winter, 47–50. Pasadena, CA: Institute of International Studies, 2009.

———. "The Kingdom Strikes Back." In *Perspectives on the World Christian Movement: A Reader*, edited by Ralph D. Winter and Steven C. Hawthorne, 209–27. 4th ed. Pasadena, CA: William Carey Library, 2009.

———. "The Last Act." Unpublished paper, n.d.

———. "Lecture 3. The Biblical Plan: Announcement of the Great Commission." 2009. Online. http://www.foundationscourse.org/uploads/documents/intros/3_lecture.pdf.

———. "Lecture 4. The Unfolding Story of Scripture: Part 1." 2009. Online. http://www.foundationscourse.org/uploads/documents/intros/4_lecture.pdf.

———. "Lecture 7. The Gospels and Christ: A Global Perspective." 2009. Online. http://www.foundationscourse.org/uploads/documents/intros/7_lecture.pdf.

———. "Missions in the Bible, Part I." *Mission Frontiers*, April 1, 1980. Online. http://www.missionfrontiers.org/issue/article/missions-in-the-bible3.

———. "Missions in the Bible, Part II." *Mission Frontiers*, August 1, 1980. Online. http://www.missionfrontiers.org/issue/article/missions-in-the-bible7.

———. "Missions in the Bible, Part III." *Mission Frontiers*, November 1, 1980. http://www.missionfrontiers.org/issue/article/missions-in-the-bible10.

———. "Seeing the Big Picture." *International Journal of Frontier Missions* 13.1 (1996). Online. http://www.ijfm.org/PDFs_IJFM/13_1_PDFs/07_Winter.pdf.

# 3

# A Theology of Creation

*Order Out of Chaos*

—BETH SNODDERLY

In beginning, God created the heavens and the earth.

As for the earth, it was destroyed and desolate (*tohu wabohu*),

> with darkness on the face of the deep (*tehom*),

> but the Spirit of God (*ruach elohim*) stirring over
> the face of the waters.

Then God said, "Let there be light," and there was light! And God
saw that the light was good (*tob*) (Gen 1:1–4a, author's translation).

THE IMAGES IN THE first few verses of Genesis set the tone and theme for the
entire Bible as we see the Spirit of God hovering over the feared unknown
of the darkness and deep, ready to stir it to life-giving status. Similarly, in
the Gospel of John we see the tradition of an angel stirring up the waters
of Bethesda, making them life-producing and healing. These images illustrate the biblical theme of cosmic battle introduced in Genesis 1:2: setting
right what is not right, something destroyed and desolate, something that
is not compatible with life—*tohu wabohu*. God's response is to overcome
evil with good, and, when necessary, to start over—and over, and over.
Consider Seth, Noah, Abraham, the Exodus, the return from Exile, Jesus,
and someday the new heaven and new Earth.

## Interpretive Summary of Genesis 1

In one of God's new beginnings God re-fashioned everything in nature, as the author of Genesis knew it, because the land had been destroyed and left desolate after the disastrous consequences of conditions contrary to God's will. But God had not given up on the land and its people. The Spirit of God was stirring over the deep chaos that was blanketed by darkness. This darkness—a common biblical symbol of evil—is the first thing God corrected as he set about overcoming evil with good. At the right time God said, "Let there be light," and there it was! God saw that the light was good and he separated the light from the darkness. He called the light "day" and the darkness "night."

The next thing God did was to make some basic structural divisions, to be followed later by filling in the details. God wasn't in a hurry to get everything ready at once. Instead, God worked within the framework of evenings and mornings toward his goal of making a land habitable for humans, who could then work with God to fulfill God's purposes. Each day saw increasing order brought out of the chaos. Within the rhythm of evening followed by morning, God divided the upper and lower waters, undoing their mingling and making it possible to distinguish what was good and helpful from what was not conducive to life. Next, God provided for some stability by separating dry land from the lower waters. The existence of the land made it possible for basic subsistence, and now plants and fruit bearing trees were able to thrive.

Next, purpose was given to the heavenly bodies (their regular cycles had become visible as the murky atmosphere cleared) to mark the times and seasons in a predictable way—looking ahead toward the need of humans to remember how to take care of the land and to remember to honor their Creator, on whose behalf they would be stewards of the land. After that, moving creatures in the water, air, and land populated the area, with increasing degrees of ability to choose how to use their mobility.

Finally everything was ready for God's masterpiece and helper—the first humans whom God made in the image and likeness of God to continue the process of bringing order out of chaos and defeating evil. God gave our first parents freedom of choice, hoping they would choose to follow the pattern God had demonstrated in the process of making their land ready for them. The seventh day was set aside for them, and for us, to focus on God and to follow God's example of resting from work. God wanted people to reflect on God's purposes and to maintain a trusting relationship.

## Purpose in Creation

The account in Genesis 1:1—2:2 of how God made worthless land into a livable place would have served as a metaphor for the original audience to see how God was shaping them to participate in the purposes God had in mind for creation. A poetic creation account in Isaiah 45 spells out those purposes.

(A) He who fashioned and made the earth,

(A') He founded it;

(B) He did not create it to be *tohu* (*Lo tohu bera'a*)

(B') But formed it to be inhabited (*Lasebet yesara*) (Isa 45:18).

Isaiah went on to say: "Turn to me and be saved, all you ends of the earth. . . . Before me every knee will bow; by me every tongue will swear. They will say of me, 'In the LORD alone are deliverance and strength'" (Isa 45:22–24).

God wants all peoples to choose to join God in restoring the world to its original purposes. God did not create the world to be empty, formless, void, desolate, *tohu*. Rather, God formed the world for the purpose of it being inhabited and cared for by humans:

> Then God said, "Let us make mankind in our image, in our likeness, so that they may rule over the fish in the sea and the birds in the sky, over the livestock and all the wild animals, and over all the creatures that move along the ground." So God created mankind in his own image, in the image of God he created them; male and female he created them. God blessed them and said to them "Be fruitful and increase in number; fill the earth and subdue it. Rule over the fish in the sea and the birds in the sky and over every living creature that moves on the ground." (Gen 1:26–28)

But it is clear that we humans have not done a good job of fulfilling God's purpose in creating us. Something is wrong in the world; it does not reflect God's intended order. Ordinary people, like those for whom Moses wrote the book of Genesis, have always noticed that evil is mingled with good in this world. "Man has always suspected that behind all creation lies the abyss of formlessness," wrote the German Old Testament scholar, Gerhard von Rad.[1] Although Genesis 1 may have been written to simple, uneducated people who were former slaves, Moses himself was an intellectual who had been well educated in Egypt. His orderly, calm presentation in

---

1. Rad, *Genesis*, 52.

Genesis 1 communicates to readers throughout the ages that God is good, and not the author of evil.

A biblical theology of creation needs to account for the role of the evil one, in order to avoid attributing evil to God. Tony Campolo summarized the role of the evil one this way:

> Since Satan's fall, he and his followers have been at work perverting and polluting all that God created. Before Adam and Eve were ever created, Satan worked to create havoc throughout creation. One of the consequences of Satan's work is that the evolutionary process has gone haywire. That is why we have mosquitoes, germs, viruses, etc. God did not create these evils. They evolved because Satan perverted the developmental forces at work in nature.[2]

## What Would Moses' Audience Have Understood in Hearing Genesis 1:1–3?

Many evangelicals object to the concept of an evolutionary process, thinking it conflicts with the Genesis 1 account of Creation. But far from being ready for a science lesson on how God created the world, Moses' audience would have had their recent harrowing escape from slavery foremost in their minds. From their experiences they were well aware of chaos and disorder. The creation story introduced in Genesis chapter 1 shows that God wanted people to know God is the creator of everything good. The story of creation was preparing the emerging nation of Israel to understand Moses' explanation of their dramatically changing identity from slaves in Egypt to "a kingdom of priests" (Exod 19:6) in what Walton describes as God's "cosmic temple" within creation.[3]

But in the second verse of Genesis 1, both the words, "darkness"/ *hosek,* and "deep"/*tehom,* would no doubt have sent shivers of remembered horror down the spines of Moses' listeners. They had just escaped from abusive slavery (societal *tohu wabohu*) in the land of Egypt where the plague of darkness had helped change Pharaoh's mind about letting them

---

2. Campolo, *How to Rescue the Earth*, 38. Editors' Note: Regarding the evolutionary process not reflecting God's good intentions, see chapter 18, "An Enemy Did This: A Cosmic Conflict Understanding of 'Natural' Evil." Some readers may have a different understanding of the timing and process of creation, but that should not undermine the value of these important theological perspectives.

3. Walton, *Lost World of Genesis,* 84.

go. Finally, the people had escaped from Pharaoh's pursuing army and from the "deeps" of the feared sea by the *ruach*/spirit/wind of God (Exod 15:10) separating the water and making a dry path for their escape. There is no doubt but that the imagery conjured up by the phrases in Genesis 1:2 would have meant to Moses' listeners that something had gone wrong, was out of order, contrary to God's intentions, before God had begun setting things back in order, as recorded in Genesis 1.

The third phrase in Genesis 1:2 points ahead to God's intention to correct the chaotic conditions described as *tohu wabohu*, dark, deep, not life-sustaining: "the Spirit of God was hovering over the waters" (Gen 1:2). God had never left the land (or the people) without the presence of God's spirit. In the creation account of Genesis 1, the people could see that God had brought order and goodness to the earth or "land" that was *tohu wabohu*—destroyed and desolate, turned upside down. "That's like us!" they would have recognized.

## Significance of *Tohu Wabohu*

The Hebrew figure of speech, *tohu wabohu*, startles the listener or reader with its rhyming quality and calls attention to the fact that something surprising and significant is being said, possibly something unexpected that will throw the reader and listener off balance. Most people are used to the King James translation of "formless and void." But this does not convey nearly enough of the negative connotations of the term, *tohu wabohu*, to be a helpful translation. Throughout the Old Testament, each occurrence of the word *tohu* is in the context of a state of the land or of humans that God wants to see corrected. It implies the existence of evil, of opposition to God's will.

Consequences (or judgment) for wrongdoing are always part of the context for the eighteen other occurrences, besides Genesis 1:2, of the word "*tohu*." This is especially true for the two other occurrences in the Hebrew Bible where *tohu* is paired with *bohu*. In Isaiah 34:11 we see the imagery of a measuring line of chaos/confusion (*tohu*) and a plumb line of desolation (*bohu*). The tools for building construction are being put to the opposite of their intended use: the tearing down of a civilization and the resulting emptiness of a howling desert. In Jeremiah 4:23 the prophet "looked at the earth, and it was [*tohu wabohu*]; and at the heavens, and their light was gone." It sounds like creation being undone. The context shows the prophet is warning that God will send an agent from the north to destroy the cities because God's people have foolishly refused to know and obey him. Their moral values are completely reversed and upside down. "They are skilled in doing evil; they know not how to do good" (Jer 4:22). In this passage we see that the land had been darkened, shaken, and ruined—it was *tohu wabohu*—a consequence of God's withdrawal of blessing, allowing evil to run its course.

It seems logical to assume, then, that the first occurrence of the word *tohu*, and the full term, *tohu wabohu*, in Genesis 1:2, would have had the same connotation of judgment on circumstances contrary to God's will. In fact, it could have been the original use of the term the other writers of Scripture had in mind when using the term. A thorough word study demonstrates that *tohu* implies chaos, desolation, meaninglessness, wastefulness, and emptiness.[4]

The question, then, would be, what could have been desolate and chaotic, that God would have seen a need to judge, before the Genesis 1 creation account? Ralph Winter often mentioned Dallas Seminary professor Merrill Unger's conservative evangelical understanding that the first verses of Genesis may speak of a judged Earth that is about to be re-created:

> God did not create the earth in the state of a chaos of wasteness, emptiness, and darkness. It was reduced to this condition because it was the theater where sin began in God's originally sinless universe in connection with the revolt of Lucifer and his angels (Isa 14:12–15; Ezek 28:13; Rev 12:4). The chaos was the result of God's judgment upon the originally sinless earth.[5]

Perhaps the unusual rhyming sound of *tohu wabohu* would have given a playful and reassuring twist to the depiction of anti-creational chaos. Job seems to do something similar in his description of the feared chaos monster, Leviathan, in Job 41:1, 5: "Can you pull in Leviathan with a fishhook? . . . Can you make a pet of it?" Perhaps by the very sound of the words he was inspired to choose, *tohu wabohu*, Moses was reassuring the people that God has chaos under control and that even conditions contrary to God's will can be turned to good purposes.

A whimsical metaphor that could have occurred to Moses during his years of wandering in the desert gives further comic relief to the dark picture described in the second verse of Genesis. In describing the creation of the world, the Lord asks Job, "Have you ever given orders to the morning, or shown the dawn its place, that it might take the earth by the edges and shake the wicked out of it?" (Job 38:12–13). This sounds like an allusion to a tent-dwelling nomad shaking the bed bugs out of his sleeping blanket in the morning. Think about that as part of what Moses may have had in mind, as a nomad himself, when he reported God saying "Let there be light"! The

4. See Snodderly, "Word Associations."
5. Unger, *Unger's Commentary*, 5.

circumstances calling for a new beginning, as well as the chaotic aftermath of judgment—"shaking the wicked"—reflect the meaning of *tohu wabohu*—namely, people and societies operating contrary to God's intentions for the world and experiencing the consequences.

The solution to the problem of evil, and our response to it, is built right into a Hebrew play on words in Genesis 1:2–4. As Sailhammer notes, by bringing order out of chaos in the process of creation, God was overcoming evil with good (*tohu wabohu* becomes *tob*/good).[6]

## Creation as Cosmic Battle: God Overcomes Evil with Good

We are well aware that the first humans chose to go against God's will, with the result that we live in a world that "lies in the power of the evil one" (1 John 5:19 ESV). A number of scholars, literary greats, such as C. S. Lewis and J. R. R. Tolkein, as well as the post-apostolic church fathers, agree that God's good creation has been deliberately distorted by evil intelligent beings. Pastor-theologian Gregory Boyd summarizes apocalyptic tradition that "under the leadership of Satan (or some corresponding figure), [his] angels work to afflict the world with earthquakes, famines, hailstorms, diseases, temptations, and many other things that are not part of God's design for his creation."[7] C. S. Lewis wrote, "It seems to me . . . a reasonable supposition, that some mighty created power had already been at work for ill on planet Earth, before ever man came on the scene."[8]

Along this line, scientist/pastor Bruce McLaughlin wrote in the journal of the American Scientific Affiliation:

> According to Scripture, the universe was originally good and the glory of God is still evident in it (Rom 1:20). But something else—something frightfully wicked—is evident in it as well. Of their own free will, Satan and other spiritual beings rebelled against God in the primordial past and now abuse their God-given authority over certain aspects of creation. Satan, who holds the power of death (Heb 2:14), exercises a pervasive, structural, diabolic influence to the point that the entire creation is in bondage to decay. The pain-ridden, bloodthirsty, sinister, and hostile character of nature should be attributed to Satan and

6. Sailhamer, *Genesis Unbound,* 63.

7. Boyd, *God at War,* 206.

8. Lewis, *Problem of Pain,* 138.

his army, not to God. Jesus' earthly ministry reflected the belief that the world had been seized by a hostile, sinister lord. Jesus came to take it back.[9]

Erich Sauer, a German theologian with an Open Brethren background, postulated that Satan's area of power had been granted to him legally before his fall and that God's plan to take the rulership of the world back from him had to be done "legally" in order to reflect God's justice.[10] This meant, according to Sauer, that God would have to take the rulership of the world back, without force, through the free choices of neutral beings who would have to decide for themselves which ruler to follow. This was obviously a big risk for God, as Greg Boyd points out.[11] In effect, by creating humans and putting them in charge of a particular part of the world, God was setting up a counter kingdom and throwing out a challenge to Satan. Sauer wrote that God's purposes for the new inhabitants of the Earth, to join God in taking it back from the devastations of the evil one, required that humans have freedom of will.[12] The serpent's insinuation to Eve was Satan's initially successful response to that challenge. But God struck back with a long-term plan, first mentioned in Genesis 3:15, to defeat the dark prince of this world and restore the world to what it was originally intended to be, under the rule of the Creator-King—the promised Messiah. In the battle for the rulership of this planet, God is deliberately overcoming evil with good until, in the end, Jesus will reign in his kingdom of *shalom*.

## Genesis 1: Responsibility of God's People to Demonstrate God's Purposes for Creation

But until God ushers in that final perfect new heaven and new Earth, there is a need for believers to engage intentionally in efforts to demonstrate God's will for people, for societies, and for God's good creation. Jesus' followers serve as God's display window, showing what Jesus' reign is meant to look like. As Boyd says, "As Christ gave his all for us, so we are called and empowered to give our all for others. As we abide in Christ and participate in the love of the self-sacrificial God, our lives are to manifest the self-sacrificial love of God to others."[13]

9. McLaughlin, "From Whence Evil?," 237.
10. Sauer, *King of the Earth*, 73.
11. Boyd, *Satan*, 86.
12. Sauer, *King of the Earth*, 73.
13. Boyd, "Living In, and Looking Like, Christ," 407.

God's way of dealing with the physical condition of the Earth described in Genesis 1:2 gives direction for dealing with the roots of human problems at spiritual, personal, community, and physical levels, including disease. God's people have the privilege of allowing God's Spirit to work through them to demonstrate God's good character by fighting back against *tohu*—the conditions societies and individuals encounter when they are in opposition to God's will. We have seen that the conditions described as *tohu wabohu* are against God's original, best, and ultimate intentions for creation, and that God wants to work by the Spirit and through God's people to correct these conditions. "Be fruitful and increase in number; fill the earth and subdue it" (Gen 1:28). As Boyd writes, "Humans are made in the image of God and placed on earth so that they might gradually vanquish this chaos."[14] We further know that "our struggle is not against flesh and blood, but against the rulers, against the authorities, against the powers of this dark world and against the spiritual forces of evil in the heavenly realms" (Eph 6:12). As Christ's followers, we have this mandate: "Do not be overcome by evil, but overcome evil with good" (Rom 12:21).

## Conclusion

In all cultures throughout history, disease is one form of the chaos and evil that is always waiting in the wings to overtake and destroy. AIDS, cancer, malaria, tuberculosis, COVID-19—these are not evidences of a life-giving Creator's intentions for creation. The context in which the concept of *tohu wabohu* is introduced precisely at the beginning of Scripture, shows God's purpose is to correct conditions that are contrary to his will. Genesis 1 shows God preparing the land for a new humanity, made in God's image for the purpose of working with him to bring order out of chaos and to defeat the opposition of the adversary. Anything humans do to bring order out of chaos fights back against the forces of evil that result in *tohu wabohu*. This is the origin of a theology of disease—which is the opposite of ease, the opposite of order; it is entropy, disintegration, *tohu wabohu*, at the cellular level.

Working to overcome physical and societal chaos, including disease, gives a foretaste of God's ultimate intention for *shalom* (health, wholeness, peace) to characterize this world. Isaiah foresaw that the *shalom* at the end of history included salvation from feared enemies in the realm of nature (which could also represent disease micro-organisms that were unknown at that time): "The wolf will live with the lamb, the leopard will lie down

---

14. Boyd, *God at War*, 107.

with the goat, . . . and a little child will lead them. . . . They will neither harm nor destroy on all my holy mountain, for the earth will be filled with the knowledge of the LORD as the [good] waters [*mayim*] cover the [feared] sea [*yam*]" (Isa 11:6, 9).

In a final new beginning, when God makes everything new, God will dry even the smallest amounts of salty water, the tears spoken of in Revelation 21:4. The troubles and chaos the ancient Hebrew people traditionally associated with the sea will be gone. There will be no more death, disease, crying, or pain. Darkness and night will be permanently replaced with "good" light (Rev 22:5). In this vision of the future, relationships are healed: with creation, with one's self (a new heart), with other humans, and, most importantly, with God. The river of life in the heavenly city waters the tree of life on each side of the river, "and the leaves of the tree are for the healing of the nations" (Rev 22:2).

> Then I heard every creature in heaven and on earth and under the earth and on the sea, and all that is in them, saying:
>
> "To him who sits on the throne and to the Lamb
>
> be praise and honor and glory and power, for ever and ever!" (Rev 5:13)
>
> "The kingdom of the world has become the kingdom of our Lord and of his Messiah, and he will reign for ever and ever." (Rev 11:15)

## Bibliography

Boyd, Gregory A. *God at War: The Bible and Spiritual Conflict*. Downers Grove, IL: InterVarsity, 1997.

———. "Living in, and Looking Like, Christ." In *Servant God: The Cosmic Conflict Over God's Trustworthiness*, edited by Dorothee Cole, 409–18. Loma Linda, CA: Loma Linda University Press, 2013.

———. *Satan and the Problem of Evil: Constructing a Trinitarian Warfare Theodicy*. Downers Grove, IL: InterVarsity, 2001.

Campolo, Tony. *How to Rescue the Earth without Worshiping Nature: A Christian's Call to Save Creation*. Nashville: Thomas Nelson, 1992.

Lewis, C. S. *The Problem of Pain*. New York: HarperCollins, 1940.

McLaughlin, Bruce. "From Whence Evil?" *Perspectives on Science and the Christian Faith* 56 no. 3 (2004) 237.

Rad, Gerhard von. *Genesis: A Commentary*. Translated by John H. Marks. Philadelphia: Westminster, 1973.

Sailhamer, John H. *Genesis Unbound: A Provocative New Look at the Creation Account*. Sisters, OR: Multnomah, 1996.

Sauer, Erich. *The King of the Earth: The Nobility of Man According to the Bible and Science*. Grand Rapids: Eerdmans, 1962.

Snodderly, Beth. "Word Associations in Context with Tohu (and Bohu)," n.d. Online. https://static1.squarespace.com/static/5b3157f3b40b9d21a8096625/t/5e6670582 7360a0a03af1590/1583771737080/Tohu+Context+Chart.pdf.

Unger, Merrill. *Unger's Commentary on the Old Testament*. Chicago: Moody, 1981.

Walton, John H. *The Lost World of Genesis One: Ancient Cosmology and the Origins Debate*. Downers Grove, IL: InterVarsity, 2009.

# 4

# Early Church Perspectives on the Cosmic Conflict[1]

—SIGVE K. TONSTAD

CHRISTIANS IN THE EARLY church saw the Earth as the stage of a cosmic conflict that involved God, human beings, and Satan—a fallen angel. His fall happened before the fall of human beings. When Satan fell, he played a crucial role in breaking up the relationship between human beings and God. This story, which the early Christians found in the Bible, was at the core of their belief.

Celsus, a non-Christian philosopher writing around the year 175 CE, was mystified by Christians who departed from what he called the "divine enigmas"—the true mystery of God. In his eyes, the figure of Satan was unthinkable for what it said about God.

> But they [the Christians] show how utterly concocted these ideas are when they go on to say that the highest god in heaven, desiring to do such and such—say, confer some great gift on man—cannot fulfil his purpose because he is opposed and thwarted by a god who is his opposite. Does this mean that the Son of God can be beaten by a devil?[2]

"What is this," we fairly hear Celsus shout, "portraying God as though he has an opponent that limits him! What is this but a God who is a pushover and a weakling!" God, in Celsus's view and in the view of the best philosophical

---

1. This chapter consists of excerpts from the author's chapter, "Early Church Perspectives on the Cosmic Conflict," originally published in the book, *Servant God: The Cosmic Conflict Over God's Trustworthiness.* Used by permission.

2. Celsus, *On the True Doctrine*, 99.

tradition of the second century, should be a sovereign God. He should be the undisputed boss. God's defining attribute is his power. There should be no other power within sight that challenges God. It is blasphemy to say that when the greatest God indeed wishes to confer some benefit upon men, he has a power which is opposed to him, and so is unable to do it.[3]

Unlike intellectuals in the twenty-first century, Celsus's objection to the reality of Satan was not because he couldn't believe in anything beyond the human sphere. His primary opposition to the Christian teaching was squarely because of what it said about God.

A worldview that made room for Satan put at risk the notion of God's sovereignty, the doctrine that was most sacred to Celsus. The power relation between Jesus and Satan was turned on its head in the Christian message. Jesus, who should be strong if he was to do any good at all, seemed the weaker party. To Celsus's mind this meant that there could not be any connection between Jesus and God. No God who took his dignity seriously would consent to being treated abusively and kicked around the way that Jesus was. Who in their right mind would even want a God like that?

The basic principle of good theology, in the eyes of Celsus, was to project the power of God and his sovereignty. There should be no "ifs, ands, or buts." Celsus thought the Christian belief painted God as a being that no sane person could respect. What the writers of the New Testament praise as good news, never tiring of this term, is news that made Celsus cringe in utter revulsion. He dismissed Christianity, because he considered it an insult to God.

## Explaining and Defending the Christian Belief

### 1. The Christians and the Being That Is Opposed to God

The author of the Christian reply to Celsus was Origen of Alexandria (185–254 CE), and the title of the book was short and to the point: *Against Celsus*. Origen believed that Celsus's attack on the Christian message was unjustified. He could have left it at that, saying nothing. The fact that he wrote a lengthy book, discussing Celsus's arguments point by point, should be taken to mean that Celsus's book was having an impact against the influence of Christianity.

Origen is remembered as one of the most devout and learned men in the history of the Christian church. Today he is known somewhat in the Roman

3. Origen, *Contra Celsum* 6.42.

Catholic Church, hardly remembered at all in the Protestant world, but he remains the most influential theologian in the Eastern Church.

Origen certainly affirmed the cosmic conflict perspective that riled Celsus, and he explained it in conspicuous detail. "The name Devil, and Satan, and Wicked one, is mentioned in many places of Scripture, and he who bears it is also described as being the enemy of God."[4]

We find this message everywhere in Origen's books; in fact, so much so that Origen has been called the greatest diabolist in the history of the Christian church. The theme of cosmic conflict constitutes the framework for his understanding of God, and it bears on the most puzzling elements in God's story. Origen never lets his readers forget it.

> He who was Lucifer and who arose in heaven, he who was without sin from the day of his birth and who was among the cherubim, was able to fall with respect to the kindness of the Son of God before he could be bound by chains of love.[5]

Origen was not in the slightest shaken by the ridicule Celsus heaped on the Christian cosmic conflict story. Christians in the third century, like the Christians in the first and the second centuries, believed in "a being who is opposed to God." Origen defended the belief. He pointed to its source in the Bible. He pursued its explanatory power, pressing the point home. And he took on Celsus for the flaws in his view of God and human reality.

## 2. The Source of Christian Belief

The source of the Christian belief, of course, is the Bible—the Old Testament as well as the New. Texts in the Old Testament that on the surface refer to a human power or king, such as "the king of Babylon" in Isaiah (Isa 14:12) or "the prince of Tyre" in Ezekiel (Ezek 28:12), have a meaning that looks beyond the human factor. A larger figure is projected on the screen, a figure that does not have a human referent only. This insight is basic to the Christian interpretation of the Old Testament, and Origen defended it vigorously. His discussion of the text describing "the prince of Tyre" in Ezekiel 28:12–19 is a case in point.

> Who is there that, hearing such sayings as this, "Thou wast a signet of likeness and a crown of honour in the delights of the paradise of God," or this, "from the time thou wast created with the cherubim, I placed thee in the holy mount of God," could

---

4. Origen, *On First Principles* 1.5.2.

5. Origin, *Commentary on Romans*, 377.

possibly weaken their meaning to such an extent as to suppose them spoken of a human being, even a saint, not to mention the prince of Tyre? Or what "fiery stones" can he think of, "in the midst" of which any man could have lived? Or who could be regarded as "stainless" from the very "day he was created," and yet at some later time could have acts of unrighteousness found in him and be said to be "cast forth into the earth"? This certainly indicated that the prophecy is spoken of one who, not being in the earth, was "cast forth into the earth," whose "holy places" also are said to be "polluted."[6]

Perfection of the kind envisioned in Ezekiel is not found in the human realm, especially when the one who fell originally was counted among the cherubim. Indeed, to suggest that a historical "prince of Tyre" at some point was "the signet of perfection" (Ezek 28:12) is to miss the mark entirely. Ezekiel, Origen contends, is concerned about a figure that surpasses anything found on the human horizon.

Origen was soft-spoken and humble on behalf of his own effort, but he did not harbor the slightest doubt that the Bible tells the story of a cosmic conflict or that it traces footprints of evil back to a non-human point of origin.

If anyone with the time to examine the holy Scriptures were to collect texts from all the sources and were to give a coherent account of evil, both how it first came to exist and how it is being destroyed, he would see that the meaning of Moses and the prophets with regard to Satan has not even been dreamt of by Celsus or by any of the people who are dragged down by this wicked daemon and are drawn away in their soul from God and the right conception of Him and from His Word.[7]

## 3. God in the Christian Belief

The biblical account, as explained and defended by Origen, does not deal with Satan for his own sake. What makes Satan such an important figure is that he is the one who initially distorted the truth about God and who continues to do so. This subject is the all-important one. Origin's statement on the scriptural basis for the role Christians attribute to Satan, quoted above, goes to the heart of the problem. People "are dragged down by this wicked

6. Origen, *On First Principles,* 411–13
7. Origen, *Contra Celsum* 6.44.

daemon and are drawn away in their soul from God and the right conception of Him and from His Word."[8]

We cannot afford to miss this point. If we were assigned the task of summarizing the story of the temptation and fall in the Garden of Eden, we could not state it more succinctly than Origen did nearly eighteen hundred years ago. The serpent began by misrepresenting God, distorting God's warning into a command of severity and restriction (Gen 3:1). Next, the serpent directly attacked God's credibility, alleging that God knowingly was not telling the truth (Gen 3:4–5). The seed of misrepresentation sprouted the plant of distrust, and the plant of distrust matured into conscious alienation (Gen 3:6). Alienation yielded the terrifying fruit of fear, now manifested in the relationship between God and human beings and expressed in the most grief-stricken sentence in the Bible: "I heard you in the garden, and I was afraid because I was naked; so I hid" (Gen 3:10).

All of this is captured in Origen's succinct summary—it is Satan's goal to entice human beings to misread God and to draw them away from "the right conception of Him."[9] Thus, the problem facing the human family—and the core issue in cosmic conflict theology—centers on the character of God.

The God Celsus believed in must be an undisputed sovereign who would not allow anything or anybody to stand in his way. Divine sovereignty was, in his system, the most important and sacred doctrine. What, we might therefore ask, is the most important doctrine in Christianity? If it is not divine sovereignty, what is it? How does Origen defend the Christian teaching on this point?

## 4. Evil and Freedom

Celsus could not understand the God of the Christians, because he neither understood nor valued freedom. The very ideas that were a stumbling stone to Celsus are to Origen the cornerstone. Crouzel calls Origen "the supreme theologian of free will."[10] Evil arose in the context of freedom; there could not be evil in the absence of freedom. And yet freedom only provides the opportunity and is not the cause of evil. Freedom is the value that God will not surrender even in the face of sin.

God has, as it were, taken upon himself to pay the price for freedom rather than to solve the problem of sin by abolishing freedom. The power of

---

8. Origen, *Contra Celsum* 6.44.

9. Origen, *Contra Celsum* 6.44.

10. Crouzel, *Origen*, 21.

the cross suffices for the healing not only of the human plight but also reaches to heavenly powers and orders. This may sound strange to us today, but it was not strange to Origen, because to him and to the early church, the power that was opposed to God was above all a non-human power.

## 5. Salvation as Healing

Cosmic conflict theology describes salvation as healing. We cannot fail to notice Origen's emphasis on this point. Jesus' death on the cross is the healing remedy that dwarfs all others, because it shows God to be a giving person (John 12:23–32), making null and void the misrepresentation that "the prince of this world" has been promoting. The effect of the cross is so great that "it suffices for the healing and restoration not only of the present and the future but also of past ages,"[11] and its influence also extends to the non-human realm. Far more than I can show here, Origen saw in the teachings of the Bible a message of healing. He understood salvation in medical, more than in legal terms. He was concerned to show how the life and death of Jesus heals human misperception of God.

Coercion, the method that Celsus was more than eager to see God deploy, was anathema to Origen. Not only is coercion incompatible with freedom, but if used, it will compound rather than solve the problem of evil. In God's wisdom, God allows good and evil to develop and to run their respective courses until each side has declared itself.

God's remedy is not compulsion but revelation; it is persuasion, not force.

## The Christian Story Today

In light of the Bible, the source that informs and obligates Origen's account, the story that is told has a triangular shape, involving God, human beings, and a third order of being. While the story gives rise to many questions, it provides the framework for the questions that need to be raised.

Origen admits that he tells a story that he knows "by inspiration of God" that the Bible makes clear "what are evils" and that the Bible tells how evils "came to exist," and "how they will be removed."[12] In this account, evil has a beginning, and it will one day end.

---

11. Origen, *Commentary on Romans* 5.10.16.

12. Origen, *Contra Celsum* 4.65.

Origen is not well known in large circles of the Christian church. His account of evil has fallen on hard times. Eric Osborn writes that with the conversion of Constantine in the fourth century, "theodicy gave way to triumphalism."[13] This means that the church felt less need to tell the biblical story of the origin of evil, because it was in a position to command belief. It no longer had to engage the world from a position of weakness. In the days of Origen, Christianity was a persecuted minority. Origen had recourse only to persuasion. After the conversion of Constantine, the church could resort to coercion when persuasion came up short.

Osborn describes this transformation as a process of contraction. The field of vision narrowed from the big story of the rebellion of Satan to the smaller story of personal salvation and to doctrines such as the Trinity and the nature of Christ.[14]

I write this under the conviction that the time has come to return to the larger story—the one espoused by the New Testament and by believers such as Origen. In his answer to Celsus, Origen said, "No one will be able to know the origin of evils who has not grasped the truth about the so-called devil and his angels, and who he was before he became a devil, and how he became a devil, and what caused his so-called angels to rebel with him."[15]

If we relearn the larger story, we will not simply find the foot that fits the shoe that has left the devastating footprints of evil in human history. We may also be able to engage more meaningfully the contemporary person to whom the existence of evil is an obstacle to faith, as are misconceptions of the God who permitted it to happen.[16]

## Bibliography

Celsus. *On the True Doctrine: A Discourse against the Christians.* Translated by R. Joseph Hoffmann. New York: Oxford University Press, 1987.

Crouzel, Henri. *Origen.* Translated by A. S. Worrall. Edinburgh: T&T Clark, 1989.

Origen. *Commentary on Romans.* Translated by Thomas P. Scheck. Vol. 103 of *The Fathers of the Church.* Washington, DC: Catholic University of America Press, 2001.

———. *Contra Celsum.* Translated by Henry Chadwick. Cambridge, MA: Cambridge University Press, 1965.

———. *Homélies sur Ézékiel.* Translated by Marcel Borret. Paris: Les Éditions du Cerf, 1989.

13. Osborn, "Apologist Origen," 58.
14. Osborn, "Apologist Origen," 58.
15. Origen, *Contra Celsum* 4.65.
16. Tonstad, "Theodicy," 202.

————. *On First Principles.* Translated by George W. Butterworth. London: Society for Promoting Christian Knowledge, 1936.

Osborn, Eric. "The Apologist Origen and the Fourth Century: From Theodicy to Christology." In *Origeniana Septima*, edited by Wolfgang A. Bienert, 52. Louvain: Leuven University Press, 1999.

Tonstad, Sigve K. "Theodicy and the Theme of Cosmic Conflict in the Early Church." *Andrews University Seminary Studies* 42 (2004) 169–202.

5 _____

# Sin and the Etiology of Disease

—Daniel W. O'Neill

## Scientific and Theological Integration

THE SCIENCE OF MEDICINE is premised upon the discovery of the root causes (etiologies) of disease processes and the application of preventive, palliative, restorative, and curative care. The science of public health seeks the common good through researching disease origins and injury prevention, and detecting, preventing, and responding to infectious diseases. Though some diseases are mediated through microorganisms, some of which can now be detected and treated, the full scope of disease is much more complex than infectious diseases. As Western science is built upon the post-enlightenment rational presupposition of materialist causation, modern health care and public health practice tend to neglect spiritual, moral, or metaphysical causes to human problems like disease. This truncated approach has been recognized as insufficient for addressing deep human need, especially when over 80 percent of the world continues to hold a religious world view.[1] Integrating these approaches for enhancing human and planetary health, countering the works of evil, and glorifying God as healer, is a necessary pursuit.

## Addressing Complexity and Limitations

It is clear that disease has a diabolical nature. Many diseases have similar characteristics to the evil described in the Bible: invasion, deception,

1. Pew Research Center, "Global Religious Landscape."

mimicry, destruction, disintegration, contagion, resistance, and chaos. Disease is subversive, occult, invasive, despair-generating, disabling, life-compromising, and un-dignifying. It is an intrinsic part of the final common pathway to natural death. Though ubiquitous, it is variable in its effect among every people group and among all social and economic strata. It tends to manifest more profoundly in persons, communities, and nations who have limited knowledge of, disregard for, or have forgotten God and his ways. Though direct linear etiologies can be elusive, and there are plenty of innocent collateral casualties, some of the disease processes are brought on or magnified by the individual through their own willful move away from God's best intentions for them, regardless of their knowledge of it being an offense to God. Examples include unbridled and misdirected passions, chasing fantasies, sloth-induced impoverishment, unchecked appetites, breaches of hygiene, self-loathing, etc. However, disease is also induced or magnified by the impoverishing effects of *others*, through traceable human action (or inaction) such as oppressive governments, some cultural-religious frameworks, unjust economic systems, ecological disregard, human exploitation, gender-based violence, systemic racism, abuse, neglect of children, and intellectual ignorance. Many of these practices get embedded in generations, systems, and communities, and thus are perpetuated or even normalized.

## The Disease: Sin as Etiology

There are few who would argue that human activity is not a well-recognized cause of disease. The fallout resulting from sin and rebellion by free moral agents against God's original design and his intention for the world affects not just human beings, but the whole ecological system, and the whole cosmos, permeating everything. Howard Snyder identifies disease as a root biblical metaphor for sin, which he describes as a complex ecology of alienations: "Viewing sin as a deadly disease, a fatal infection, helps us grasp what sin is and how it affects humans and all creation."[2] Though not a popular subject in the secular world, I wish to make the case that sin can be viewed as the proximate cause of all human disease, the up-stream problem. I do not refer, as some may suppose, to one's sin in particular but to the ecology of sin—that is, celestial, original, individual, and generational/systemic sin, namely, rebellion against God. How do we begin to understand these often overlapping four-fold etiologies?

2. Snyder, *Salvation Means Creation Healed*, 67.

Bernard Ramm, along with Blaise Pascal, highlighted the way the concept of sin has been rejected by the *intelligentcia* as an "offense to reason."[3] But without the doctrine of sin "much of human life and history remains forever opaque."[4] I would add that the same is true regarding disease and death. Paul develops the understanding of the effects of sin in chapter 8 of his letter to the Romans. "The creation was subjected to frustration . . . by the will of the one who subjected it, in hope" (Rom 8:20). The subject of this phrase is ambiguous, possibly because the point is not so much *who* subjected the creation but that *there is hope* in liberation from the bondage to decay. In individuals as well as societies, "although the body is dead because of sin, the Spirit is life because of righteousness" (Rom 8:10 ESV). So disease and early death can be magnified by sin, or mitigated by righteous living and by the Holy Spirit. Sin can be perpetrated onto innocent victims, or fomented by the individual onto himself or herself. Sin can affect the fabric of the created but cursed world in what seems like random, uncaused afflictions. Plantinga notes, "*Shalom* is God's design for creation and redemption; sin is blamable human vandalism of these great realities and therefore an affront to their architect and builder."[5] The corrupted Earth, legions of fallen spiritual beings, and the vagaries of human persons and whole societies bent toward sin, are all subject to the law of sin and death and lead to its just consequences, which include the chaos of "sword, famine, and plague" (Jer 14:12; 24:10; Rev 6:8; see Ezek 7:15). In one sense, this is natural, a consequential cause-and-effect, as well as a manifestation of the justice of God's laws which he does not fail to warn humanity about from the time of Genesis 2. In another sense, it is unnatural in that it was not and is not the Creator's best intentions or ultimate plans for his creation, and therefore remains an enigma, a theodicy.

The question arises then, whose sin was Paul referring to in Romans 8? The sin of rebellion of the fallen angels including Satan, or the original sin of Adam and Eve, or the sin of the parents visited upon their children for generations (i.e., embedded in corrupt systems), or an individual's personal sin? In the case of the man born blind recorded in John 9, Jesus rejected the latter two options (which were common Deuteronomic presuppositions and the opinion of Job's friends), but he did not explicitly reject the former two possibilities. All four of these options are due to actions or inactions of *created moral agents* in time and space.

---

3. Ramm, *Offense to Reason*, 163.

4. Ramm, *Offense to Reason*, 163.

5. Plantinga, *Not the Way It's Supposed to Be*, 16.

For Jesus, speculating about causation in individual cases was not as fruitful as displaying the works of God through healing intervention. "*We must do the works of him who sent me*" (John 9:4). In the case of the man born blind, healing was mediated through material means (mud) and the man's trusting activity (washing in the pool of Siloam). But it was, at its root, a visible work of God to release an afflicted person from the effects of sin (of whatever origin). Messer and others have pointed out that philosophical theodicies which seek to identify specific sources of the problem of evil, pinning it on a singular moral agent, especially implicating the one afflicted, can themselves compound the problem. Blaming God for the design and implementation of disease and death is also a common misunderstanding of the texts of Scripture, even among Pentecostals.[6] Though God may permit affliction for greater purposes than individual human health, and use the matrix of suffering to teach important lessons, he is not its author nor implementer. A distinctly Christian approach addresses identifiable mediators and origins of suffering through *resistance*, but as Messer points out, this will also include lament, forgiveness, thoughtfulness, and hospitality among those suffering, regardless of the causative moral agent or our ability to resist.[7] An analysis of the four categories of sin by created moral beings helps us frame an approach to disease which integrates spiritual elements, moral aspects, and material intermediaries.

## Celestial Sin

The biblical narrative of the rebellion of Satan and the other fallen angels gives a reason for destructive activities perpetrated by the sin of these created moral agents. The devil "has been sinning from the beginning," and Jesus' *raison d'être* was to destroy the devil's nefarious works (1 John 3:8). As spiritual beings banished to Earth, demons seek embodiment (Matt 8:31–32; 12:43–45) in both humans and animals, and perhaps in microorganisms. Their ends are depicted as violence, destruction, deception, corruption, and distortion. Satan holds the power of death (Heb 2:14) and has been a killer from the beginning (John 8:44). However, it does not necessarily follow that *all* disease is caused by demons. In Wilkinson's detailed analysis of the biblical accounts, only six cases of demon possession were noted among the twenty-six cases in which Jesus healed diseases.[8] He suggests that the woman bound by Satan (Luke 13:16) and Paul's thorn

6. Thomas, *Devil, Disease, and Deliverance,* 291–96.

7. Messer, *Flourishing,* 131.

8. Wilkinson, *Bible and Healing,* 71.

the flesh (2 Cor 12:7–10) indicate that disease *can* be the direct activity of Satan.[9] Jesus healed all those oppressed by the devil (Acts 10:38), but distinguished the demon-possessed from those with other afflictions such as epilepsy when he healed, and when he commissioned the disciples to follow suit (Matt 4:24; 10:1).

Though often de-emphasized and allegorized in modern Western theology, the reality of demons as personalities is indicated in the biblical narrative by their having names, being spoken-to, and by being part of the experience of early and modern divines. Jesus' teaching in Matthew 12:27–29, about driving out demons as a sign of the kingdom, and binding the strong man (Beelzebul—lord of the flies[10]), means two things about the evil one: (1) he is strong ("the prince [*archōn*] of this world" [John 12:31]), and (2) he can be bound (Matt 12:29). In the biblical narrative, angels of light are against the demons of darkness, which are vying for power in the human realm. One promotes life as messengers of God's healing purposes in the world, the other promotes disease and death as Satan's messengers of opposition. But that does not mean it is easy to trace out those associations. In the parable of the wheat and tares, Jesus explained that the enemy (the devil) sows corruption in the field of the world, and the harvesters (the disciples) may not have the capacity to eradicate the tares. "Let them both grow together until the harvest" (Matt 13:30).

Disease and health, then, continue to exist side by side in this present epoch of world history. Getting to a state of health can mean different things in different cultures. Health in a Middle Eastern culture emphasizes states of being rather than abilities of function as in the West. Illness then, in Jesus' context, leads to more of a disvalued state, a shameful position which disrupts life in many domains. The felt need in Jesus' time would have been for the *oppressiveness* associated with afflictions to be removed. Medical anthropologist John Pilch suggests that a healer or therapist becomes a mediator of culture to restore meaning and purpose in living. He suggests that demons are not the cause of disease, and that "Jesus' exorcisms are thus symptomatic rather than etiologic therapies."[11] Jesus' healing "reduces and removes the experiential oppressiveness associated with such afflictions . . . meaning is restored to life and the sufferer is returned to purposeful living."[12] Following Jesus' pattern, according to Pilch, the contemporary healer or therapist becomes a mediator of culture, using symbolic bridges, relating to the "mythic

9. Wilkinson, *Bible and Healing*, 141, 227–32.

10. Black, *Mark*, 110.

11. Pilch, *Healing*, 13.

12. Pilch, *Healing*, 14.

world," using transactional symbols to guide a "therapeutic change in the sick person's emotional reactions" and pursuing confirmation of success in restoring a valued state of being.[13]

Pilch represents the thinking of many in the West who are incredulous toward the reality and influence of demonic forces on disease processes, and who prefer a more allegorical hermeneutic.[14] However, using biblical angel and demon terminology with sincerity amid suffering humanity creates touch points to many current tribal or primal cultures, as well as to most of the people who practice the world's religions. Eschewing these ancient views in the modern world by demythologizing them as a cause or treatment of disease through scientific rationalism based on purely materialist assumptions, or based on higher textual criticism, or overly allegorical biblical hermeneutics, does not build bridges for mutual transformation or meaning-making with most of the world's population. Frederick Gaiser notes that, "cold rationality cannot always do justice to the complexity, or perhaps the darkness, of the world in which we live."[15] Even in modern Western countries, active confrontation with evil powers is not always seen as archaic. For example, expelling (*ekballo*) demons individually and witnessing to the powers (*exousiai*) in systems is a dual praxis against evil as expounded by Swartley's latest work.[16]

## Original Sin

In the Genesis narrative, the consequences of the Fall were a cursed serpent and Earth. Human beings consequently faced relational disruption, shame, health-impairing conditions such as excessive pain, troublesome procreation, and a biosphere which became difficult to tend. Paul develops the concept of the first man (Adam) being of the dust and subject to death due to willful disobedience in the Garden, which was inherited for all humanity (Rom 5:12). "Your body is subject to death because of sin," Paul writes (Rom 8:10). Disease is a final common pathway to ubiquitous natural death. The initial law was in place and consequences expressed by God prior to the temptation and rebellion in Eden. "The sting of death is sin, and the power of sin is the law" (1 Cor 15:56). Thus, God retains his moral integrity as his justice is manifest through disease by being true to the law of sin and death, which he established when sin entered the world. "The soul who sins shall die" (Ezek 18:20

13. Pilch, *Healing*, 33.

14. See Hiebert, "Flaw of the Excluded Middle," 414–21.

15. Gaiser, *Healing in the Bible*, 131.

16. Swartley, *Jesus, Deliver Us*.

ESV). Human corruption and barred access to the health-sustaining tree of life were consequences of Adam's willful disobedience. Plantinga notes that "Sin is disruption of created harmony and then resistance to divine restoration of that harmony."[17] Martin Lloyd-Jones writes, "Man's real problem is not simply that he is sick, but that he is a rebel."[18] In light of the COVID-19 pandemic, N. T. Wright notes that people who are called to be partners in restoring creation are "themselves 'carriers' of the disease that has infected the whole human race, the proto-virus called 'idolatry and injustice' which is killing us all."[19] The concept of sin is not unique to Hebrew or Christian understanding, as Bernard Ramm points out. "The fracture of the self and the breakdown of society are universal problems."[20] If one rejects the doctrine of the Fall, then sin must be defined as a necessary aspect of creation, which, "in turn makes God the author of sin,"[21] and consequently, I would add, corruption and disease. This would be contrary to God's character and purpose, and thus cannot be so.

## Individual Sin

There is a connection between moral evil (sin), Gods wrath, and natural evil (disease and death), but many see it as a "highly porous" relationship[22] which does not follow a "simple formula."[23] Likewise, there is a relationship between righteousness, forgiveness, health, longevity, and healing expressed through poetic symmetry in the Law, the Prophets, and the Writings (see Deut 32:39; Jer 17:14; Ps 103:3; 104:29–30; 107:17–22), which highlight the pervasive Hebrew understanding of human responsibility in the causation of disease or the promotion of healthy human life. "I have set before you life and death, blessings and curses. Now choose life, so that you and your children may live" (Deut 30:19). Yet, Job and Ecclesiastes express the mystery of non-linear causality, and the unpredictability of human and non-human moral agency. Causation is not always easy to trace, nor is it formulaic, and it is often reciprocal and multi-faceted.

Some of Jesus' healings were linked with forgiveness of an individual's sins (Matt 9:2; Mark 2:5; Luke 5:20–23), but not most of them. History is

17. Plantinga, *Not the Way It's Supposed to Be*, 5.

18. Lloyd-Jones, *Healing and the Scriptures*, 64.

19. Wright, *God and the Pandemic*, 13.

20. Ramm, *Offense to Reason*, 61.

21. Ramm, *Offense to Reason*, 80.

22. Messer, *Flourishing*, 117.

23. Bruckner, *Healthy Human Life*, 160.

replete with examples of assumptions of disease being attributed to direct divine justice or blamed on the moral infractions of the afflicted, such as blaming the victims of the cholera epidemics in 1830 to 1832 in New York City, when others traced the blame instead to the human injustice of exploitation of black and immigrant workers.[24] In either case, the etiology is tied to the actions (or inactions) of created moral agents. Tracing upstream etiologies can assist in developing strategies to address disease, but theological or sociological arguments to cast or shift blame, especially in order to abrogate personal responsibility, are narrow, self-serving approaches, which compound the consequences. These overly-confident presuppositions about etiology could also become triumphalist or fatalistic in the extremes. The one who becomes smug by only speculating about the deeper causes without *engaging* in the work of God and looking forward to healing in the present and future, is not following Jesus' supreme example.[25]

Much of disease (or health) is determined by human thoughts and actions. "The mind governed by the flesh [*sarx*] is death, but the mind governed by the Spirit is life and peace" (Rom 8:6). Hotz and Mathews note that Paul's use of *sarx* was to describe an orientation (or disorientation) of the whole person toward sin, and thus being subject to the law of sin and death.[26] It is well-established that abusive words harm a person's self-image and affect generations and whole cultures in their collective conscience. Words matter, and by them we are judged (Matt 12:36–37), and through repentance (*metanoia*—a changed mind) we are forgiven. "Gracious words are a honeycomb, sweet to the soul and healing to the bones" (Prov 16:24). But cruel words are like deadly arrows (Ps 64:3), and deceptive words are worthless (Jer 7:8). Jesus was quite clear that everyone will have to give an account for every empty word spoken (Matt 12:36).

## Generational and Systemic Sin

The prophets directly connected wicked ways in a causative way to afflictions of "sword, famine, and plague" in Israel and other nations (Ezek 6:11), and the prophets were held accountable for not warning them in a timely fashion (Ezek 3:18; 33:8). In contrast, blessings, peace, and renewal of the land are contingent upon righteous obedience to the law that gives life (Ezek 11:17–20; 36:24–28).

---

24. Harrison, *Disease and the Modern World,* 107.

25. Wright, *God and the Pandemic,* 17.

26. Hotz and Mathews, *Dust and Breath,* 41–42.

There is now heightened understanding that human health and disease is inextricably linked to planetary conditions and the ecological environment.[27] Human health can no longer be considered in isolation, as climate change affects more and more deserts and shorelines, especially on small island nation-states, with increased infectious disease outbreaks like dengue and cholera in areas of extreme weather and forced migration. What humans burn and what they eat matter for human and planetary flourishing. The church has a key role which she is starting to play in addressing these ecological challenges using complex systems thinking.[28]

Hotz and Mathews write that "Stewardship of the good bodies God has given us calls us to think big, to look for the 'something else' that is going on when bodies break down, and to wrestle with the demons lodged in our institutions."[29] Intellectual ignorance, as the "shroud that enfolds all peoples" (Isa 25:7), is a major cause of disease. Because people did not retain the knowledge of God, he "gave them over to a depraved mind" to go against God's best intentions for the world (Rom 1:28). Though "those who do such things deserve (*axios*—are worthy of) death, they not only continue to do these very things but also approve of those who practice them" (Rom 1:32). This foments disease regionally, generationally, and systemically. In the Prophets, God is said to bring disaster and disease upon faithless Israel and other nations, as an expression of God's justice, when weighing their deeds in the balance. However, disease is also expressed as a natural consequence: "The fruit of their [own] schemes" (Jer 6:19), and "Whoever digs a pit will [or may] fall into it" (Prov 26:27; see Eccl 10:8). Wickedness ultimately self-destructs. This (bad) fruit can be visited upon succeeding generations (Num 14:18), especially during the vulnerable first one thousand days of life,[30] and can affect the whole course of one's life. Indeed, it can affect the development of whole nations (Deut 18:12; 1 Kgs 14:24).

## The Treatment: Christ as Remedy

If the sin of created moral agents is, indeed, the root cause of disease, and God's grace and presence leads to human health and flourishing, what should be the remedy applied today? "Healing demands compassion, not

27. See chapter 7, "A Theology of Ecology: Earth Care and Health."

28. Mitchell and Grills, "Historic Humanitarian Collaboration," 87–94.

29. Hotz and Mathews, *Dust and Breath*, 70.

30. Angulo and Losada, "Emerging Health Paradigm," 113–28.

curiosity . . . action not discussion," writes Wilkinson.[31] N. T. Wright concurs: "Out of lament must come fresh action."[32] The actualization of our intentions that align with God's redeeming work to "reconcile to himself all things" (Col 1:20) in all of groaning creation, *requires a mediator, needs power, and is universal in scope.*

Why did Jesus dwell with tax-collectors, sinners, lepers, Gentiles, outcasts, and the poor? Why did he spend so much of his brief life and ministry healing all who came to him with afflictions? His answer: "It is not the healthy who need a doctor [*iatrou*], but the sick. I have not come to call the righteous, but sinners to repentance" (Luke 5:31–32). The literary parallelism is not incidental. Jesus equated "the healthy" with "the righteous" and "the sick" with "sinners." He took on mortal flesh, healed, taught, and died a wretched death, appearing "once for all at the culmination of the ages to do away with sin by the sacrifice of himself" (Heb 9:26). Jesus' suffering was provocative, not passive, and "calls the church to work for justice so that structures of constraint are replaced by structures of opportunity and liberation."[33] In the atonement, death and disease give way to the hope and promise of abundant life in the continuum of redemptive history. The Earth was subjected to futility, "in hope that the creation itself will be liberated from its bondage to decay and brought into the freedom and glory of the children of God" (Rom 8:21–22). The wise woman from Tekoa said to King David, "Like water spilled on the ground, which cannot be recovered, so we must die. But that is not what God desires; rather, he devises ways so that a banished person does not remain banished from him" (2 Sam 14:14). This is good news indeed. The church, being planted in every remote people group, empowered by the Spirit, becoming a healing community, proclaiming and demonstrating the freedom from sin and death through the gospel of the kingdom of Messiah, and working toward justice, is the hope for the healing of all nations.

## Bibliography

Angulo, Jose Miguel de, and Luz Stella Losada. "The Emerging Health Paradigm in the Twenty-First Century: The Formative First One Thousand Days of Life." *Christian Journal for Global Health* 3.2 (2016) 113–28.

Black, C. Clifton. *Mark*. Abingdon New Testament Commentaries. Nashville: Abingdon, 2011.

31. Wilkinson, *Bible and Healing*, 152.
32. Wright, *God and the Pandemic*, 64.
33. Hotz and Mathews, *Dust and Breath*, 56.

Bruckner, James K. *Healthy Human Life: A Biblical Witness*. Eugene, OR: Cascade, 2012.

Chan, Simon. *Grassroots Asian Theology: Thinking the Faith from the Ground Up*. Downers Grove, IL: InterVarsity Academic, 2014.

Gaiser, Frederick J. *Healing in the Bible: Theological Insight for Christian Ministry*. Grand Rapids: Baker Academic, 2010.

Harrison, Mark. *Disease and the Modern World: 1500 to the Present Day*. Cambridge: Polity, 2004.

Hiebert, Paul. "The Flaw of the Excluded Middle." In *Perspectives on the World Christian Movement: A Reader*, edited by Ralph D. Winter and Steven C. Hawthorne, 414–21. 4th ed. Pasadena, CA: William Carey Library, 2009.

Hotz, Kendra G., and Matthew T. Mathews. *Dust and Breath: Faith, Health, and Why the Church Should Care About Both*. Grand Rapids: Eerdmans, 2012.

Lloyd-Jones, Martyn. *Healing and the Scriptures*. Nashville: Oliver-Nelson 1988.

Messer, Neil. *Flourishing: Health, Disease, and Bioethics in Theological Perspective*. Grand Rapids: Eerdmans, 2013.

Mitchell, Robert B., and Nathan J. Grills. "A Historic Humanitarian Collaboration in the Pacific Context." *Christian Journal for Global Health* 4.2 (2017) 87–94. Online. https://journal.cjgh.org/index.php/cjgh/article/view/160/437.

Ott, Craig, and Harold A. Netland, eds. *Globalizing Theology: Belief and Practice in an Era of World Christianity*. Grand Rapids: Baker Academic, 2006.

Pew Research Center. "The Global Religious Landscape." December 18, 2012. Online. https://www.pewforum.org/2012/12/18/global-religious-landscape-exec.

Pilch, John J. *Healing in the New Testament: Insights from Medical and Mediterranean Anthropology*. Minneapolis: Fortress, 2000.

Plantinga, Cornelius, Jr. *Not the Way It's Supposed to Be: A Breviary of Sin*. Grand Rapids: Eerdmans, 1995.

Ramm, Bernard. *Offense to Reason: A Theology of Sin*. Vancouver: Regent College Publishing, 1985.

Snyder, Howard A., and Joel Scandrett. *Salvation Means Creation Healed: The Ecology of Sin and Grace*. Eugene, OR: Cascade, 2011.

Swartley, Willard M. *Jesus, Deliver Us: Evil, Exorcism, and Exousiai*. Eugene, OR: Cascade, 2019.

Thomas, John Christopher. *The Devil, Disease, and Deliverance: Origins of Illness in New Testament Thought*. Cleveland, TN: CPT, 2011.

Wilkinson, John. *The Bible and Healing: A Medical and Theological Commentary*. Grand Rapids: Eerdmans, 1998.

Wright, N. T. *God and the Pandemic: A Christian Reflection on the Coronavirus and Its Aftermath*. Grand Rapids: Zondervan, 2020.

# 6

# A Theology of Health for the Nations[1]

—Daniel Fountain

## Prologue: The Problem of Lions: An African Parable

ONCE UPON A TIME there was a big village situated in a large forest in Africa. Many lions roamed this forest. Often the lions would attack the people of the village when they worked in their fields outside the village or when they went to the stream for water or to bathe. At night the lions would even come into the village and attack the people in their houses. Many were wounded; some were killed. This was a great problem for the people of this village.

One day the village leaders sat down together to discuss what they could do about this problem. Someone suggested that they try to get rid of the lions. They discussed this idea at length, but there were many objections. Who would kill the lions? How could they do it? There were many lions in the forest, and they were dangerous animals. Furthermore, they had always been in the forest because God had put them there. So they concluded they would have to live with the problem as best they could.

Then someone suggested that they could at least help the people whom the lions had wounded. This seemed like an excellent idea. To do so, they would need a small hospital, some equipment, and people trained to help the wounded.

The village people set to work and began to build a small hospital. They contributed money to buy some equipment, and they asked friends from other villages far away to help them with this. When they had finished building the hospital, they hired a doctor and some nurses to work there. The

1. This article consists of excerpts from Daniel Fountain's monograph, *Health, the Bible, and the Church*. Used by permission.

doctor and the nurses were very busy, because every day lions attacked one or more persons, wounding some and killing others. But the people felt they had done all they could to solve the problem of the lions.

The lions continued to come into the village at night to attack people in their houses. The people had no safe place to live or to sleep. So the village leaders called another meeting to discuss this matter. How could they stop the lions from coming into the village at night? In that way people could at least sleep in peace. But lions are very powerful. They can climb trees and jump very high. Who could build a fence high enough or strong enough to keep out the lions when they were hungry?

Nevertheless, a fence around the village seemed to be the only possible means of protection, so the people set to work. Many long logs were cut and tapered at one end to make a sharp point. They drove these logs into the ground very close together to form a stockade completely around the village. They placed heavy doors at each end of the village so they could go out during the day to their fields and to the stream to bathe and get water.

Now the people felt better. The lions could no longer come into the village to attack the people there. They could sleep peacefully at night So they held a big feast to celebrate this major triumph. But had they indeed solved the lion problem?

A few days later a woman went to her fields with two of her children. Suddenly a lion attacked them and ran off with one of the children. The woman ran screaming back into the village. "A lion has just killed my child! What good is your fence? I still have to work in the fields outside and go to the stream for water. Why can't you get rid of the lions?"

Again the leaders called a meeting. The discussion was long and difficult, for now they realized that there was only one solution to the problem. They must get rid of the lions, and they must do it themselves. So they called for volunteers among the young men to begin training in the techniques of lion hunting.

After some weeks, when all was ready, teams of young lion hunters went out into the forest. Three days later they killed the first lion, and there was great rejoicing in the village. Soon more lions were killed and the hunters went further into the forest. Lions wounded some of the hunters who were brought back to the hospital in the village. Two of the hunters were killed and there was much sadness. However, after many months the hunters returned to the village singing songs of victory. The last lion had been killed, and there were no more left in the forest. The problem of lions was finished!

* * *

This bit of African wisdom speaks volumes to us. We have spent vast resources in hospitals and clinics to care for the sick and to treat those who have fallen victim to the "lions" of disease. We have invested some effort and resources in preventing certain infectious diseases and have had a few notable successes. But we seem quite inept in promoting health and in "driving the lions from the forest."

What are these lions? They are not just viruses, or bacteria, or parasites. Rather they are primarily our habits and behavior patterns that make us susceptible to diseases. They are the stress factors of our lifestyle that produce excessive wear and tear on our lives. They are the social, economic, and political structures that confine millions of people to conditions unfavorable to health and keep them from participating in the full benefits of an abundant life.

That is what this chapter is all about: lions that destroy health and what we can do about them. We must become thoroughly familiar with lion-hunting weapons and techniques and how to use them. We must know these lions: where they live, what are their habits, and how we can get at them. Then we must see how to move out into the "forest" and do battle against all the lions that diminish or destroy our health.

## A Biblical Worldview

To think biblically about health, we must understand the essential elements of the Christian faith that underlie our beliefs, values, and actions, and that give meaning and purpose to all that we do.

We can function effectively as followers of Jesus Christ only if we learn to think God's thoughts as he has revealed them to us. Jesus Christ came to save the whole of persons, society, and the created world, and this includes physical, psychological, and spiritual healing or restoration as well as the restoration of wholeness to communities and society. If we cling to a fragmented view of the person, the community, and the created world, we will not be able to restore wholeness to persons or to society. We can do so only after a radical housecleaning of our thinking, in short, by renewing our minds according to God's Word and the Spirit of Jesus Christ within us.

The central elements of the biblical worldview and their relationship to health include our beliefs in:

1. God, the Maker of heaven and Earth, who is sovereign, good, and the Giver of life and health

2. The created world, which is good, . . . and with which we must live in a relationship of responsible caring

3. The human person as the image of God in the world, created for life with God, responsible service for others, and community interaction

4. Evil as an aberration of God's plan, a real force bent on the destruction of God's creation, and which we can combat with God's help

5. A complex relationship between health and behavior

6. Jesus Christ, God's son, who came to make possible the radical restoration of wholeness, and who demonstrated the principles on which we must build our ministries of health and the restoration of wholeness.

Put quite simply, God's plan for the world is this: that all persons everywhere, in every nation, know God's saving health and be delivered from disobedience, disruption, despair, disease, and all that would destroy our wholeness.

## God Desires Our Health and Wholeness

The God of Abraham, Isaac, and Jacob, the God and Father of our Lord Jesus Christ is the God who heals, saves, restores, and makes whole. He is the God of Good News, of health, and of life. Until we have an adequate understanding of our faith and beliefs, and until we are comfortable and proficient in the use of "weapons for hunting the lions of poor health," we will not succeed in overcoming the problems that still destroy the life and health of so many of us. We will look at these weapons (beliefs) carefully in order to understand their importance to health. With the biblical perspective underlying our efforts to promote health through education and the motivation of changes in behavior, we will be able to help persons and communities deal with the lions that threaten their health.

God is the giver of life, not death. In spite of the disease and disorder which so buffet our lives, we believe that God desires our health and wholeness. What is the biblical evidence for this affirmation of faith?

## 1. The Original Creation.

When God created the world, he placed man and woman in the Garden of Eden. An implication in this account is that there was no sin, suffering, disease, or death in this original state of human existence. But were there *tubercle bacilli* in the Garden? Was the malaria parasite there? Did mosquitoes bite Adam and Eve and live on their blood? The record does not answer these questions for us, but it does make clear that health was God's plan for his human creatures and that disease and death were not part of the original human condition. The God who created the morning star and the lily of the valley is not the God who dispatches cancer to this one, or a malaria-bearing anopheles mosquito to that one.

## 2. God Is Our Healer

The Old Testament portrays God as our healer. "I am the LORD, who heals you" (Exod 15:26). God's saving health is to be proclaimed among the nations (Ps 67:2). Health is a blessing; disease is a curse (Lev 26; Deut 28). Health is therefore good, and it is God's intention for his people.

## 3. Jesus Healed

Jesus said, "I have come down from heaven not to do my will but to do the will of him who sent me" (John 6:38). When he came, he "went throughout Galilee . . . healing every disease and sickness among the people" (Matt 4:23). Healing must therefore be God's will, and all disease, be it physical, mental, spiritual, or social, is a violation of God's plan for our lives.

## 4. Eternity

At the end of human history, God will unite all his people together in the eternal realm. "There will be no more death or mourning or crying or pain" (Rev 21:4).

## 5. Jesus Commanded Us to Heal

At the beginning of human history and at its culmination, disease, destruction, and death are excluded. During the present painful interlude, disease, destruction, and death represent the presence of evil in the world.

But "the reason the Son of God appeared was to destroy the works of the devil" (1 John 3:8 ESV), including disease. The Son of God trained his followers to carry on his work of reversing the devil's work until the culmination of history.

## What God Says about Evil

How then do we cope with the frightful reality of evil and the many unanswerable questions it poses to us? We must start from God's perspective. We cannot deduce the nature of God from what we observe in the world. So as we wrestle with the problem of evil, our starting point is the goodness of God and not the evil we see around us in the world.

A mother lies in bed, tortured by the agony of terminal cancer. Is this God's desire for her and for her family? A young man whose liver is completely scarred by cirrhosis gasps for breath because his lungs are full of the liquid of edema. Does this come from the Giver of every good and perfect gift? Surely our minds recoil from such thoughts. Yet why, then, do we pray, "Father, if it be your will, heal this person?"

The prayer for healing qualified by "if it is your will" is, in effect, a cop-out. Perhaps our efforts to heal have proved inadequate, or perhaps we are afraid they will be inadequate. Rather than admit our inadequacy or commit ourselves to work and pray for healing in the face of possible disappointment or failure, we wash our psychological hands of the burden by implying that it is all up to God. If healing as we desire it does not occur, it then is God's fault, not ours. If God is unwilling, we certainly cannot fight against God!

I am a physician, trained in the science and technology of healing. Am I fighting against God as I give life-saving chloroquine to a malarious child, or work to overcome the causes of malnutrition and cirrhosis, or remove an inflamed appendix from a young man? The answer is no. Rather, God has commissioned me to fight against the causes of disease and to heal in his name.

What does God have to say about evil—the works of the devil?

1. There was no evil, disorder, pain, or disease in the original creation. Goodness is therefore an essential part of creation and of our human nature, but evil is not.

2. God permits evil and works somehow through it to accomplish his good purposes in us.

3. Evil came after creation when Satan rebelled against God and then succeeded in inciting our ancestors to rebel (Isa 14:12–15; Gen 3). Evil is an aberration of the good and comes when good things are used for destructive purposes. It is not an essential part of creation but is a distortion that has come into creation.

4. Evil is that which separates us from God and therefore from life. Evil is morally wrong because it destroys life and leads to death—eternal and spiritual death.

5. We are to resist evil. However, we cannot combat it with our strength alone because evil is within us and its power is vastly greater than our own. We can combat it effectively only with our faith in God and with the power he makes available to us through Christ (1 John 5:3–5). Repeatedly in the gospels (e.g., Matt 10:8; Luke 9:2) Jesus charged his disciples to heal the sick and cast out demons in his name. Does he still give the same direction to his followers?

6. Evil confronts us with a choice, the choice to succumb or to overcome. The manifestations of evil which confront us in suffering, disease, or tragedies, bring us to a moral decision: do I succumb or do I seek to overcome it by bringing good out of it? My response determines whether I move toward life and wholeness, or whether I permit the power of evil to destroy me as a person. Disease may destroy much or all of my body but I can choose between life or death for my person.

In the Bible evil is personified. The Bible gives many names to the "person" of evil: the serpent, Satan, the Devil, Lucifer, the ruler of the spiritual powers in space. As Satan had no power over Christ, so we can resist his power by our faith in Christ. John tells us that Jesus came to destroy the devil's work (1 John 3:8). The devil is trying to destroy the image of God within us. Yet the devil cannot accomplish this without our permission and cooperation any more than God can make us follow him without our consent and cooperation.

The devil had destroyed the image of God in the man who lived in the burial caves in the region of the Gerasenes (Mark 5:1–5). This man lived an animal existence and even mutilated his own body. The devil had destroyed the image of God in the boy with a convulsive disorder (Mark 9:14–29). The child was non-communicative, was the victim of uncontrollable seizures, and on occasion fell into the fire. The devil was attempting to destroy his body as well as his mind and spirit. In each of these cases, Jesus overcame the works of the devil and restored mental, spiritual, and physical health to both persons.

To put this in biblical terms, we live in a world that has been corrupted by evil. This evil has produced disorder in the natural environment, and we are part of this environment. Although this evil and disorder will ultimately be eliminated, they are nevertheless frightfully real for us now. What about leprosy, Down's syndrome, devastating droughts, and the innumerable diseases and disasters that continue to plague us—are these the works of the devil? Most certainly they are. We can affirm that they are the works of the devil because they can potentially destroy the image of God within us.[2]

## The Origin of Diseases

Image-destroying diseases in general come from a variety of sources. Furthermore, a specific case of disease may have more than one factor involved in the cause. Throughout history we have often erred by assuming that all diseases come from one general source.

The ancient Hebrews believed that all diseases came because of sin and were a punishment from God for sin. Many traditional religions ascribe disease to disruptions in the social order. Illness comes because of the curse of another person who is angry with the sick person, or from ancestral spirits because of neglect of traditional regulations or values.

In modern times, with the development of our sciences of bacteriology, biology, chemistry, and others, we came to believe that all diseases have natural causes: bacteria, viruses, chemical imbalances in the body, and other physical problems. Some believe they can explain all diseases as the result of nutritional imbalances. Others believe the basic problem to be skeletal mal-alignment. Still others believe that illness is due to negative mental and psychological processes, with healing coming from a change in thinking.

There is truth in all of these beliefs. A relationship does exist between health and behavior. Disorders of social relationships, of nutrition, of thoughts, emotions, and feelings can all cause illness. And the germ theory has not been disproved! Viruses, bacteria, and parasites are present throughout nature and some of them can install themselves in us and cause disease. Genetic defects produce a variety of congenital abnormalities. We can consider some sicknesses and disasters as resulting from the effects of disorder in the natural realm, such as drought that can cause famine or malnutrition for thousands, making them susceptible to numerous diseases.

2. Editors' Note: We would disagree with Dr. Fountain that diseases, disasters, and the devil can "destroy" the image of God in humans. They may "tarnish" or "distort," but the *Imago Dei* is an irrevocable part of human essence even when burdened with disabilities and sickness and even when steeped in sin.

## Believers' Obligation to Cooperate with God

By his power, God seeks to restore order to what has become disordered. God is the owner of the whole creation but he has put the Earth at our disposition. He can work through all who, in faith and in active submission, become available to him as channels of his power. He has delegated us to be his managers and to exercise authority over the Earth according to the patterns he has established and revealed to us. God will not do for us what he has equipped us to do for ourselves. In vain do we seek a miracle for something which we are quite capable of doing for ourselves.[3] So the very practical question is, how can we cooperate with God in his activity in the world?

God has given all humans sensory skills and intelligence to discern and analyze the patterns according to which he has created all things. God has given us the power to change and improve some of these things for our benefit. Cooperation with God thus requires us to make full use of the wisdom and power he has given us and to continue to explore and analyze our world to discover new patterns beneficial to us. We cannot expect God to work with us if we neglect or deny the gifts he has already given us.

Science and the Christian faith both affirm an inherent understandable order in nature, the ability of human intelligence to experiment and discern that order, and the cultural mandate of humankind to discover, organize, and make use of the natural world. Our study of the natural environment gives us an understanding of the physical world around us which can enable us to make changes favorable to health. As our understanding of the natural world progresses, we acquire greater possibilities for the improvement of the health and well-being of all humankind. We understand a great deal about many diseases and how as communities and individuals we can protect ourselves from many of them and even eliminate certain disease-producing hazards.

A biblical understanding of nature, of God who sustains her, and of the abilities and responsibilities God has given us, equips us for the promotion of health. It enables us to replace resignation with initiative, passivity with activity, despair with hope. We cannot control all of nature but we can manage certain aspects of the natural world for our benefit.

The orderly pattern of nature plus the intelligence with which God has endowed us enable us to work for health and for healing. In our health sciences we study disease and attempt to discover and understand what goes wrong, both in the person and in the community. We can then seek ways to

---

3. Editors' Note: Along this line, Ralph Winter used to humorously say, "Don't ask God to paint the back fence!"

restore the person and the community to health. We develop "tools" to build health and to restore health to those who are ill. Ampicillin, laser surgery, and the principles of sanitation are examples of such life-changing discoveries. These are gifts from God, coming because of the orderly patterns in the world he has created and the intelligence God has given us to discern and utilize these patterns for our benefit. By using these gifts for health and healing we are cooperating with God who intends our health and who has made these things possible for us.

By restoring order where there is disorder, we can facilitate healing and the restoration of persons and communities. We must use every means at our disposal to combat the viruses and bacteria, the biochemical imbalances in the body, and the nutritional deficiencies of the sick person.[4] This includes the many technical means we have to overcome the disease process and its noxious effects, and the psychological, social, and spiritual support necessary for restoring wholeness. We also need to use the means of protection we have or are developing to prevent some of these conditions from occurring. All of this is legitimate because God intends us to be healthy, is working actively for our health and wholeness, and has given us these means to combat disease. Our whole ministry of bringing health and wholeness to the world exists because we know that disease, pain, and death are real but that good can triumph over them. Evil, pain, and sin are very real and are part of our daily existence. So we must deal with them.

God has created the human self in his own image and that image is good. The human self is good and is worth saving and restoring. Because health is the intention of God for all persons, God's people are to promote health and to bring healing until that Day when God will bring all things together again with Christ as Supreme Lord over all.

---

4. Editors' Note: See chapter 15, "A Scientist's Perspective on Disease and Death" for an example of a new nano-technology being used to kill antibiotic-resistant bacteria and potentially even the virus responsible for COVID-19.

# 7

## A Theology of Ecology

*Earth Care and Health*

—SIGVE K. TONSTAD

HOW TIME FLIES! How fast the years went by! And yet how immeasurably vast the distance between then and now!

By the time I graduated from medical school in 1979, I had heard many lectures on the disease challenge that lay behind us and the task ahead. Behind us was the Era of Infectious Disease. Ahead lay the Era of Lifestyle Diseases. Infections, for centuries the main killer and reason for shortened life expectancy, had been conquered by improved hygiene, better nutrition, the development of vaccines, and the discovery of antibiotics. Smallpox, a major scourge, was gone. Poliomyelitis, a significant threat even after World War II, was no longer a threat in developed countries. Beginning with penicillin, antibiotics held out the prospect of recovery even for the most serious bacterial infections. Nobel Prizes in Medicine were routinely awarded to researchers who made the conquest of infections their priority: Ronald Ross in 1902 for his work on malaria; Robert Koch in 1905 for discoveries in relation to tuberculosis; Sir Alexander Fleming, Ernst Chain, and Sir Howard Florey in 1945 for the discovery of penicillin and its curative effect on bacterial infections; Max Delbrück, Alfred D. Hershey, and Salvador Luria in 1969 for discoveries concerning the replication and structure of viruses; Baruch Blumberg and D. Carleton Gajdusek in 1976 for discovering new mechanisms for dissemination of infectious diseases, with the dreaded hepatitis B virus as the main case in point.[1]

---

1. See "Ronald Ross"; "Robert Koch"; "Sir Alexander Fleming"; "Max Delbrück"; "Baruch S. Blumberg."

The twentieth century gives proof of unprecedented progress in the struggle against infections to bring the era to an end in the developed world. This is not to say that advances had stopped by the time I was in medical school. Progress has continued in the form of a vastly expanded understanding of the immune system and ways to harness—and suppress—it. Vaccines for prevention of the most common forms of hepatitis are now widely in use as are medications that promise to cure these dreaded diseases when already established. These advances testify to the triumph of science over ignorance, and hope over despair.

My generation of physicians had good reasons to prepare for a lifetime of combatting so-called Lifestyle Diseases like hypertension, diabetes, heart disease, and cancer. Or, as lesser problems, mood disorders (depression) and gastroesophageal reflux disease. The label stuck even though it is imprecise. Is diabetes truly a disease of "lifestyle"? Is it not also a disease conditioned by inheritance and environment—truly a Disease of Civilization? Similar caveats apply to hypertension and heart disease. Smoking is the main cause of lung cancer and a huge contributor to heart disease. For many other cancers, the link between lifestyle and the cancer remains tenuous. Imprecise labels notwithstanding, these are the health problems that have loomed large throughout my medical career.

For these diseases, too, the past forty years have seen tremendous advances. My wife, a medical school classmate, dedicated her life to the prevention of heart disease, working mostly on lipid disorders, type two diabetes, smoking, hypertension, and obesity. Who can forget the excitement when Joseph Goldstein and Michael Brown in 1985 received the Nobel Prize in Medicine for their discovery of the LDL-receptor (low density lipoprotein receptor)? Who will disparage the subsequent development of cholesterol-lowering drugs, that, in the reckoning of some experts, are medications that have saved more lives than any other known drug? Or what about laws imposing constraints on the predatory ways of the tobacco industry? Or, lest we forget, the discovery that peptic ulcer disease, once thought to be a disease of lifestyle, is caused by a bacterium known as *Helicobacter pylori*? This discovery was so counter-intuitive and unexpected that those who made the discovery were awarded the Nobel Prize in Medicine in 2005.[2]

And yet, it is not wrong to call these decades the Era of Lifestyle Diseases.

Until now—until COVID-19.

2. "Nobel Prize in Physiology."

## Medicine at a Loss

COVID-19 is an infectious disease that will be more of a landmark than the Spanish flu in 1918, inflicting a greater global disruption. As I write this, the United States has recorded almost six million cases in the course of just seven months. More than two hundred thousand people have died of this disease in the United States during the same period.[3] Some survivors are left with significant long-lasting disabilities. Global travel is at a standstill. Robust economies are crashing, with predictions indicating a slow crawl back to pre-COVID levels. It already seems that the Era of Lifestyle Diseases was a brief interlude and that the Era of Infections is back with a vengeance.

This is not to say that infections ever went away. In a global perspective, what I have called the Era of Lifestyle Diseases was never quite that; it was never as though infections ceased to be a threat. It is enough to mention the persistence of malaria, tuberculosis, diarrheal disease, hepatitis, parasitic diseases, and HIV to realize that infections could not fully become secondary concerns. While COVID-19 struck suddenly, warnings of a new era in the making had been ample in the form of SARS (severe acute respiratory syndrome) from 2002 to 2004, MERS (Middle East respiratory syndrome) in 2012, and Ebola hemorrhagic fever from 2012 to 2014.[4] Like SARS-CoV-2, which causes COVID-19, SARS-CoV-1 and MERS-CoV are coronaviruses, so named because of their shape. The two predecessors to COVID-19 set off a global scare less for the numbers infected (8,400 for SARS;[5] 2,500 for MERS[6]) than for the high fatality rate (from 0 percent to 50 percent depending on the age group affected, with an overall estimate of case fatality of 14 percent to 15 percent for SARS;[7] 34 percent for MERS[8]).

A pattern has emerged. First, the new infections are caused by viruses. Viruses are tiny "organisms" that are, in important respects, "incomplete," dependent on their ecological environment since they cannot live or replicate except inside cells of other organisms.[9] "It mooches. It steals," says David

---

3. During the publication process, deaths from COVID-19 have grown to over half a million and continue to rise.

4. Quammen, *Spillover*. The first documented case of Ebola infection in humans happened in 1976.

5. "SARS (Ten Years After)."

6. "MERS Monthly Summary."

7. "Update 49."

8. "MERS Monthly Summary."

9. Editors' Note: For additional details about viruses, see chapter 15, "A Scientist's Perspective on Disease and Death."

Quammen.[10] Once inside the cell, the virus harnesses the cellular mechanisms of the host for its own replication and survival. As proof that most viruses are not welcome, the host mobilizes a massive immune response to rid itself of it. With COVID-19, in elderly people and persons with pre-existing conditions, it is the severity of the immune response that dooms the patient, not the virus itself. The mechanism, still poorly understood, is that age brings out a mismatch between "on" and "off" in the immune response, with the "off" signal too weak. The ravages to the human lung of this virus are by now legendary in the medical community.

SARS-CoV-2 is a single-stranded RNA-virus. This makes it a simple virus, but it also makes it unstable and prone to mutations. The propensity to mutate confers possibilities, including the possibility that the virus can "spill over" to infect species other than the original host. The discovery that SARS-CoV-1 had its original habitat in Chinese bats appeared to show that bats and the virus get along: the virus does not trigger an immune reaction. Moreover, direct transmission from bats to humans has not been demonstrated. The virus needs an intermediary "amplifying" host. For SARS-Cov-1, one of the amplifying hosts is thought to be the masked palm civet,[11] a racoon-like or skunk-like wild animal that is defined as its own species and is native to the Indian Subcontinent and Southeast Asia. According to the current thinking, SARS CoV-2 (the virus responsible for COVID-19) is similar to SARS-CoV-1. It, too, has had a stable, non-adversarial habitat in Chinese bats. Its pathway to become a human pathogen may have gone by way of pangolins, an odd-looking wild mammal also known as "scaly anteater" for its panzer-like exterior and food preference. The pangolin is a nocturnal animal, shy and solitary in its manner of operation, with the ability to roll itself up in a ball. Pangolins are threatened by poaching and heavy deforestation of their natural habitat—and, not to be missed—they are "the most trafficked mammals in the world."[12] They are bred in captivity in China, the meat sold in the open meat markets in cities like Wuhan. According to the best hypothesis for the COVID-19 pandemic, the virus mutated and spilled over from the bat to pangolins and from pangolins made the jump to become a devastating human pathogen.[13]

Second, COVID-19 is a zoonosis, an infection acquired from animals before there was human-to-human transmission. Just like viruses

10. Quammen, *Spillover*, 267.

11. Shi and Hu, "Review of Studies on Animal Reservoirs."

12. Goode, "Struggle to Save the Scaly Pangolin." See also Quammen, "Did Pangolin Trafficking Cause the Coronavirus Pandemic?"

13. Cyranoski, "Did Pangolins Spread."

depend on ecology for survival inside cells, ecology plays a crucial role in transmission. Humans have encroached on habitats that were previously left undisturbed. This virus did not come to us. We came to the virus. "Human-caused ecological pressures and disruptions are bringing animal pathogens ever more into contact with human populations, while human technology and behavior are spreading those pathogens ever more widely and quickly," says Quammen.[14] He elaborates that human activities "are causing the disintegration of natural ecosystems at a cataclysmic rate."[15] This has brought civilization in close contact with millions of hitherto un-known creatures, including viruses. "Students of virology now speak of the 'virosphere,' a vast realm of organisms that probably dwarfs every other group."[16] A virus, the tiniest of organisms, the character of which hardly counts as "alive," now sidles up to the center of world health concerns to make *ecology* the *sine qua non* of health.

Third, let *ecology* now stand alone, as a separate word, although it is already present in the world of viruses for their need of the cells of other creatures for survival. COVID-19 must be understood in *ecological* terms. We face a scenario that "the disruption of natural ecosystems seems more and more to be unloosing such microbes into a wider world."[17]

*Health* that misses the ecological dimension can, on this logic, not count as health. Ecology is the science of relationships, and health must be, too. This is anticipated in the writings of Wendell Berry, addressing the dis-connection between the farmer in the field and the physician in the hospital. The *relational* and thus *ecological* tenor of Berry's outlook is pervasive.

> A medical doctor uninterested in nutrition, in agriculture, in the wholesomeness of mind and spirit is as absurd as a farmer who is uninterested in health. Our fragmentation of this sub-ject cannot be our cure, because it is our disease. The body cannot be whole alone. Persons cannot be whole alone. It is wrong to think that bodily health is compatible with spiritual confusion or cultural disorder, or with polluted air and water or impoverished soil.[18]

I read this in Berry's book the year I graduated from medical school, but it is only now, spurred by the COVID-19 pandemic, that I see its true relevance and urgency. A similar line of thought is embraced by the most

14. Quammen, *Spillover*, 40.
15. Quammen, *Spillover*, 40.
16. Quammen, *Spillover*, 40.
17. Quammen, *Spillover*, 41.
18. Berry, *Unsettling of America*, 102.

influential medical journal in the world, *The Lancet*, with a new publication dedicated to *Planetary Health*, and it is coming to the fore in the concept of *One Health*: the health of humans cannot be separated from animal health or the health of the Earth.[19]

## Theology Also at a Loss

Despite spectacular advances, modern medicine is outgunned and outmaneuvered by COVID-19. It seems trite to say that medicine has been too individualistic, disease-focused, and cure-oriented, but it is necessary to check "all of the above" to acknowledge the deficits. The contrast would be a system that is ecological, health-focused, and prevention-oriented. CO-VID-19 is an ecological moment of truth, a time to recognize neglected interactions and inter-dependencies. During the most acute phase of the pandemic in Italy and slightly later in New York, efforts concentrated on "flattening the curve" in the hope that hospital resources would not be overwhelmed. In some places, it was not enough. Colleagues report harrowing scenes from intensive care units overflowing with patients on respirators, fewer than half of whom would survive.

This grim picture in medicine is dwarfed by a grimmer picture in theology. It, too, has been at a loss. It, too, even more than medicine, has been complicit in habits of thought that have been individualistic rather than communal, ecological, and global. If medicine has been preoccupied with the "salvation" of individual human bodies, Christian theology has further narrowed the scope to concern for the individual human soul—even in the absence of care for the body. In the most extreme version of this outlook, Origen of Alexandria (185–254) implied that the material world and the human body were not part of God's original plan and would, he surmised, eventually disappear. "God therefore made the present world and bound the soul to the body as a punishment," said Origen.[20] As for the future, he envisioned a state without matter and bodies. "For if all things can exist without bodies, doubtless bodily substance will cease to exist when there is no use for it," he held.[21] Other Christian thought leaders were less extreme than Origen, but the separation of the soul from the body and the priority of the soul over the body has been a staple of

19. Mackenzie, "One Health," 163–89; Mackenzie and Jeggo, "One Health Approach."

20. Origen, *On First Principles* 1.8.1.

21. Origen, *On First Principles* 2.3.2.

Christian theology until our time.[22] In an influential book on the history of medicine, Roy Porter puts it this way:

> Western thinking about the human condition long hinged on the union of two contrasting elements, body and soul. At least from the time of Plato (c. 428–c. 348 BC), models of their relationship—complementary but conflictual—promoted a dualism which, once given the blessing of Christianity, proved durable, persuasive, and dominant. A grasp of the emergence of those ideas is essential for understanding later developments.[23]

Porter sees the emerging Christian outlook as an alien element and a contrast to the earth- and-body-embracing outlook of the Old Testament. Thus, "the soul-body dualism which became fundamental to Christian theology was derived not from the Hebrew heritage but from admixtures of Levantine theosophy and Greek philosophy."[24] W. H. C. Frend captures the same monumental transformation from the point of view of church history. "Basically," he says, "nothing could be more opposed than the Jewish and Greek [Platonic] views of God, of creation, of time and history, and of the role of humanity in the universe."[25]

The consequence of the dualistic outlook for health and medicine is beyond computation. Why take an interest in the body when it is the soul that matters? Why study the Earth when, in the life to come, life is to be celestial, and the redeemed will never see the Earth again? These sentiments ushered in an era of ignorance and neglect of the body and the Earth that lasted well over a thousand years and in some respects got worse as the influence of Christianity increased.[26] It is too simplistic to say that the era culminated with the Black Death pandemic in the fourteenth century (1347–1351), but it is not an exaggeration to see that pandemic as emblematic for the ignorance that marked the period.[27] Philip Ziegler is not the only writer to make ignorance and neglect of the natural world a reason for the paralysis that prevailed when the Black Death unleashed its fury on Europe.

> From the tiny patch of fitful light which played within the circle of their comprehension our forefathers stared aghast into the darkness. Strange shapes were moving, but what they were they

---

22. Tonstad, *Letter to the Romans*, 23–48.

23. Porter, *Flesh in the Age of Reason*, 28.

24. Porter, *Flesh in the Age of Reason*, 35.

25. Frend, *Rise of Christianity*, 368.

26. Tonstad, *Lost Meaning*, 330–53, 376–98.

27. Tonstad, *Lost Meaning*, 332–38.

did not know and hardly dared to speculate; strange sounds were heard, but who could say from where they came? Everything was mysterious, everything potentially dangerous; to stand still might be perilous, to move fatal.[28]

The Christian civilization of Europe in the fourteenth century was incapacitated by lack of understanding of *relationships*—and thus *ecology*—with respect to hygiene, contagion, and treatment. By this criterion, the Black Death was a paradigm-breaking event. Alexander Solzhenitsyn captured it succinctly when he told the graduating class at Harvard University in 1978 that "the Middle Ages came to a natural end by exhaustion, having become an intolerable, despotic repression of man's physical nature in favor of the spiritual one."[29]

It took time to recover from such a blow. In one of my classes, I use the date 1543 as a marker on the road to recovery. That year, some twenty years after Martin Luther's Protestant Reformation, witnessed the publication of Andreas Vesalius's *Fabrica* (*On the Fabric of the Human Body*), a masterpiece on human anatomy, and Copernicus's *De revolutionibus* (*On the Revolution of the Heavenly Spheres*), a book showing that the sun and not the Earth is at the center of our solar system. An Era of Neglect (500–1500) was about to give way to an Era of Domination (1500–present). The script for this era was sketched by Francis Bacon (1561–1626), sometimes called the father of empiricism and the architect of the scientific method.[30] He envisioned a new era not only of *discovery* but also of *conquest*, not only of *investigation* but also of *domination*. If COVID-19 becomes to the Era of Domination what *Yersinia pestis* (the bacteria that caused the Black Plague) was to the Era of Neglect, the respective diseases represent a diagnostic challenge in medical terms and a *diagnostic reckoning* for human civilization, as well. Both are emblems of ecology—*Yersinia* for the preceding centuries of neglect of the natural world, COVID-19 for centuries of domination and predation.

The footprint of COVID-19 is not yet fully measurable, but its ecological character is. We see the wounds and blotches of disruption and fragmentation, in character with Wendell Berry's assessment that things may change outwardly and yet be traced to the same source: the legacy of the Era of Neglect carries over into the Era of Domination. "This separation of the soul from the body and from the Earth is no disease of the fringe, no aberration, but a fracture that runs through the mentality of institutional religion like a geologic fault," says Berry. There is no letting up because "this rift in the

---

28. Ziegler, *Black Death*, 275.

29. Solzhenitsyn, *World Split Apart*, 49.

30. See Leiss, *Domination of Nature*; Bauckham, *God and the Crisis of Freedom*.

mentality of religion continues to characterize the modern mind, no matter how secular or worldly it becomes."[31]

Notice words like "separation," "fracture," "geologic fault," and "rift." These terms describe an ecological landscape that is also influenced by theology. Again, in Berry's words, "the Bible's aim . . . is not the freeing of the spirit from the world. It is the handbook of their interaction. It says that they cannot be divided: that their mutuality, their unity, is inescapable: that they are not reconciled in division but in harmony."[32]

## Remedial Action

I will now list six items that, in my view, are essential to a "Theology of Ecology"—remedial actions aiming to heal the fractures.

### 1. An Ecological Perspective of Scripture

First, it will be necessary to restore to Scripture the ecological perspective that interpretation has taken away.[33] Ecology is not alien to Scripture; it is a mystery why it has gone missing. On this logic, an ecological reading is textual, exegetical, and theological. It is not a task driven by an alien or anachronistic ideology. Ecology is Scripture's native language in the creation stories; in the Sabbath ordinance, the Sabbath Year, and the Jubilee; and in the prophets' call for an end to predation and disease and their hope of a world restored (Isa 11:1–10; 65:16–17). We need an ear attuned to ecology to hear (non-human) creation groaning in labor pain until now in Paul's letter to the Romans (Rom 8:22), and we need ecological eyesight to perceive the indivisibility of theology and ecology in Revelation's vision of the world to come: "And I heard a loud voice from the throne saying, 'Look! God's dwelling place is now among the people, and he will dwell with them. They will be his people, and God himself will be with them and be their God'" (Rev 21:3).

If humans at some point are removed from Earth to heaven, here they are returned. Earth, not heaven, is the address at journey's end. God, too, relocates to Earth, in John's vision of Earth and of God as *earthling!* Centuries earlier, in the book of Exodus, Moses had asked God to identify himself, disclose his innermost self, his name. "Suppose I go to the Israelites and

31. Berry, *Unsettling of America*, 108.

32. Berry, *Unsettling of America*, 109.

33. Tonstad, *Letter to the Romans*, xi.

say to them, 'The God of your fathers has sent me to you,' and they ask me, 'What is his name?' Then what shall I tell them?" (Exod 3:13).

The answer has confounded most readers for centuries and still does. "God said to Moses, 'I AM WHO I AM.'" He said further, "This is what you are to say to the Israelites, 'I AM has sent me to you'" (Exod 3:14; cf. Rev 1:4).

"I AM."

Does it mean "God, the self-existent One"?

"I AM THAT I AM."

Does it mean "God, the enigma, the unknowable"?

It means none of the above. "It is not the idea of eternity which is primary when the Israelites pronounce the name Yahweh, but that of presence . . . God is he who is *with* someone," says Edmond Jacob.[34] The expression is *relational*. God returns a *relational* answer to Moses' question, "What is his name?" "I AM THAT I AM" means that God is first and foremost the One who *is with you*. God is not the "I AM" in the sense of splendid aloneness or the "I AM" of inscrutable remoteness. When Revelation says that "God himself will be with them" (Rev 21:3), it presents a familiar God, God as God is, God as God has always been. On the logic that ecology is the science of relationships,[35] theology and ecology are inseparable. God—the One who is *with* someone—underwrites ecology. Theology and ecology are two sides of the same coin. In Revelation's perspective, there is God, and Earth, and community in an ecological vision that is also theology coming home to itself (Rev 21:3–4).

And yet the remedial work cannot be limited to how we read *texts*. The distance between the agrarian context in which the text originated and the reader who reads the text today is too great. It can be bridged to some extent by soliciting the help of *contemporary agrarians*, as Ellen F. Davis perceptively points out.[36] New awareness of the text must go hand in hand with new awareness of non-human creation and the Earth. For the latter, we need the help of people who have that awareness even if their orbit is not related to the Bible. Davis claims that "the mutually informative relation between ecological awareness and biblical study rests not only on the land-centeredness of the Bible but also on the nature of the ecological crisis, which is principally moral and theological rather than technological."[37] The person who is attuned to "the Book of Nature" might have a head start on

34. Jacob, *Theology of the Old Testament*, 52.

35. Leopold, *Sand County Almanac*, 209–10.

36. Davis, *Scripture, Culture, and Agriculture*.

37. Davis, *Scripture, Culture, and Agriculture*, 9.

the person who has "the Book" only;[38] the reader of "the Book of Nature" can serve as a mentor to better readings of the Book.

> Agrarianism, as described by Wendell Berry, is no small, whittled-down philosophy for rural folks. It is, rather, a full-blown philosophy rooted in the realities of soil and nature as "the standard" by which we also come to judge much more. It is grounded in farming but is larger still. The logic of agrarianism in Berry's work, "unfolds like a fractal through the divisions and incoherence of the modern world."[39]

This leads to what Davis calls her "stronger and riskier claim: Reading the work of the contemporary agrarians can make us better readers of Scripture."[40] There is no quick fix in this, as though everything can be reduced to *reading* only. "If agrarianism were a technique of literacy criticism, even a hermeneutic, I might more quickly become adept," says Davis. "But it is a mind-set, a whole set of understandings, commitments, and practice that focus on the most basic of all cultural acts—eating—and ramify into virtually every other aspect of public and private life."[41]

Will theology be open to such a dramatic turn—to make food, care for non-human creation, and the Earth legitimate *theological* concerns? An influential book covering five hundred years of Protestant history, coinciding with the five hundredth anniversary of the Reformation, suggests a prospect that is surprisingly hopeful. Alec Ryrie depicts Protestantism in a state of decline in the world in which it originated and once flourished. Nevertheless, he credits it with an ability to reinvent itself and return stronger. And then, unexpectedly, he envisions a scenario that is unabashedly *ecological.* "What new causes will animate and divide the next generation of Protestants?" he asks. His answer is likely to surprise because it has an ecological tenor.

> My guess is that some Protestants will rediscover the spiritual importance of food. . . . This may be justified on health grounds, as a way of honoring the bodies God gave us. It may be justified with reference to the Old Testament dietary laws, for which some Protestants have always hankered. It may be justified on the grounds of the environmental damage or the misuse of scarce food resources that are associated with animal husbandry.

38. Editors' Note: Ralph Winter wrote along this line: "God has given us two 'books' of revelation (1) the Bible which is His Book of Scripture, and (2) nature, which is His Book of Creation" (Winter, "Twelve Frontiers of Perspective," 35).

39. Davis, *Scripture, Culture, and Agriculture*, 17.

40. Davis, *Scripture, Culture, and Agriculture*, 22.

41. Davis, *Scripture, Culture, and Agriculture*, 22.

It may be justified on animal-centered grounds, whether the specific cruelties of industrialized farming or the wider intuition that consuming fellow creatures is wrong. It will also be opposed, both on classic grounds of Christian freedom [based on biblical concessions to meat-eating in the post diluvian era] and also, of course, because many people like eating meat.[42]

## 2. Retrieve Materiality

Second, we must retrieve materiality. This should not be hard to do because Scripture bursts at the seams with materiality from the first pages of creation in Genesis to the last pages of re-creation in Revelation. It will be difficult, nevertheless, because of the entrenched conceptions and habits of thought mentioned earlier. In the middle, between the beginning and the ending, is the story of one who "was a descendant of David, and who through the Spirit of holiness was appointed the Son of God in power by his resurrection from the dead: Jesus Christ our Lord," as Paul tells it in his letter to the Romans (Rom 1:3–4).[43] This is not the story of escape from the world or denigration of materiality. It is the exact opposite, a story of God bringing the world into existence with a commission to thrive and flourish (Gen 1:20–31)—and then, when things went awry—committing to its restoration at high cost to himself (Isa 11:1–10; 52:13–15).

## 3. The Faithfulness of God

Third, for such a relation between God and the world, the tenor of the Bible's language of faith must be *the faithfulness of God* and not only *human faith*. I say this so as not to miss out on the dramatic change taking place in scholars' understanding of the faith-language in Paul's letters—from "faith in Jesus" to "the faithfulness of Jesus Christ."[44] In this reading, Paul declares that he is "not ashamed of the gospel" because God has not put the believer and the world to shame (Rom 1:16; cf. Isa 28:16; 50:7).[45] Echoing Habakkuk, who decried God's apparent absence and un-faithfulness (Hab 1:2–4), Paul adopts God's promise to Habakkuk as the program text in Romans. "For in

42. Ryrie, *Protestants*, 461–62.

43. Tonstad, *Letter to the Romans*, 16–22.

44. Hays, *Faith of Jesus Christ*; Tonstad, "Πίστις Χριστοῦ," 37–59; *Letter to the Romans*, 12–16.

45. Tonstad, *Letter to the Romans*, 72–80.

the gospel, God's right-making is revealed, *from* faithfulness *for* faithfulness, as it is written, 'The righteous shall live by (my) faithfulness'" (Rom 1:17, author's translation; cf. Rom 3:22–26; Hab 2:3–4).[46]

The Earth and non-human creation, too, shall live by God's faithfulness. They, too, await redemption, as Paul puts it when he writes that "the [non-human] creation waits with eager longing . . . that the [non-human] creation itself will be set free from its bondage to corruption . . . that the whole [non-human] creation has been groaning together in the pains of childbirth until now" (Rom 8:19–22 ESV).[47] This is ecology leaning hard on theology, counting on God to deliver on God's promise. *Faith* has not disappeared, but God's *faithfulness* is inclusive and ecological in a way that *faith*, in its traditional conception, cannot be. This new perspective on Paul extends a hand to ecology, the appreciation for which is still in its infancy.

## 4. A New Vision of Community

Fourth, remedial action has a new vision of *community*. This is not limited to human community that is so endearingly described in Romans 16:1–16.[48] The notion of community that accommodates an ecological vision looks beyond human community to what Richard Bauckham calls "the community of creation."[49] Human beings are unique for being created in the image of God, but we are members of "the community of creation," a community that does not exist only for our whim and benefit. "Humans are not demi-gods with creative power, set like God above creation," says Bauckham, "but creatures among other creatures, dependent, like other creatures, on the material world of which they are part, and immersed in a web of reciprocal relationships with other creatures."[50] The non-human members of this community have *rights* (Gen 1:20–23); they are even afforded *protection* in the Sabbath commandment and the Sabbatical Year in Exodus (Exod 20:8–11; 23:10–11). Paul's attunement to the groaning of creation in Romans is proof that non-human creation has *hope* even though, as I read the passage, it "waits with eager longing for the revealing of the sons [and daughters] of God" (Rom 8:19 ESV).[51]

46. Tonstad, *Letter to the Romans*, 12–16, 72–80, 135–39.

47. Tonstad, *Letter to the Romans*, 238–60.

48. Tonstad, *Letter to the Romans*, 49–68.

49. Bauckham, *Bible and Ecology*, 64.

50. Bauckham, *Bible and Ecology*, 27–28.

51. Tonstad, *Letter to the Romans*, 242–57.

A rights-based, protection-based, and hope-based view of ecology will respond more quickly and earnestly to the plight of non-human creation than one that is based on human self-concern. "Ecological" readers will not reduce creation to "the environment." Kathryn Greene-McCreight says perceptively:

> The only warrant that the secular world gives us to care for the "environment" is a thinly veiled version of self-concern: our children will suffer unless we change our habits. Divorcing creation from redemption leaves us alone in the world with ourselves as our only companion. The message of ecologists is far more powerful when framed in terms of the biblical narrative: the waters we pollute and the land we poison were created by the One who made, reconciles, and redeems us."[52]

## 5. Sabbath

Fifth, the Sabbath may well be the most potent resource and corrective in a *theology of ecology* because it mandates *cessation*, and *cessation* is ecology's most neglected working principle (Gen 2:1–3; Exod 20:8–11; Deut 5:12–15).[53] Cessation sets a limit to production and productivity; indeed, it makes something other than productivity the measure of plenitude. The cessation mandated by the weekly Sabbath benefits everyone, but the most vulnerable, the slave, the resident alien, and the toiling beast, are specifically mentioned. In the Exodus version of the Ten Commandments, we read that cessation is to include male and female servants, "your animals, [and] any foreigner residing in your towns" (Exod 20:10). In Deuteronomy, the range of beneficiaries is expanded and more detailed, and the tenor of economic relief is more explicit: "The seventh day is a sabbath to the LORD your God. On it you shall not do any work, neither you, nor your son or daughter, nor your male or female servant, nor your ox, your donkey or any of your animals, nor any foreigner residing in your towns, so that your male and female servants may rest, as you do" (Deut 5:14). As Walter Brueggemann wryly notes, "How strange to use the most airtime at the mountain on the Sabbath command!"[54]

The principle of cessation extends to the Sabbath "outposts" in the Old Testament, the Sabbath Year (Exod 23:10–11; Lev 25:1–7) and the Jubilee

---

52. Greene-McCreight, "Restless," 234–35.
53. Tonstad, *Lost Meaning*, 376–98.
54. Brueggemann, *Sabbath as Resistance*, 27.

(Lev 25:8–24). The Sabbath Year is designated in overtly ecological terms as a Sabbath for the land—"For six years you are to sow your fields and harvest the crops, but during the seventh year let the land lie unplowed and unused" (Exod 23:10–11). Leviticus repeats the stipulation, saying that "The land is to have a year of rest" (Lev 25:5). Beyond land rest, the Sabbath Year makes a gesture of mercy to the underprivileged—"then the poor among your people may get food from it"—and to wild animals— "the wild animals may eat what is left" (Exod 23:11). These are tantalizing conceptions for a time that sees human civilization advancing relentlessly, resulting in deforestation, loss of biodiversity, and the threat of ecosystem collapse. In the paradigm of the Sabbath Year, advance is interrupted by retreat; expansion is tempered by a time of retrenchment. It is even possible to imagine boundaries that protect the interests of non-human creatures, seen and unseen. During the Sabbath Year, it is as if "the wild animals" retake lost territory. Here, the COVID-19 pandemic comes to mind, as if nature protests uninterrupted and reckless predation, the dissolution of an ecosystem compelling the human predator to take notice.

Was God serious about the Sabbath Year? The prophets certainly thought so. Indeed, the logic they invoke suggests that the sabbatical institutions are a matter of divine commitment and not only divine commandments. Regarding the land Sabbath, God keeps his commitment if the people fail to do so. When the Israelites head into captivity in Babylon, failure to respect the Sabbath Year is given as the reason for the captivity or at least the rationale for its length: "to fulfill the word of the LORD by the mouth of Jeremiah, until the land had enjoyed its Sabbaths. All the days that it lay desolate it kept Sabbath, to fulfill seventy years" (2 Chr 36:21 ESV; cf. Jer 25:11–12; 29:10; Dan 9:2). "Seventy years," that is, to make it up to the land for 490 years of non-observance of the Sabbath Year.

The Jubilee adds another plank to the ecological texture of Sabbath theology. "Consecrate the fiftieth year and proclaim liberty throughout the land to all its inhabitants," we read. "It shall be a jubilee for you; each of you is to return to your family property and to your own clan" (Lev 25:10). This is radical economics and hugely consequential for ecology. Land should not be made into a commodity and accumulated indefinitely. "The land must not be sold permanently, because *the land is mine* and you reside in my land as foreigners and strangers" (Lev 25:23). The Jubilee functions as a reversal button, a reset, a return. Norman Habel calls it "economic amnesty."[55] Jacob Milgrom sees a mechanism that prevents "the ever-widening gap between the rich and the poor which Israel's prophets can only condemn, but which

---

55. Habel, *Land Is Mine*, 104.

Israel's priests attempt to rectify in Leviticus 25."[56] In this conception, land is not "real estate" that can be accumulated, sold, and resold in a never-ending spiral. Where proprietors are close to the land and conscious of being "aliens and tenants," respect for the land will be greater, as will the obligation to faithful stewardship. Brueggemann has this in mind when he warns of "a *sabbathless* society in which land is never rested, debts are never canceled, slaves are never released."[57] His call to take the Sabbath into account and to restore the connection between the Sabbath and the care of the land also counts as a form of *resistance*. "People who keep Sabbath live all seven days differently," he says.[58]

## 6. Compassion and Grace

For a sixth and final remedy, will it be possible to restore *compassion* to our way of thinking and practice? Can *grace* reassert itself, not as a theological formula but as a way of living and relating to vulnerable ecosystems? How did it come to pass that so many who claim to believe in the Bible have a nihilistic attitude toward non-human creatures and the Earth and show so little willingness to reflect God's mercy? Jacques Derrida says that "war is waged over the matter of pity," and we are entering a critical phase.[59] Perhaps the absence of compassion is nowhere more seen than in the mass confinement of domestic animals for a meat industry that has ceased to treat the animal as a sentient creature. Matthew Scully, writing as a political conservative, dissects the detachment, the genetic manipulation, and the violation of the animal's instincts in one of the most searing books on the subject to date.[60] "Factory farming isn't just killing," he says. "It is negation, a complete denial of the animal as a living being with his or her own needs and nature. It is not the worst evil we can do, but it is the worst evil we can do to them."[61]

Slaughterhouse practices are similarly bereft of compassion. How can they be compassionate when the goal is to kill and process countless animals as cheaply as possible to enable a level of meat consumption that is unsustainable and contrary to nature? Timothy Pachirat went undercover in a slaughterhouse in Omaha, Nebraska, to study how the industry

56. Milgrom, "Leviticus 25," 32.

57. Brueggemann, *Land*, 60.

58. Brueggemann, *Sabbath as Resistance*, 43.

59. Derrida, *Animal*, 29.

60. Scully, *Dominion*.

61. Scully, *Dominion*, 289.

attempts to combine efficient killing with the least possible exposure to the cruelty even for the workers at the facility.[62] Would it help if slaughter-houses had glass walls? he asks.

An increasingly globalized food economy has disregard of compassion written on it. Raj Patel describes its *hourglass shape*, millions of producers at one end being squeezed (starved), millions of consumers at the other end being stuffed, with a few corporations at the narrow part of the hourglass controlling market access for the growers and product selection and quality for the consumer.[63] Such a system has little concern for ecological matters, whether as financial benefit to the producer or for the health of the consumer.

The apostle Paul exhorts believers in Rome to live "by the mercies of God" (Rom 12:1 ESV). I have elsewhere offered suggestions for how this might look in an ecological perspective—how to bring mercy back to the way we regard seeds, animals, and land.[64] In this, too, ecology brings a return to theology. Is not the economy of seeds in Genesis a reflection of God as a *giving* Person, a God of *grace*, which, when we peel away the doctrinal accretions, is just another word for *gift*? "Then God said, 'Let the land produce vegetation: seed-bearing plants and trees on the land that bear fruit with seed in it, according to their various kinds.' And it was so. The land produced vegetation: plants bearing seed according to their kinds and trees bearing fruit with seed in it according to their kinds. And God saw that it was good" (Gen 1:11–12; cf. 1:29).

"Seeds" are emblems of plenitude, renewal, and profusion. While we cannot have our cake and eat it too, with respect to many things in life, we can with respect to seeds. In the seeds of the plant we eat is the source of the new plant. Concealed from us, removed from the land as most of us now are, ecology is inscribed with theology, the story of God who gives and sustains, and who yearns for all creation to flourish.

## Closing Thoughts

Had I written this chapter another time, the emphasis would not be different, but the sense of urgency might have been less. COVID-19 is a before-and-after moment in history. It must be understood in ecological terms in its origin, transmission, and dissemination. It strikes the world at a time when

---

62. Pachirat, *Every Twelve Seconds*.
63. Patel, *Stuffed and Starved*.
64. Tonstad, *Letter to the Romans*, 286–308.

nations and cultures are intricately linked: a virus can travel in no time from Wuhan to Washington or Warsaw or Winnipeg. Is COVID-19 already "the Next Big One," the virus David Quammen prognosticated in his remarkable book in 2012? "Will the Next Big One be caused by a virus?" he asked. "Will the Next Big One come out of a rainforest or a market in southern China? Will the Next Big One kill 30 or 40 million people?"[65] Quammen even had the prescience to ask whether the Next Big One, when it comes, will have high infectivity preceding notable symptoms, thus helping it "to move through cities and airports like an angel of death."[66]

The question for the person in-the-know was *when*, not *if*. Quammen adds that the emerging viral pandemics "reflect things that we're *doing*, not just things that are *happening* to us."[67]

The temptation to call COVID-19 a *China* virus should be resisted, in part because the *spillover* of the virus from animals to humans is plausible for any country and in part because viruses are notoriously elusive and mobile. Stigmatizing the country of the origin of the human disease caused by the virus this way does not add to a nation's sense of virtue if that nation is guilty of treating domestic animals as badly or worse than pangolins are treated at the point of origin of SARS-CoV-2. While the virus has taken a greater toll on the elderly and most vulnerable in society, it has also taught a lesson in human terms. Can health care be differentiated and portioned out selectively, with an advantage for the more well-to-do, against a virus that is indiscriminate with respect to who it will infect? Will I be safe, ensconced within my bubble of privilege, if you, living outside the bubble, are not? I am asking this in awareness that the virus treats such bubbles as figments of the imagination.

Reactions to COVID-19 come from voices that see the problem mostly in utilitarian terms, stirred by the devastating consequences. Ecological theology, or theology-informed ecology, is not indifferent to consequences, but it is proactive in ways that reactions motivated by consequences cannot be. It knows that God in the beginning conferred on non-human creatures a blessing and the right to flourish in words quite like God's commission to human beings (Gen 1:20–22, 28–29). It knows that God places human beings in the Garden "to *serve* and *preserve*," as we ought to translate the commission in Genesis (Gen 2:15).[68] It knows from the very first pages of the Bible that theology is ecology and ecology, theology.

65. Quammen, *Spillover*, 42.

66. Quammen, *Spillover*, 208.

67. Quammen, *Spillover*, 515.

68. Sarna, *JPS Torah Commentary*, 20; Tonstad, *Letter to the Romans*, 301.

# Bibliography

"Baruch S. Blumberg: Biographical." *NobelPrize.org*, n.d. Online. https://www. nobelprize.org/prizes/medicine/1976/blumberg/biographical.

Bauckham, Richard. *The Bible and Ecology: Rediscovering the Community of Creation.* Waco: Baylor University Press, 2010.

———. *God and the Crisis of Freedom: Biblical and Contemporary Perspectives.* London: Westminster John Knox, 2002.

Berry, Wendell. *The Unsettling of America: Culture and Agriculture.* New York: Avon, 1977.

Brueggemann, Walter. *The Land: Place as Gift, Promise, and Challenge in Biblical Faith.* Minneapolis: Fortress, 2002.

———. *Sabbath as Resistance: Saying No to the Culture of Now.* Louisville: Westminster John Knox, 2014.

Cyranoski, David. "Did Pangolins Spread the China Coronavirus to People?" *Nature*, February 7, 2020. Online. https://www.nature.com/articles/d41586-020-00364-2.

Davis, Ellen F. *Scripture, Culture, and Agriculture: An Agrarian Reading of the Bible.* Cambridge: Cambridge University Press, 2009.

Derrida, Jacques. *The Animal That Therefore I Am.* Translated by David Wills. New York: Fordham University Press, 2008.

Frend, W. H. C. *The Rise of Christianity.* Philadelphia: Fortress, 1984.

Goode, Emilia. "A Struggle to Save the Scaly Pangolin." *New York Times*, March 31, 2015.

Greene-McCreight, Kathryn. "Restless Until We Rest in God: The Fourth Commandment as Test Case in Christian 'Plain Sense' Interpretation." In *The Ten Commandments: The Reciprocity of Faithfulness*, edited by William P. Brown, 223–36. Louisville: Westminster John Knox, 2004.

Habel, Norman C. *The Land Is Mine.* Minneapolis: Fortress, 1995.

Hays, Richard B. *The Faith of Jesus Christ: An Investigation of the Narrative Substructure of Galatians 3:1—4:11.* 1983. Reprint, Grand Rapids: Eerdmans, 2002.

Jacob, Edmond. *Theology of the Old Testament.* Translated by Arthur W. Heathcote and Philip J. Allcock. London: Hodder & Stoughton, 1971.

Leiss, William. *The Domination of Nature.* Montreal: McGill-Queens's University Press, 1994.

Leopold, Aldo. *A Sand County Almanac: With Essays on Conservation from Round River.* New York: Ballantine, 1970.

Mackenzie, John S., et al. "One Health: From Concept to Practice." In *Confronting Emerging Zoonoses: The One Health Paradigm*, edited by Akio Yamada, 163–89. Tokyo: Springer, 2014.

Mackenzie, John S., and Martyn Jeggo. "The One Health Approach—Why Is It So Important?" *Tropical Medicine and Infectious Disease* 4.2 (2019) 88. Online. https://www.mdpi.com/2414-6366/4/2/88/htm.

"Max Delbrück: Biographical." *NobelPrize.org*, n.d. Online. https://www.nobelprize. org/prizes/medicine/1969/delbruck/biographical.

"MERS Monthly Summary." *World Health Organization*, November 2019. Online. https://www.who.int/emergencies/mers-cov/en.

Milgrom, Jacob. "Leviticus 25 and Some Postulates of the Jubilee." In *The Jubilee Challenge: Utopia or Possibility? Jewish and Christian Insights,* edited by Hans Ucko, 28–32. Geneva: WCC, 1997.

"The Nobel Prize in Physiology or Medicine 2005." *NobelPrize.org,* n.d. Online. https://www.nobelprize.org/prizes/medicine/2005/7693-the-nobel-prize-in-physiology-or-medicine-2005-2005-6.

Origen. *On First Principles.* Translated by George W. Butterworth. London: Society for Promoting Christian Knowledge, 1936.

Pachirat, Timothy. *Every Twelve Seconds: Industrialized Slaughter and the Politics of Sight.* New Haven: Yale University Press, 2011.

Patel, Raj. *Stuffed and Starved: The Hidden Battle for the World Food System.* New York: Melville, 2012.

Porter, Roy. *Flesh in the Age of Reason: How the Enlightenment Transformed the Way We See Our Bodies and Our Souls.* London: Penguin, 2003.

Quammen, David. "Did Pangolin Trafficking Cause the Coronavirus Pandemic?" *New Yorker,* August 31, 2020.

———. *Spillover: Animal Infections and the Next Human Pandemic.* New York: Norton, 2012.

"Robert Koch: Facts." *NobelPrize.org,* n.d. Online. https://www.nobelprize.org/prizes/medicine/1905/koch/facts.

"Ronald Ross: Biographical." *NobelPrize.org,* n.d. Online. https://www.nobelprize.org/prizes/medicine/1902/ross/biographical.

Ryrie, Alec. *Protestants: The Radicals Who Made the Modern World.* London: William Collins, 2017.

Sarna, Nahum. *The JPS Torah Commentary on Genesis.* Philadelphia: JPS, 1989.

"SARS (Ten Years After)." *Centers for Disease Control and Prevention,* March 3, 2016. Online. https://www.cdc.gov/dotw/sars/index.html.

Scully, Matthew. *Dominion: The Power of Man, the Suffering of Animals, and the Call to Mercy.* New York: St. Martin's Griffin, 2003.

"Sir Alexander Fleming: Biographical." *NobelPrize.org,* n.d. Online. https://www.nobelprize.org/prizes/medicine/1945/fleming/biographical.

Shi, Zhengli, and Zhihong Hu. "A Review of Studies on Animal Reservoirs of the SARS Coronavirus." *PMC,* April 23, 2007. Online. https://www.ncbi.nlm.nih.gov/pmc/articles/PMC7114516.

Solzhenitsyn, Alexander. *A World Split Apart.* New York: Harper & Row, 1978.

Tonstad, Sigve K. *The Letter to the Romans: Paul among the Ecologists.* Earth Bible Commentary. Sheffield: Sheffield Phoenix, 2017.

———. *The Lost Meaning of the Seventh Day.* Berrien Springs, MI: Andrews University Press, 2009.

———. "Πίστις Χριστοῦ: Reading Paul in A New Paradigm." *Andrews University Seminary Studies* 40 (2002) 37–59.

"Update 49—SARS Case Fatality Ratio, Incubation Period." *World Health Organization,* May 7, 2003. Online. https://www.who.int/csr/sarsarchive/2003_05_07a/en.

Winter, Ralph D. "Twelve Frontiers of Perspective." In *Frontiers in Mission: Discovering and Surmounting Barriers to the Missio Dei,* edited by Ralph D. Winter, 28–39. 4th ed. Pasadena, CA: William Carey International University Press, 2008.

Ziegler, Philip. *The Black Death.* New York: Harper, 1971.

8 _____

# A Theology of Love in the First Epistle of John

—Lizette Acosta

On a National Day of Lament, on June 1, 2020, leaders from various faith groups gathered to remember the deaths of over one hundred thousand people in the US alone due to the coronavirus. COVID-19 has reminded us, in painful ways, of the effect of sin in our world and world systems. As the church seeks ways to respond to this crisis, the First Epistle of John offers a vital response: love, as the means to join God in promoting life and destroying the works of the devil (1 John 3:8). While the devil's works can be summarized as bringing death—both physical (resulting from disease or societal chaos) and spiritual (resulting from unbelief and sin)—the Son of God appeared to give life (4:9). The appearing of the Son of God resulted in works and characteristics that are the opposite of those associated with the works of the devil, thus nullifying or destroying them.

To understand how 1 John contributes toward a theology of disease, this chapter is organized as follows:

1. A description of the state of world systems vs. God's desire for the world

2. God's character as light and love

3. Implications for God's children whose lives must be grounded in imitation of God's character in promoting life and destroying the works of the devil

4. The way to sustain the outpouring of love, which is by abiding in God and walking in the light

5. A current example of love promoting life amidst the COVID-19 pandemic.

## World Systems vs. God's Desire for the World

The author of 1 John juxtaposes the present reality of the world (*kosmos*) with God's desire for the world and God's purpose in sending his unique Son into the world. The term *kosmos* is used twenty-three times in 1 John. Of these, several convey the corruption of the *kosmos* by human sin such as lust or pride, ignorance, hatred of the children of God, or by false prophets or antichrists (1 John 2:15–16; 3:1, 13; 4:1, 3). These descriptions can be summarized by the last occurrence: "the whole world is under the control of the evil one" (5:19). These negative statements about the world describe the condition of the world and world systems.

But these statements do not reflect the author's attitude *toward* the world. Positive statements about the world show God's concern to rescue the *kosmos*: Jesus died for the sake of the whole world (2:2); God showed his love for the world by sending his Son (4:9) to be the Savior of the world (4:14). From these uses of *kosmos* in 1 John, it is evident that the current state of the world is not God's intention for the world, and thus it is redeemable.

We find two other uses of *kosmos* in 1 John, which, in effect, stand between the current reality and God's desire for the world. These are the call for God's children to continue the work of Christ ("in this world we are like Jesus" [4:17]), and the assurance that this work will be completed ("Who is it that overcomes the world? Only the one who believes that Jesus is the Son of God" [5:5]). As Georg Strecker maintains, when we take the Son as our model, we must, "in the same way, actualize love in and for the world. . . . So it must be when the Christian community accepts its responsibility and understands its existence as *agape* in the world to be a binding obligation."[1]

Ultimately, the author of 1 John insists that God's desire for humanity in this world is life. "He sent his one and only Son into the world that we might live through him" (4:9; cf. John 10:10: "I have come that they may have life, and have it to the full.") Further we see that "the Son of God appeared . . . to destroy the devil's work" (1 John 3:8) which is contrary to life. Therefore, to join God in his work implies promoting life, which must include fighting disease.

---

1. Strecker, *Johannine Letters*, 166.

## God's Love and Ours

The primary motivation that propels us to join God in bringing about God's intention for the world is God's love *for* the world, for God *is* love (1 John 4:8, 16). God is the source and origin of love. Whether God is creating, ordering, guiding, judging, disciplining, or ruling—whatever God does, all God's activity is branded by his nature, which is love.

The evidence of love, both in God and in God's children, is through actions. It is not enough for the author to say that God is love, a truth he explicitly affirms twice (4:8, 16). God's love is not expressed in word or speech alone, but also in actions and in truth (3:18). Throughout 1 John, whenever God's love is mentioned, it is always accompanied by an action that demonstrates that love:

> "See what great love the Father has lavished on us, that we should be called children of God!" (3:1)

> "This is how we know what love is: Jesus Christ laid down his life for us. And we ought to lay down our lives for our brothers and sisters." (3:16)

> "God is love. This is how God showed his love among us: He sent his one and only Son into the world that we might live through him." (4:8, 9)

> "This is love: not that we loved God, but that he loved us and sent his Son as an atoning sacrifice for our sins." (4:10)

> "God is love. Whoever lives in love lives in God, and God in them." (4:16)

There is no mention of God's love in 1 John without a correlating deed to demonstrate that love. Moreover, God's loving activity always has the other as beneficiary. In 1 John 3:1, *we* are called children of God; in 1 John 3:16, he laid his life for *us*. In 1 John 4:9, 10, and 14, God sending the Son benefits us, and then extends to the world. Therefore, we who are God's children must express our love accordingly—in word and speech as well as in actions and in truth. Love encompasses the totality of how we are to live in the world.

## Imitation of God's Character

As has been hinted above, ethical behavior in 1 John is summarized in the call to be like Jesus/God. One way this is expressed is by the use of the adverb, *kathōs* (just as). Four of the occurrences of this term relate to being like Jesus:

> "Whoever claims to live in him must live *as* Jesus did." (2:6)

> "We know that when Christ appears, we shall be like him, for we shall see him as he is. All who have this hope in him purify themselves, *just as* he is pure." (3:2–3)

> "The one who does what is right is righteous, *just as* he is righteous." (3:7)

> "Herein is our love made perfect, that we may have boldness in the day of judgment: because *as* he is, so are we in this world." (4:17 KJV)

The author calls his readers to be in this world just as Jesus is. The implications of this last verse should not be lost, as the author raises the standard for living to the highest. His call to be like Christ sets an ideal toward which we strive even now and makes this imitation all-encompassing. All other Johannine uses of *kathōs* as imitation of Christ, converge in 1 John 4:17.

The ethical call to imitate God is also grounded in our identity as God's children. Since God is love (4:8), as God's children, we must not act contrary to the one from whom we come (3:1). Through the use of the verb *gennaō* (to give birth), the author establishes certain criteria that identify the ones born of God and the expectations (2:29; 3:9; 4:7; 5:1, 4, 18). In each of these occurrences, the one born of God reflects God's character. Everyone who proceeds from God carries God's seed of love (3:9). The statement "we are born of God," then, is a critical premise of this argument because the child should not act contrary to the parent. Therefore, our love as God's children ought to be in like manner as God's love for us. This claim carries colossal ethical expectations. God's love in action not only demands mutual love but also defines how we express that love, which necessarily includes the world.

## Abiding in God's Love and Light

The ethical call to love as God loves is humanly impossible apart from God's abiding presence. Only as we remain in God are we able to live out God's love in the world. For this reason, the verb *menō* ("I abide") is central to the Epistle. This term, in a sense, brings together other central themes in 1 John.[2] For example, in 1 John 2:6, the claim to abide (or "live" as in NIV) in God must be corroborated by the imitation of Jesus, to live as he did. In 1 John 2:10, to love is to abide or live in the light. In 1 John 4:15–16, the verb *menō* is used three times—the last uses of the verb in the Epistle. The author is emphatic about the inter-connectedness of abiding: Since God is love, to abide in love is to abide in God and for God to abide in us. Only by remaining in God can we imitate Jesus. In and of ourselves, we lack the power to do so. Moreover, the Spirit of God enables us to abide:

> "This is how we know that he lives [abides] in us: We know it by
> the Spirit he gave us" (3:24).

> "This is how we know that we live [abide] in him and he in us:
> He has given us of his Spirit" (4:13).

In general, abiding is not passive; it is not merely remaining or being still. Mutual indwelling manifests in tangible ways. For this reason, the author can speak of the evidence of abiding which is a life modeled after Christ's own life. At the heart of abiding in God is a complete dependence and trust in God to do in and through us what only God can do.[3]

Abiding or living in God's love is connected to the important theme of light's effect on darkness. In 1 John 2:8, in reference to the love-command, the passive voice of the verb *paragetai* (darkness is being "taken away"[4]) in connection with "the true light is already shining" (2:8), emphasizes the light's capacity to overcome the darkness (cf. John 1:5: "in [God] there is no darkness at all"). The fact that light is already shining is likely a reference to

---

2. For this reason, Peter Rhea Jones describes the verb as "the presiding metaphor," that is, "the master image that dominates a work," by which other key concepts are presented (Jones, "Presiding Metaphor," 181).

3. Editors' Note: Mutual indwelling is like the "exchanged life" discovered by Hudson Taylor, founder of China Inland Mission. He described moving from imitation ("I follow at such a distance and learn so slowly to imitate my precious Master") to "No longer I": "There was no thought of imitation now! It was in blessed reality 'Christ lives in me.' And how great the difference! Instead of bondage, liberty; instead of failure, quiet victories within; instead of fear and weakness, a restful sense of sufficiency in Another" (Taylor, *Spiritual Secret*, 159).

4. Wahlde, *Gospel and Letters of John*, 68.

Jesus' life on Earth, which inaugurated God's kingdom on earth.[5] In God's light and love, the light "which is Christ, scatters the darkness of sin and all the powers opposed to God which lurk behind it."[6]

The means by which we join the Son of God in promoting life and destroying the works of the devil is love. Some may find the lack of specificity frustrating and may wish for more of an applied approach to ethics and engaging the world's problems; a list of do's and don'ts. Yet the Johannine authors refuse to narrow the love command except to add that it must be "in actions and in truth" (1 John 3:18) and must be not only modeled after Christ's own life, but actually the work of Christ indwelling in the believer.

## Conclusion

Shining the light of Christ dispels the darkness of the evil one. I conclude with a story by CNN from the hospital where I work as a chaplain where a housekeeper sought to put the love command into practice. Her job technically had nothing to do with patient health. She was only responsible for keeping the rooms of COVID-19 patients free of harmful germs. But she could see that one of the patients, whose room she cleaned each day, was losing the battle against the disease. Not allowed to have visitors to encourage him in his severe, unrelenting pain, he had accepted last rites from a Catholic priest and remotely said goodbye to his family. She began to talk with him while she cleaned, and he began looking forward to those short conversations. The results were life-giving, as the COVID-19 patient expressed: "She was saving my life." All she had sought to do was treat the patient with kindness and compassion as she "put everything in God's hands."[7]

This story illustrates that any follower of Jesus can contribute toward nullifying the works of the devil in the realm of disease. While researchers, doctors, and nurses are the most visible actors in the battle against disease, those without formal training can also contribute substantially. Despite the personal risk, when someone shares love out of their connection to God's love, when their presence expresses the very presence of Christ, they can encourage a sick person's will to live with the result of victory over the evil one's influence toward death. The light of life dispels the darkness of death.

---

5. Note the use of "light" in John 12:35–36, as an indirect reference to Jesus' life on earth.

6. Schnackenburg, *Johannine Epistles*, 106.

7. Burke, "He Was a Covid-19 Patient."

## Bibliography

Burke, Daniel. "He Was a Covid-19 Patient. She Cleaned His Hospital Room. Their Unexpected Bond Saved His Life." *CNN Health*, June 11, 2020. Online. https://www.cnn.com/2020/06/11/health/orlando-hospital-coronavirus-patient-housekeeper-wellness/index.html.

Jones, Peter Rhea. "A Structural Analysis of 1 John." *Review and Expositor* 67 (1970) 433–44.

Schnackenburg, Rudolf. *The Johannine Epistles: Introduction and Commentary.* Translated by Reginald and Ilse Fuller. New York: Crossroad, 1992.

Strecker, Georg. *The Johannine Letters.* Translated by Linda M. Maloney. Minneapolis: Fortress, 1996.

Taylor, Howard, and Geraldine Taylor. *Hudson Taylor's Spiritual Secret.* Chicago: Moody, 2009.

Wahlde, Urban von. *The Gospel and Letters of John.* Grand Rapids: Eerdmans, 2010.

9

# Health and Disease

*Why Mercy and Compassion Matter*

—KEITH SO

## Introduction

THE FOCUS OF THIS chapter is to show that mercy, compassion, and advocating for those who are marginalized should be an essential attitude displayed by the church, and a basis for a theology of disease. The Democratic People's Republic of Korea (DPRK), also known as North Korea—a restricted-access, impoverished country of 25.5 million people—will serve as an example.

There has often been a judgmental attitude towards the DPRK. Such a bias has led to organizations calling out the country for human rights abuses, including accusing the country's government of neglecting the needs of its people[1] and even persecuting Christian believers.[2] There is also extreme prejudice against the country. Pew Research Center states that "Overall, 78 percent of Americans have an unfavorable view of the communist nation ruled by Kim Jong Un, with 61 percent holding a *very* unfavorable opinion."[3]

However, there is another perspective needed, especially from followers of Christ. This perspective, which must include an attitude of mercy and compassion toward the people, starts with learning and a deeper understanding of the situation in the DPRK. This is especially true in regards to public health issues. When believers understand more about the health

1. "North Korea: Events of 2018."
2. "1. North Korea."
3. Poushter, "Americans Hold Very Negative Views of North Korea."

and disease status of the country, they can be more informed about what it means to show mercy and compassion toward the people, demonstrating God's love and kingdom purposes.

## Historical Background

A little history about the Democratic People's Republic of Korea (DPRK) will help better understand why mercy and compassion are important attitudes to have in approaching the people of this country.

The first ruler of the DPRK, Kim Il-Sung (1912–1994), founded the country in September of 1948 as a response to the founding of the Republic of Korea (ROK, also known as South Korea) in May of 1948. Both nations declared sovereignty over all of the Korean peninsula, and grew antagonistic toward each other. With the backing of post-WWII powers, the ROK having the support of the US, and the DPRK having the backing of Russia, the Korean War broke out in 1950, until a stalemate in 1953. North Korea was devastated by the war with deaths of an estimated 10 percent of the population (four hundred thousand military personnel and six hundred thousand civilians[4] out of a total population of about ten million in 1950[5]). From a biblical perspective, this is precisely what Jesus prophesied as far as nations rising against nations (Matt 24:7). The people suffered as a result of these opposing powers.

After the war, under the strong leadership of Kim Il-Sung, and with the aid of its communist allies (Russia and China), the DPRK achieved rapid restoration and economic development through the 1950s. However, in the 1960s, things began to change in the DPRK. Kim Il-Sung shifted his strategy to establishing an independent version of government. He called it *woori-shik* 우리식 ("our way") of socialism. He did not want other nations to interfere in domestic matters anymore, and began to emphasize "independence" and "self-reliance."

Since the 1960s, an ideology called *Juche* 주체 ("self-reliance") has been taught to the people, starting from childhood. This indoctrinates the people into the belief in "national self-reliance and submission to the leader, that permeates North Korean culture."[6] The official webpage of the country states, "The *Juche* idea means, in a nutshell, that the masters of the revolution and construction are the masses of the people and that

---

4. "Korean War Fast Facts."

5. DESA, *World Population Prospects 2019*.

6. Holmes and Hong, "Contextualization of the Gospel," loc. 3759–61.

they are also the motive force of the revolution and construction."[7] This attitude of self-sufficiency is based on atheistic and materialist ideologies and isolationism and conflicts with biblical values such as trust in God (Prov 3:5–6) and relying on God alone (2 Cor 3:5; 12:9). The result of this deliberate rejection of God's ways is evident in the poor living standards and health of much of the country.

The communist basis of *Juche* became intertwined with a strong emphasis on Kim Il-Sung's personality. In 1977, *Juche* replaced Marxism in the DPRK constitution. There was a sense that the founder of this nation was becoming a god, "sent from heaven," as he was being addressed in the annals of their history books as "the Great Leader." In addition, his son Kim Jong-Il, who succeeded him in power in 1994, was addressed as "the Dear Leader." Citizens were expected to bow before statues and portraits of these leaders. Then, at the end of 2011, when Kim Jong-Il passed away, his son Kim Jong-un succeeded him as the "Supreme Leader."[8] To this very day (2021) he has served as the unchallenged leader of the country, and its global isolation based on *woori-shik* ("our way") and *Juche* ("self-reliance") continue. The lessons in biblical history about Nebuchadnezzar, the Pharaohs, Darius, and Caesar setting themselves up as gods are instructive about the devastating fallout of such pretension.

## Health and Disease in the DPRK

The conditions of health and disease in the DPRK can be better understood through outcomes that have been measured to some degree over time through a variety of reports. Many of these reports come from a combination of sources, from both the global health community such as the World Health Organization (WHO) and from the country's Ministry of Public Health (MoPH).

### *Lower Life Expectancies and Higher Mortality Rates*

In the early 1950s, during the time of the Korean War conflict, life expectancy was at an all-time low of about thirty-three years for men and forty-four years for women.[9] This was due to the devastating war, which included thousands of civilian casualties. Over time, life expectancies have

7. "*Juche* Ideology."
8. "Kim Jong-Un."
9. DESA, *World Population Prospects 2019.*

improved, so that these numbers have increased to about sixty-eight years for men and seventy-six years for women as of 2019. In contrast, their counterparts in the Republic of Korea (ROK), also known as South Korea, have an average life expectancy of ten years higher (seventy-nine years for men and eighty-six years for women).[10]

In order to measure the health outcomes of women and children in a country, some understanding of epidemiology is needed. The infant mortality rate (IMR) is the number of deaths at or under the age of one year for every one thousand live births. The under-five mortality rate (U5MR) is the number of deaths under age five years for every one thousand live births. And the number of maternal deaths per hundred thousand live births is known as the maternal mortality ratio, or MMR. In the DPRK the IMR was fourteen, the U5MR was eighteen in the year 2018, and the MMR was eighty-nine in 2017, according to the World Bank. In contrast, in the ROK (South Korea), the IMR and the U5MR were only three in 2018, and the MMR was only eleven in 2017. Such a difference makes it clear that, within the same people-group, if one is born or is pregnant in North Korea, the chances of survival are much less than in South Korea.[11]

## Malnutrition

The DPRK has also been consistently struggling with enough food for its people going as far back as the famine in the 1990s. Within the past thirty years, out of the current population of about twenty-six million,[12] up to two million people have died from starvation.[13] And this has been an ongoing problem for decades. According to the UN, in 2019, 40 percent of the population was in "urgent need of food aid."[14]

## Declining Conditions in Water, Sanitation, and Hygiene

In addition, there is the issue of an inadequate supply of clean water and sanitation, which are vital for the survival and development of children. UNICEF points out that "lack of access to safe drinking water and

10. "Country Comparison, GDP."
11. "Maternal Mortality Ratio"; "Mortality Rate, Infant"; "Mortality Rate, Under-5."
12. "North Korea Population (Live)."
13. Chisholm, "Food Insecurity of North Korea."
14. Sang-Hun, "North Korea Urgently Needs Food Aid."

adequate sanitation contributes to a higher incidence of diarrhoea, respiratory tract infections, and waterborne diseases."[15] However, in 2017, only 61 percent of North Korean households had access to safe water, and were under pressure to use fecal matter for fertilizer which "leads to widespread and unsafe handling of excreta in agriculture."[16]

## Disease in the DPRK

There has been much uncertainty over the actual incidence of diseases in the DPRK. Unfortunately, due to a lack of diagnostic resources, especially in the 2000s, documentation through epidemiological data has been scant. Over time, more data have been reported, despite the gaps in the public health literature.[17] An examination of the availability of essential medicines and technologies reveals a serious deficiency in the DPRK. Essential medicines are defined by the WHO as aspirin, statins, angiotensin-converting enzyme inhibitors, thiazide diuretics, long-acting calcium-channel blockers, beta-blockers, insulin, metformin, bronchodilators, and steroid inhalants. Basic technologies include blood pressure measurement devices, weighing scales, height measuring equipment, blood sugar and blood cholesterol measurement devices with strips, and urine strips for albumin assay. The DPRK has only five out of ten essential medicines and only three out of six basic technologies.[18]

### COMMUNICABLE DISEASES

Diseases related to inadequate clean water and sanitation have led to a rise in communicable diseases such as diarrhea. Tuberculosis is one illness whose numbers have been recorded in DPRK and that has therefore drawn the attention of the outside world. According to the World Health Organization (WHO), there were more than one hundred twenty thousand notified cases of tuberculosis in each of the years, 2015 and 2016.[19] An increasing number of these cases were multi-drug resistant, meaning that the mycobacterium tuberculosis organism was resistant to more than one drug. According to

15. "Water, Sanitation & Hygiene."
16. "Water, Sanitation & Hygiene."
17. Park et al., "Systematic Review," 1.
18. WHO, *Noncommunicable Diseases.*
19. Bhatia, "rGLC Country Support Mission Report," 4.

one study, more than 75 percent of the cases were identified as multi-drug resistant,[20] making treatment and control an increasing challenge.

Another major disease, malaria, is indigenous to the Korean peninsula. In the DPRK, malaria was eradicated in the 1970s but in 1997 a malaria epidemic emerged, reaching as many as three hundred thousand cases in 2001. The incidence has been declining since then, but due to missing statistics, "the exact size of the malaria epidemic in North Korea could have been underestimated."[21]

Uncertainty also exists about the presence of HIV. One author noted that there were more than eighty-three thousand cases of HIV in DPRK in 2018 in spite of the government's claim that HIV was not present.[22] But in 2019 the country officially recognized the problem, and its Ministry of Public Health (MoPH) created a National HIV/AIDS Program.[23]

NONCOMMUNICABLE DISEASES

Noncommunicable diseases (NCDs)—cardiovascular and cerebrovascular diseases, hypertension, diabetes, cancers, and respiratory illnesses—are on the rise. In fact, the WHO named NCDs to be the biggest killers of people in 2018, with low income countries (such as DPRK) having the largest number of global NCD deaths.[24] The World Health Organization states, "The rise of NCDs has been driven by primarily four major risk factors: tobacco use, physical inactivity, the harmful use of alcohol, and unhealthy diets."[25]

## The Biblical Value of Mercy and Compassion

In light of these health problems and resource disparities in the DPRK, can the global church have a heart of compassion for a country that is struggling with less capability to care for its own people? Where do we begin to address these problems with mercy and compassion toward those people-groups beset by intractable afflictions?

Throughout the Old Testament, mercy and compassion are displayed as part of God's attributes. For the people of Israel, led by Moses

20. Jung et al., "Characteristics," 1105.

21. Kim et al., "Malaria Incidence."

22. Mole, "North Korea Reveals Explosive HIV Outbreak."

23. "World AIDS Day 2019."

24. "Top Ten Causes of Death."

25. WHO, *Noncommunicable Diseases.*

in Exodus 34:6–7, God was "the compassionate and gracious God, slow to anger, abounding in love and faithfulness, maintaining love to thousands, and forgiving wickedness." Christians recognize that part of the purpose of God's mercy was so that God's people might appreciate his grace and repent of their sin, transforming their societies, and expressing mercy and compassion toward others—including the foreigner (Exod 23:9). According to Miles Van Pelt, "God's merciful character is translated into hope for sinners, and this is, without a doubt, the most important application of God's compassionate character."[26]

The prophets in the Old Testament also called for mercy. Micah warned the people of Israel to "act justly and love mercy" on behalf of those in need of it (Mic 6:8). "This is what the LORD Almighty said: 'Administer true justice; show mercy and compassion to one another. Do not oppress the widow or the fatherless, the foreigner or the poor. Do not plot evil against each other'" (Zech 7:9–10). Likewise, the Psalms show that the Lord works righteousness and justice for all the oppressed (Ps 103:6), and that God is a refuge for them in times of trouble (Ps 9:9).

In the New Testament, we see the ultimate embodiment of compassion through Christ. Jesus had compassion on the crowds who followed him (Matt 14:14; Mark 8:2–9) because they were "harassed and helpless, like sheep without a shepherd" (Matt 9:36). His compassion extended to the hungry (Mark 8:2), the sick (Matt 14:14), the foreigner (John 4; Luke 7:1–10), and the oppressed (Luke 4:18). In the Parable of the Prodigal Son, we see that just as the waiting father felt compassion and ran to embrace his lost son, God has compassion on people and accepts them when they leave their idolatry and seek a restored relationship with the Father.

## The Need for Mercy and Compassion in the DPRK

When followers of Christ view a country like the DPRK, do we see a country of oppressors or a country of the oppressed? Do we see a country whose iniquities and transgressions need to be forgiven, as we have been forgiven? Is not the church to act justly and love mercy? Is not the church to be an advocate especially to those who are hungry and sick, even if they live in other countries? Does not the global church desire to be merciful and compassionate to the people of a country whose ideologies and systems are oppressive and in need of repentance?

---

26. VanPelt, "Old Testament God of Compassion."

The country of the DPRK is one of the most impoverished nations in the world. According to the CIA, the DPRK ranks 215 out of 229 countries in terms of gross domestic product per capita.[27] Humanitarian organizations partner each year to meet some of the most urgent needs for food security and sanitation. However, the UN reports that "increased funding is needed to make a sustainable impact on the lives of the most vulnerable people in the country."[28]

Furthermore, Dr. Kee B. Park, a physician who has traveled into the country numerous times for humanitarian work, argues that, compared to other less impoverished nations, in terms of per capita GDP, the DPRK has received proportionally much less funding from the USAID office than countries like Afghanistan, Ethiopia, Syria, Kenya, and Pakistan.[29]

## Response by the Global Church

In response to these global disparities and unmet needs, how can the church respond? The DPRK is an example of what happens to a people when their leaders reject the principles God gave the Israelites for sanitation, food security, and treatment of others. God gave these principles in the Pentateuch to help people avoid consequences of the evil one's corruption of nature. God's people have a responsibility to bring the light of the gospel into dark places like the DPRK where God's Word is largely unknown or rejected.

### Willingness to Understand the People and Their Culture

DPRK is one of the most misunderstood nations of the world.[30] The Western world, in general, does not see North Koreans as people like ourselves. Instead, we tend to view them as the enemy and maintain the sort of confrontational stance that our country's politics exhibit. But God's people must make an effort to transcend political conflicts and seek to understand people who are different from themselves, especially those who are captive to evil powers and their destructive effects. It is crucial to realize that as we are crossing cultures we need to humbly learn about the culture, especially through the

27. "Country Comparison, GDP."
28. OCHA, DPR Korea.
29. Park and Kim, "Rebuttal to Mr. Katzeff Silberstein."
30. Spodek, Understanding North Korea.

lens of Scripture, and see where God is already at work.[31] Even for health care professionals who bring expertise, skills, and abilities to treat disease, it does not necessarily give them license to enter a country like the DPRK without an understanding of the culture and existing health systems. For example, in the DPRK, physicians are trained through two different philosophies: modern Western medical science (anatomy, physiology, biochemistry, etc.) and traditional medicine which includes the ancient *Koryo* system that makes use of domestic medicinal plants and acupuncture.[32]

Dr. Stephen Yoon, an American who lived in North Korea with his family for ten years, learned the North Korean medical culture, in a way that many in the Western world would have questioned, by earning a PhD from the Pyongyang Medical College of North Korea. His degree gave him entrance into people's hearts in the capital of the country, and paved the way for opportunities for ministry. His wife's book, *Discovering Joy: Ten Years in North Korea*, gives a marvelous glimpse of the culture of the DPRK.[33] The Yoons were willing to give up their comfortable life in America and dedicate themselves to living in this foreign country which has such great needs. Just as Christ humbled himself and took on the nature of a human servant (Phil 2:7–8), the Yoons laid aside their life of privilege and their cultural biases, and spent years learning the language and culture of the people of the DPRK. Because of this sacrificial attitude of learning, they were able to bridge differences, at great cost, in order to build trust in relationships.

## Advocating for the Marginalized through Prayer

God's people are called to "speak up for those who cannot speak for themselves, for the rights of all who are destitute. Speak up and judge fairly; defend the rights of the poor and needy" (Prov 31:8–9). As Christians, we can maintain an attitude of prayer for the people of the DPRK who are oppressed by their government and other principalities and powers. Even without a loud voice, we have the "confidence . . . that if we ask anything according to his will, he hears us" (1 John 5:14). This confidence leads us to trust that praying for the people of DPRK is a powerful form of advocacy. There are prayer networks around the world that believers can join and participate in to lift up the people of DPRK, including praying for their public health issues.[34]

31. Newell, *Crossing Cultures in Scripture*.
32. Sop, "*Koryo* System of Medicine in DPR Korea," 69, 72.
33. Yoon, *Discovering Joy*.
34. "Prayer."

## Meeting the Most Pressing Basic Needs

In the DPRK, ever since the famine in the 1990s, millions have been affected by inadequate food supply and chronic malnutrition. However, just as Christ's ministry was marked by "healing every disease and sickness among the people" (Matt 4:23), Christian organizations have been at the forefront of addressing the basic issues of hunger and disease in the DPRK. For instance, the Quaker-affiliated American Friends Services Committee has been involved in North Korea since the days of the famine through an agricultural development program.[35] Since 2010, the Eugene Bell Foundation has been using modern diagnostic tools to detect drug resistance against tuberculosis (TB). Christian Friends of Korea (CFK) has worked with local government health officials to create the first national TB Reference Laboratory. Such a lab allows specimens from patients to be tested for drugs that can treat TB.[36] Due to contributions from the Eugene Bell Foundation, patients with multi-drug resistant TB were able to receive the necessary treatment and supportive care to be cured.[37] Due to this and other initiatives, the prevalence of TB dropped from one hundred twenty thousand in 2015 to less than one hundred eight thousand in 2017.[38] In addition, World Vision has been working in the country since 2007, addressing the needs for clean water, nutrition, and disaster relief.[39] More recently, the Ignis Community has started a spine rehabilitation facility in Pyongyang, the capital city of DPRK, in reaching out to children with special needs, including cerebral palsy. This was accomplished despite the numerous barriers to providing funds and supplies for building and maintaining the facility.[40]

## Health Related Work and the Gospel

While our goal, as believers, and especially as health care professionals, is to align with God's work of healing, we must accept the limitations of even our greatest labors. We realize that this world is fallen, corrupted, disordered, and can only be redeemed by our loving Savior's work on the cross, who came to set the oppressed free (Luke 4:18). We have faith in God's process

35. "Strawberries in Winter."
36. "CFK Team Completes Fall 2019 Visit"; "What We Do."
37. Seung and Linton, "Growing Problem."
38. Bhatia, "rGLC Country Support Mission Report," 4.
39. "Randall Spadoni."
40. "Pyongyang Spine Rehabilitation Center."

of reconciling all things to himself (Col 1:20) through God's people. For example, an American physician who has traveled into the country to see patients with hepatitis B has found that many of these patients have advanced cirrhosis which could have been prevented with vaccination against hepatitis B or antiviral treatments against the infection. However, as this doctor lamented, because of the limited resources he could only be comforted by the words of Scripture, "Many are the plans in the mind of a man, but it is the purpose of the LORD that will stand" (Prov 19:21 ESV).[41] It is through painful situations like these, where we are not being able to cure diseases leading to premature death, that we can help people trust in the sovereignty of God in all things and share the hope of abundant life and eternal life that is found in Jesus Christ.

## The Strategic Value in Being a Restorer

Scott Moreau proposes six different possible roles that a person can take in presenting the gospel to people who have not experienced it: Facilitator, Guide, Herald, Pathfinder, Prophet, and Restorer. Of these six, Holmes and Hong believe that the Restorer can be the most effective role to use in contextualizing the gospel for North Koreans.[42]

> The Restorer comes to heal or deliver people from bondage of any type. For an individual, this may involve psychological, physical, or spiritual healing. On behalf of a group, it may involve social, systemic, or environmental restoration. Whereas the prophet denounces or discerns what is under the surface and exposes it, the restorer attends to the needed healing or restoration.[43]

Perhaps this is where Christian health care workers can make a difference within a culture of disbelief in the metaphysical and with high levels of human affliction. Christian health care workers understand and practice physical healing (through the traditional disciplines of Western medicine), psychological healing (through the disciplines of behavioral and mental health), and social healing (through addressing the social determinants of public health). In addressing physical, psychological, and social aspects of disease through healing, we can meet the deep spiritual needs of the people and build bridges of understanding in the *Juche* cultural context for spiritual healing and liberation. Biblical concepts of Jesus as advocate and

41. "CFK Team Completes Fall 2019 Visit."
42. Holmes and Hong, "Contextualization of the Gospel," loc. 3685.
43. Moreau, *Contextualization*, 299.

defender against demonic accusation, the required penal substitutionary atonement, and God as Supreme Father have been proposed as keys for bridge-building in DRPK.[44] Other approaches might include a celebration of the uniqueness of Korean culture and expanding that nationalistic identity to be incorporated into the global multi-ethnic covenant identity of the church. Seeing God as healer and reliable provider could perhaps awaken those experiencing disease-riddled pain to a dissatisfaction with the deception and empty promises of the Kim dynasty (as well as with the limitations of the secular international aid community).

## Conclusion: Hope for North Korea

We thank the Lord for organizations and individuals who are compassionately laboring for and advocating for the marginalized and oppressed people of the DPRK. They are seeking justice and defending the oppressed (Isa 1:17), and have been sent by God (Isa 6:8) into this country of such great need as a testimony to the God who heals. The structures of a *Juche* culture of self-reliance, corrupted power at the government level, communist ideologies, despotism, suppression of free speech, religious persecution, isolationism, and human rights abuses have significant effects on human health. International economic sanctions and prejudicial programs for aid because of opposition to the regime have also affected the economic stability and, in turn, the health status of the people. While the "principalities and powers" behind these practices are difficult to define, it is clear that, as in every other country in the world, human-centered cultural practices, power structures, and materialist ideologies that are antithetical to biblical revelation of our merciful and compassionate God, restrain human flourishing.

Christians and faith-based organizations, through their mercy ministries and advocacy, are courageously addressing physical and spiritual needs. Some are refurbishing hospitals and clinics. Others are bringing in sorely needed medicines and medical equipment. Some have focused on bringing in food to those who most need it, and offering other essential relief services. Courageous Christians are needed who actuate the mercy and compassion of God, seeing the people as harassed and helpless, like sheep without a shepherd, but also precious people with redeeming qualities as image-bearers. Aid workers, development specialists, church planters, and health care professionals, have a great opportunity to participate with the many committed believers within the country in offering help as part of the

---

44. Holmes and Hong, "Contextualization of the Gospel," loc. 3699.

wholistic message of the gospel to the people of the DPRK. This would be a prime opportunity to show the value of the Lausanne Covenant's article 5 on Christian social responsibility:

> We affirm that God is both the Creator and the Judge of all men.
> . . . Because men and women are made in the image of God,
> every person, regardless of race, religion, color, culture, class,
> sex, or age, has an intrinsic dignity because of which he or she
> should be respected and served, not exploited. Here too we ex-
> press penitence both for our neglect and for having sometimes
> regarded evangelism and social concern as mutually exclusive.
> Although reconciliation with other people is not reconcilia-
> tion with God, nor is social action evangelism, nor is political
> liberation salvation, nevertheless we affirm that evangelism
> and socio-political involvement are both part of our Christian
> duty. For both are necessary expressions of our doctrines of
> God and Man, our love for our neighbor and our obedience to
> Jesus Christ. The message of salvation implies also a message
> of judgment upon every form of alienation, oppression, and
> discrimination, and we should not be afraid to denounce evil
> and injustice wherever they exist. . . . The salvation we claim
> should be transforming us in the totality of our personal and
> social responsibilities. Faith without works is dead.[45]

Let us be called to our duty to share the gospel (evangelism) and actuate social concern as part of our full and effective witness to the people
of DPRK, who, in many ways, are held captive in an oppressive system,
but who retain deep longings for well-being and can experience liberation
and healing.

## Bibliography

"1. North Korea." *Open Doors*, n.d. Online. https://www.opendoorsusa.org/christian-persecution/world-watch-list/north-korea.

Bhatia, Vineet. "rGLC Country Support Mission Report: Democratic People's Republic of Korea." *World Health Organization*, October 23–30, 2018. Online. https://www.who.int/docs/default-source/searo/tuberculosis/pmdt-report-dprk-2018.pdf?sfvrsn=40806ddf_2.

"CFK Team Completes Fall 2019 Visit to DPRK." *Christian Friends of Korea*, Winter 2019. Online. https://static1.squarespace.com/static/57912287e58c628876d9e31d/t/5d e7fb0f6509bf0b18ae93a1/1575484185113/2019+Winter+Newsletter.pdf.

45. "Lausanne Covenant."

Chisholm, Paul. "The Food Insecurity Of North Korea." *NPR*, June 19, 2018. Online. https://www.npr.org/sections/goatsandsoda/2018/06/19/620484758/the-food-insecurity-of-north-korea.

"Country Comparison, GDP." *CIA World Factbook*, n.d. Online. https://www.cia.gov/the-world-factbook/field/gdp-per-capita-ppp/country-comparison.

Department of Economic and Social Affairs (DESA), United Nations. *World Population Prospects 2019*. New York: United Nations, 2019. Online. https://population.un.org/wpp/Publications/Files/WPP2019_Highlights.pdf.

"History." *Eugene Bell Foundation*, n.d. Online. https://www.eugene-bell.org/our-story/history.

Holmes, Robert, and Eunice Hong. "Contextualization of the Gospel for North Korean Ideology: Engaging with North Korean Refugees." In *Practicing Hope: Missions and Global Crises*, edited by Jerry M. Ireland and Michelle L. K. Raven, loc. 3759–61. Kindle ed. Pasadena, CA: William Carey Publishing, 2020.

"*Juche* Ideology." *The Democratic People's Republic of Korea*, 2011. Online. https://www.korea-dpr.com/juche_ideology.html.

Jung, Jihee, et al. "Characteristics of Drug Resistant Tuberculosis in Sanatoria of North Korea." *Journal of Korean Medical Science* 32 (2017) 1105–10. Online. https://doi.org/10.3346/jkms.2017.32.7.1105.

Kim, Jong-Hun, et al. "Malaria Incidence of the Regions Adjacent to the Demilitarized Zone in the Democratic People's Republic of Korea, 2004–2016." *Journal of Korean Medical Science* 34 (2019). Online. https://www.ncbi.nlm.nih.gov/pmc/articles/PMC6753370.

"Kim Jong-Un Biography." *Biography*, April 2, 2014. Revised August 21, 2020. Online. https://www.biography.com/dictator/kim-jong-un.

"Korean War Fast Facts." *CNN*, December 8, 2020. Online. https://www.cnn.com/2013/06/28/world/asia/korean-war-fast-facts/index.html.

"The Lausanne Covenant, Section 5: Christian Social Responsibility." *Lausanne Movement*. Online. https://www.lausanne.org/content/covenant/lausanne-covenant#cov.

"Maternal Mortality Ratio, Modeled Estimate (Per 100,000 Live Births)." World Bank, n.d. Online. https://data.worldbank.org/indicator/sh.sta.mmrt.

Mole, Beth. "North Korea Reveals Explosive HIV Outbreak—After Claiming to Be Disease-Free." *ArsTechnica*, June 25, 2019. Online. https://arstechnica.com/science/2019/06/north-korea-reveals-explosive-hiv-outbreak-after-claiming-to-be-disease-free.

Moreau, A. Scott. *Contextualization in World Missions: Mapping and Assessing Evangelical Models*. Grand Rapids: Kregel, 2012.

"Mortality Rate, Infant (Per 1,000 Live Births)." *World Bank*, n.d. Online. https://data.worldbank.org/indicator/sp.dyn.imrt.in.

"Mortality Rate, Under-Five (Per 1,000 Live Births)." *World Bank*, n.d. Online. https://data.worldbank.org/indicator/sh.dyn.mort.

Newell, Marvin. *Crossing Cultures in Scripture: Biblical Principles for Mission Practice*. Downers Grove, IL: InterVarsity, 2016.

"North Korea: Events of 2018." *Human Rights Watch*, n.d. Online. https://www.hrw.org/world-report/2019/country-chapters/north-korea.

"North Korea Population (Live)." *Worldometer*, July 21, 2020. Online. https://www.worldometers.info/world-population/north-korea-population.

Office for the Coordination of Humanitarian Affairs (OCHA), United Nations. *DPR Korea: Needs and Priorities 2020*. New York: United Nations, 2020. Online. https://reliefweb.int/sites/reliefweb.int/files/resources/2020_DPRK_Needs_and-Priorities_Plan.pdf.

Park, J. J., et al. "Systematic Review of Evidence on Public Health in the Democratic People's Republic of Korea." *BMJ Global Health*, March 9, 2019. Online. https://gh.bmj.com/content/4/2/e001133.

Park, Kee B., and Eliana E. Kim. "Rebuttal to Mr. Katzeff Silberstein." *38 North*, December 19, 2018. Online. https://www.38north.org/2018/12/kparkekim121918.

Poushter, Jacob. "Americans Hold Very Negative Views of North Korea Amid Nuclear Tensions." *Pew Research Center*, April 5, 2017. Online. https://www.pewresearch.org/fact-tank/2017/04/05/americans-hold-very-negative-views-of-north-korea-amid-nuclear-tensions.

"Prayer: Moving Forward on Our Knees." *REAH International*, n.d. Online. https://www.reah.org/get-involved/prayer.

"Pyongyang Spine Rehabilitation Center." *Ignis Community*, n.d. Online. https://igniscommunity.org/pysrc.

"Randall Spadoni." *The National Committee of North Korea*, n.d. Online. https://www.ncnk.org/member-directory/randall-spadoni.

Sang-Hun, Choe. "North Korea Urgently Needs Food Aid after Worst Harvest in Decade, UN Says." *New York Times*, May 3, 2019. Online. https://www.nytimes.com/2019/05/03/world/asia/north-korea-food.html.

Seung, Kwonjune J., and Stephen W. Linton. "The Growing Problem of Multidrug-Resistant Tuberculosis in North Korea." *PLOS Medicine* 10.7 (2013). Online. https://pubmed.ncbi.nlm.nih.gov/23935457.

Sop, Choe Thea. "*Koryo* System of Medicine in DPR Korea." In *Traditional Medicine in Asia*, edited by Ranjit Roy Chaudhury and Uton Muchtar Rafei, 69–74. New Delhi: World Health Organization, 2001.

Spodek, Joshua. *Understanding North Korea: Demystifying the World's Most Misunderstood Country*. Self-published, 2011.

"Strawberries in Winter: AFSC's Program in North Korea." *American Friends Service Committee*, July 15, 2013. Online. https://www.afsc.org/story/strawberries-winter-afscs-program-north-korea.

"The Top Ten Causes of Death." *World Health Organization*, May 24, 2018. Online. https://www.who.int/news-room/fact-sheets/detail/the-top-10-causes-of-death.

VanPelt, Miles. "The Old Testament God of Compassion and Mercy." *Tabletalk Magazine*, December 1, 2010. Online. https://www.ligonier.org/learn/articles/old-testament-god-compassion-and-mercy.

"Water, Sanitation & Hygiene." *UNICEF*, n.d. Online. https://www.unicef.org/dprk/water-sanitation-hygiene.

"What We Do." *Christian Friends of Korea*, n.d. Online. https://www.cfk.org/what-we-do.

"World AIDS Day 2019, Democratic People's Republic of Korea." *World Health Organization*, December 1, 2019. Online. https://www.who.int/dprkorea/news/detail/01-12-2019-world-aids-day-2019.

World Health Organization (WHO). *Noncommunicable Diseases: Country Profiles 2018*. Geneva: World Health Organization, 2018. Online. https://apps.who.int/iris/bitstream/handle/10665/274512/9789241514620-eng.pdf.

Yoon, Joy. *Discovering Joy: Ten Years in North Korea*. Honolulu: Klug, 2018.

# 10

## The Concept of Disease in the Pentecostal Tradition

—Daniel D. Isgrigg

One of the central tenets Pentecostals inherited from the mid-nineteenth-century evangelical four-fold gospel, was the passionate proclamation that "Jesus is Healer."[1] So universal is this commitment that some scholars suggest that healing—rather than speaking in tongues—has become the most recognized distinctive across all Spirit-filled communities throughout the last two centuries.[2] The pentecostal tradition traces its roots to the Azusa Street Revival in Los Angeles in 1906 led by William Seymour.[3] This revival began as holiness evangelicals discovered a sanctifying and empowering work they identified as the baptism in the Holy Spirit with speaking in tongues. But even today, healing has overtaken the baptism in the Holy Spirit as the most notable characteristic of global Spirit-empowered Christianity.[4]

Embedded in the pentecostal theology of healing is the recognition that sickness and disease is not from God. From the beginning of the movement, Pentecostals believed that the battle between healing and sickness was a divine drama of God verses Satan. This theology was based upon two primary theological assertions. First, Pentecostals recognized that both sin and

1. Walle, *Heart of the Gospel,* 221–22.

2. Dayton, *Theological Roots,* 115. This view is shared by Brown, *Global Pentecostal Healing,* 6–13.

3. Robeck, *Azusa Street.*

4. Green, "Appendix Two," 335–37. The Pew Forum survey revealed that more Spirit-empowered communities around the globe experienced healing personally than speaking in tongues.

sickness had the same origin in the fall of creation. When the first humans fell, the physical world was affected, resulting in not only death, but in the diseases that cause death in the physical body. William Seymour comments, "Man in the garden of Eden was pure and happy and knew no sickness till that unholy visitor came into the garden, then his whole blood system was poisoned."[5] For Seymour, the spiritual reality of sin had equally significant biological consequences on the human body, resulting in sickness and disease. This meant the nature of sickness ultimately was tied to the rebellion of man, rather than the purposes of God. The second assertion is the converse side of the first. If Jesus came to save humanity from the effects of the fall, then both sin and sickness were dealt with through Christ's atoning death. As Seymour again proclaims, "All sickness is the work of Satan, and we have just as much right to look to Jesus for the health of our bodies as for the saving and sanctifying of our souls."[6] To assert that God put sickness upon people would be counter to Jesus' clear mission.

Not only did sickness enter into the world through sin and the fall, but as Kimberly Alexander points out in her book, *Pentecostal Healing*, Pentecostals believe sickness was the present work of Satan himself.[7] As Seymour declares, "every sickness is of the Devil."[8] Alexander notes that one early pentecostal leader, F. J. Lee, believed that germs themselves were "allies to Satan."[9] In this way, the practice of pentecostal healing was considered to be a direct application of Christ's victory over the power of the devil. As Joseph Williams notes, "Pentecostals engaged in spiritual hand to hand combat with Satan on the battlefield of their bodies."[10]

At the same time, Alexander notes, although Pentecostals believed there were demonic origins of disease, "Pentecostals were able to hold in tension the fact that some were sick as a result of natural circumstances."[11] Suffering was a natural and biological consequence of the fallen world. Satan could use sickness as a means of afflicting humanity, but sickness was also embedded in the "natural, but cursed" system of the world.[12] Either way, Pentecostals believed sickness and the suffering that sickness produced had its origins outside of Gods will. The process of determining whether a sickness

---

5. Seymour, "Precious Atonement," 2.

6. Seymour, "Salvation and Healing," 2.

7. Alexander, *Pentecostal Healing*, 101.

8. Seymour, "Precious Atonement," 2.

9. Alexander, *Pentecostal Healing*, 101.

10. Williams, *Spirit Cure*, 28–29.

11. Alexander, *Pentecostal Healing*, 76.

12. Alexander, *Pentecostal Healing*, 76.

was a result of the fallen nature, sin, or the demonic required Pentecostals to exercise the charismatic gift of discernment by the Spirit.[13]

## Pentecostals and Medicine

Faith in Christ's atonement as the remedy for disease placed Pentecostals in a precarious situation with the medical community. As was the case with their evangelical forbearers, Pentecostals recognized that medicine had value, but believers had a better way through faith in the Great Physician as their healer. One Pentecostal noted that medicine was "all right for the children of the world, but not for God's children."[14] Joseph Williams notes that for Pentecostals, disease was spiritual and therefore required spiritual remedies. He says, "For many Pentecostals, reliance on human aid seemed antithetical to their understanding of the spiritual nature of disease; sickness's origin in spiritual realities necessitated otherworldly solutions far removed from physicians' prescriptions."[15] Some Pentecostals, like those who came out of John Alexander Dowie's Zion community, forbade relying upon doctors and medicine. One such believer crowed, "I have not had doctors, or medicines, or remedies of any kind for about eighteen years."[16]

Beyond the issue of faith, many Pentecostals were deeply suspicious of turn of the century medical practices, which at the time relied upon experimental and often contradictory practices even among medical professionals.[17] One Pentecostal explains,

> Some who claim to trust God fully for their bodies are constantly tampering with natural remedies. They think it no harm to use lemonade for a cold, or hot water for pain or bruise, a plaster for aches, and ask if it is not right to apply alcohol for weakness, not seeking to understand that the use of the natural interferes with the work of the supernatural, always retarding and sometimes preventing healing.[18]

Furthermore, some Pentecostals believed that medicine had "satanic origins." The use of medicines, which they called "pharmaceutics," they saw as

---

13. Alexander, *Pentecostal Healing*, 103.
14. Burpee, "Hints Regarding Divine Healing," 6.
15. Williams, *Spirit Cure*, 31.
16. Flower, "Editorial," 1.
17. Williams, *Spirit Cure*, 34–35.
18. Burpee, "Hints Regarding Divine Healing," 6.

akin to sorcery and witchcraft which were often found in the pagan cultures pentecostal missionaries were trying to reach.[19]

One of the biggest critics of medicine was a converted doctor, Lillian B. Yeomans, MD. After her conversion to the pentecostal faith, Yeomans declared, "All human remedies are necessarily futile."[20] The problem with medicine for Yeomans was that doctors had the wrong starting point. She quotes a famous doctor saying, "back of disease lies a cause, and that cause no drug can reach." If sin is the problem, then no human remedy could possibly be the answer. Also, from her own education and training, she recalled that most medical practices came from pagan traditions such as the Egyptian and Chinese healing traditions. But her final objection was that medicine at the time was "changeable, fluctuating, uncertain, and unreliable." How could any claim to solving the problem of disease come from such uncertainty? She concludes, "No; God's way of healing is One, even Christ Jesus."

Beyond the imprecise nature of medicine, Pentecostals were pragmatists and recognized medical remedies were simply ineffective. The altars of pentecostal missions were filled with countless believers who came for prayer because medical treatment had failed to provide any relief. One pentecostal woman testified in 1910 that for eight months she suffered dozens of seizures per night. She reports, "During these months I was under the physicians' care, but got no relief. . . . Two brethren and a sister who were conducting the service rebuked the trouble in the name of the Lord. And on the twenty-first of the same month I was instantly healed by the power of God through the prayers of the workers."[21]

For many Pentecostals, taking medicine was not necessarily perceived as a "lack of faith," although some certainly held that view. Noted pentecostal historian, Vinson Synan, points out that the 1911 Pentecostal Holiness denomination statement on healing declares, "We do not consider it an evidence of sin or a mark or divine displeasure because a person is sick or employs a medical aid."[22] In general they viewed God's healing as a better healing and represented a "shorter way" of attaining what may be received naturally through biological or medical means.[23]

Second generation Pentecostals began to shift their attitudes about medicine and science as Pentecostals experienced greater upward educational and

19. Alexander, *Pentecostal Healing*, 102.

20. Yeomans, "Divine Healing," 5.

21. Woods, "Remarkable Healing," 3.

22. Synan, "Pentecostal Roots," 293.

23. Alexander, *Pentecostal Healing*, 44–46. The "shorter way" concept was adopted from the higher life "finished work" views of salvation, sanctification, and healing applied by faith as opposed to Weslyan-holiness emphasis on process.

social mobility and as medical technologies and treatments also improved.[24] By the 1930s to 1940s, Pentecostals had a growing awareness that science and medicine could bring about effective treatment and breakthroughs with diseases like polio.[25] By the 1950s, pentecostal healing evangelists no longer denounced medicine and a new idea began to emerge that sought a new strategy for fighting disease that combined healing and medicine. This idea came from pentecostal healing evangelist, Oral Roberts.

## Oral Roberts and the Eradication of Disease

To give an example of pentecostal views on sickness and disease, I will examine the theology of one of the pentecostal tradition's most famous healing evangelists, Oral Roberts. According to Roberts's biographer, David Harrell, the two most important figures in mid-century Christianity were Billy Graham and Oral Roberts.[26] Roberts is particularly important to this study because he was not only a healing evangelist, but his whole-person perspective of healing led him to make forays into the realm of medicine when he founded a medical school, hospital, and medical research center on the campus of Oral Roberts University (ORU) in Tulsa, Oklahoma in the 1970s to 1980s. At ORU, Roberts's embarked on a mission to eradicate the same diseases he encountered in the 1950s in his healing crusades, only this time, instead of only prayer, he would seek out cures through medical science.

To understand Roberts's interest in eradicating disease, we have to begin with the story of his own struggles with disease as a child. Roberts was born into the home of a Pentecostal Holiness evangelist in 1918. Throughout his early life, he struggled with poverty, lack of education, and bullying because of a stuttering problem.[27] To add to his misery, Roberts came face to face with the reality of disease when he contracted tuberculosis at the age of sixteen. For one hundred sixty days, Roberts was bedridden and without any relief from medical professionals, as treatment for tuberculosis was still a decade from being discovered.[28] Despite the many different doctors and the abundance of medicines he was prescribed, Roberts was well aware that the medical profession was unable to relieve his suffering or cure his disease.[29] He remembers

24. Williams, *Spirit Cure*, 56.
25. Synan, "Pentecostal Roots," 295.
26. Harrell, *Oral Roberts*, 170.
27. Isgrigg, "I Tried Poverty."
28. Roberts, *Expect a Miracle*, 169–77.
29. Roberts, *Expect a Miracle*, 24.

his doctors prescribed "milk with eggs beaten in it" and other remedies to try to help him. Roberts's parents were preparing to send him to a sanitarium for isolation where he was assuming he would likely die. Even so, Roberts had great respect for his doctors and lamented that there were not better medical treatment for people who suffered as he did.[30]

In his darkest moments in August of 1935, Roberts was taken to a tent meeting outside of Ada, Oklahoma, where a bold pentecostal evangelist laid hands on his head and said, "Thou cursed disease, I command you in the name of Jesus Christ, come out of this boy's lungs, loose him and let him go."[31] Instantly he was healed. Roberts had never seen someone who boldly spoke to the disease itself and cast it out. If the name of Jesus can expel disease, then surely God was not the author of disease, he realized. It was also in this experience that Oral Roberts believed that God told him, "You are to take my healing power to your generation. You are to build me a university on my authority and on the Holy Spirit."

## A Ministry of Deliverance from Disease

In 1947, Roberts launched into a "ministry of deliverance" focused on bringing healing to his generation. Roberts believed deliverance ministry was God's process of delivering humanity "from demon-power, from sickness, and disease, and their very cause: sin."[32] Roberts drew his model of ministry from the summary of Jesus' ministry in Acts 10:38: "Jesus . . . went around doing good and healing all who were under the power of the devil, because God was with him."[33]

Oral Roberts's view that disease was not from God originated from his own experience of disease. Roberts recalls that while he was sick, many Pentecostals who came to pray for him told him that it was God who made him sick because he was not following the Lord. But Roberts vehemently rejected this idea. How could God who saves from sin also be the God of sickness? He recounts, "One Sunday afternoon, I got mad. The room was crowded with people and they were all trying to get me saved while in the same breath they were telling me God had afflicted me." Roberts finally sat up and said, "I don't believe it. I don't want to hear any more of it."[34] Rob-

---

30. Roberts, *Expect a Miracle*, 23–24.

31. Roberts, *Oral Roberts*, 21; *Expect a Miracle*, 33.

32. Roberts, *Valley of Tombs*, 10.

33. Roberts, "Highlights of Healing," 1–3.

34. Roberts, *Oral Roberts*, 18.

erts refused to validate the idea that the God who saves is also a God who punishes through sickness and disease.[35] Secondly, like most Pentecostals, Roberts accepted the position that healing was in the atonement of Jesus Christ. Yet, he still struggled with the view that God was distant and unconcerned with anything but the soul. It was not until he discovered 3 John 2 in 1947 that his view of God changed.[36] Roberts realized that God is by nature a good God and therefore he is a healing God because he is good. This realization changed everything and ignited his healing ministry. If God is good, he must also be against sickness, suffering, and disease.

Roberts's experience of suffering as a child gave him a hatred of disease that compelled him to minister to the needs of others. He believed it was God's mission to eradicate disease from the human experience through deliverance ministry. As God was putting the healing ministry in his heart, he recalls,

> God gave me several dreams or visions. I re-lived my deathbed struggles. Once more I felt the body shooting pains and the salty blood from my lungs. Then I heard it. The call of the sick and suffering. It came from a distance, then very near and I could see them! Bloodshot eyes, parched lips, quivering hands, wasted bodies—stricken humanity.[37]

These visions launched Roberts into ministry to proclaim boldly that sickness was not from God. Rather, it was from the devil, and God came to bring deliverance from sickness and disease. For the next decade, Roberts held hundreds of crusades and millions of people received deliverance from disease through the healing power of God. Roberts saw his ministry as a direct assault on disease. He says, "God placed me before the types of people of which few men of God had faced in such increasingly large number, and with such diverse diseases and sins."[38] He even claimed that through the Spirit, he would sometimes "feel the impact of the disease" in his own body as he prayed for people.[39] Although healing ministry would take priority, Oral Roberts knew that someday he would "merge [God's]

---

35. Isgrigg and Synan, "Early Account," 174.

36. Roberts, *Expect a Miracle*, 73; "Dear friend, I pray that you may enjoy good health and that all may go well with you, even as your soul is getting along well" (3 John 2).

37. Roberts, "How God's Healing Power Came to Me," 2.

38. Roberts, *Expect a Miracle*, 103.

39. Roberts, "Your Healing," 3.

healing streams of prayer and medicine," because he recognized that "all true healing power is His."[40]

## The Medical Stream of Healing

Oral Roberts always had great respect for the medical profession. He did not elevate healing above science and medicine as did early Pentecostals. In crusades he often would comment, "There is no conflict between God's healing power wrought through faith and prayer and the doctors efforts to being a cure though earthly means."[41] During his crisis with tuberculosis, Roberts appreciated the care and diligence of his physicians, even though there was little they could do to help. This reality made Roberts all the more aware that although God could heal, breakthroughs in medicine were needed to stop the suffering that disease inflicted upon humanity. As one who spent his life bringing healing to people suffering from disease, Roberts appreciated that the medical community shared a similar mission. He commented,

> One thing I have always appreciated about physicians is that they are against disease and they work to bring healing. . . . When you come into a doctor's office, everything there is designed to stamp out disease. . . . They do everything within their power to kill germs.[42]

When ORU began in 1963, Oral Roberts wanted to emphasize "whole person" education. This meant that for Roberts, there was no dichotomy between spiritual and physical; he believed that God wanted humanity to be whole in body, mind, and spirit. This wholistic approach could be applied to any professional field, including medicine. For Roberts, healing the body was part of God's desire for wholeness. Disease was simply "dis-ease" or a lack of true biological, mental, and spiritual wholeness. He recognized that disease attacked that wholeness, not only in the body, but also in torturing the mind and the spirit with mental torment and spiritual discouragement.[43] As the school grew, Roberts became increasingly interested in starting graduate programs, including a medical school.

By 1975, plans were under way to open the ORU graduate School of Medicine built on the concept of the "whole person."[44] In addition to

40. Roberts, *Expect a Miracle*, 251–52.

41. Roberts, "Your Healing," 10.

42. Roberts, "Why I Know," 4.

43. Roberts, "God Delights," 2, 9.

44. Crouch, "Healing through Prayer and Medicine," 191–203.

his plans to train Spirit-filled doctors in the medical school, Roberts announced in 1977 that he would open a three-tower medical research complex called the City of Faith. The impulse to build the City of Faith had been in his heart since he shared with a group of Christian doctors in 1964 that he had a dream that ORU would have a medical school committed to "research and stamping out disease."[45] Roberts believed doctors and ministers were both committed to dealing with the effects of disease at work in the body. But both approaches to disease were reactionary, treating the one who was already sick. Because diseases were more than spiritual, biological research was needed to understand and destroy the germs that caused sickness and disease.[46] This would require research from Spirit-filled medical doctors and PhD's who could find cures for diseases. The City of Faith was to be a place for the sick to get well through prayer and medicine and breakthroughs in research would take place.

## God's Eradication of Cancer

The announcement of the medical school came with a particular focus on research to find cure for diseases. But what Roberts was most passionate about was finding a cure for cancer.[47] In his ministry to the sick, Roberts was acutely aware of the destructive power of disease. Although he made his name preaching supernatural healing, Roberts also recognized that prayer alone would not solve this health crisis. This "gap" in both in the field of medicine and the field of ministry needed to be closed if true eradication of disease would take place. Roberts shared what he called the "two streams" of healing: medical and prayer. The only difference between these streams of healing was the "delivery system." One through prayer and faith; the other through science and medicine. Both were from God and complemented each other.

One of Roberts's highest priorities for medical research was a cure for cancer. Roberts always had a special burden for people with cancer in his ministry. Cancer was a particularly heinous disease in his mind because of its demonic origin. Because disease had its origin in sin and disobedience, all sickness had its origin in rebellion against God. But he felt cancer's ability to afflict one fourth of the population was particularly evil, which was discernible as he prayed for people. He notes,

45. Roberts, "Healing with the Force of Dynamite."
46. Roberts, "Why I Know," 4.
47. Roberts, "I Believe," 1–2.

> There is an odor about cancer that is different. I remember
> through the years as I preached so often on casting out demons
> . . . as I would pray for the healing of cancer and smell this ter-
> rible odor, each time I would be reminded of Beelzebub . . .
> which means the "god of corruption." . . . I did not mean the
> person with cancer is demon possessed, I meant that cancer has
> a relationship to this chief of demons.[48]

The spiritual nature of this disease meant that spiritual knowledge was
needed to find a cure. This is why the blending of the Holy Spirit and the
best of science was needed to find a cure.

The reality that one in four people in the world would have cancer
grieved him deeply. During a time of prayer, he believed the Spirit of God
told him he was "not going to put up with this much longer" and he would
provide a "breakthrough" as Spirit-filled doctors with revelation from the
Spirit would find answers to the problem of cancer.[49] Roberts believed
medical research conducted with the latest technological equipment and
the power of the Spirit was the path for breakthrough. He believed that
through the gifts of the Spirit, knowledge of the physical realm could be released and a "breakthrough" in cancer research could be achieved.[50] While
the knowledge would be supernatural, the method would be from the best
of scientific knowledge. The emphasis at the City of Faith was to be a place
where doctors could "solve the riddle" of the origins of cancer through the
best of modern technology and expert medical research.[51]

As the City of Faith opened in 1981, patients with all kinds of maladies
were finding healing through prayer and treatment. Cancer patients were
treated with a full complement of prayer, radiation therapy, chemotherapy,
and immunotherapy.[52] Cutting edge therapies, techniques, and treatments
were being developed in the research center. Testimonies of healing began to
fill the pages of Roberts's magazine, *Abundant Life*. Some accounts of healing
were supernatural. Some were reports of healing through treatment.

Although the hospital was open, it wasn't finished and criticism grew
as he tried to fund the ministry, university, and City of Faith through the
support of his partners. Some of Roberts's pleas for help were seen as sen-
sational and exploitative. By 1987, the City of Faith was in trouble and the
pleas for funds became more desperate. Finally, in 1989, the City of Faith

48. Roberts, "Winning the War Against Cancer," 21.

49. Roberts, "I Believe," 1–2.

50. Roberts, "I Will Rain Upon Your Desert," 5.

51. Roberts, "Winning the War," 20–21.

52. City of Faith, "City of Faith," 14–15.

and ORU School of Medicine closed their doors.[53] The dream of a cure for cancer was defeated.

For a variety of reasons, the City of Faith closed prematurely in 1989, but the idea of merging faith and medicine has continued to gain a place in the medical community. Roberts would eventually be appreciated for his work as a Christian evangelist who changed medicine. Dr. Harry Jonas, an official with the American Medical Association said to Roberts,

> Reverend Roberts, do not think you have failed. You have forever changed medicine and the way the medical world looks at it. . . . The idea with a focus on combining medicine with prayer, with a view toward wholeness, is an idea whose time has come. This idea has reached into virtually every doctor's office, clinic, hospital, nursing school, and nursing practice in the whole world.[54]

Roberts's emphasis on providing scholarships to students in the medical school so they could serve as medical missionaries was a radical one. Roberts envisioned "healing teams" of doctors, nurses, and other professionals that could serve as medical missionaries to at-risk peoples around the world. He believed that all nations deserved to have not only the gospel, but also quality medical care to prevent and treat curable diseases.[55] As with the City of Faith, Roberts emphasized prayer and the best of medicine, dentistry, business, and education as the path to wholeness for the nations of the world. People took notice of Roberts's vision even if they didn't agree with all of his theology or fund raising tactics. For example, missiologist Ralph Winter was complementary of Roberts's approach to not leave education and medical treatment out of the task of evangelistic ministry.[56] But each of these approaches Roberts took through ORU was fueled by the recognition of the tragedy of disease and the deep conviction from God that healing—whether by medical or spiritual means—was one of the deepest needs of humanity.

---

53. For the whole story, see Crouch, "Healing through Prayer and Medicine," 191–203.

54. Roberts, "Expect a Miracle," 300–301.

55. *Abundant Life*, 2–13.

56. Ralph D. Winter, "Editorial." It is interesting to note that Ralph Winter died of cancer the same year as Oral Roberts (2009). Editors' Note: Believers seeking to find the origins of diseases like cancer, in God's name, was what Ralph Winter was calling for in his last years. He founded the Roberta Winter Institute for this purpose.

# Conclusion

Pentecostals have always emphasized healing as a part of the full gospel they preached. Because of this, sickness and disease have been largely seen as a target of their ministry. Whether viewed as a symptom of the fallen world or as a direct manifestation of the demonic, Pentecostals have sought to utilize the resources in the gospel to address the tragedy of human suffering. This was particularly true of Oral Roberts, who because of his own experience of suffering, worked to eradicate sickness through his ministry, using both spiritual and medical means. As Roberts found out, God is a good God and that goodness should empower the church to seek to eradicate sickness in whatever realm they operate—whether through ministry and evangelism, or medical research, prevention, and treatment.

# Bibliography

Alexander, Kimberly. *Pentecostal Healing: Models in Theology and Practice*. Blandford Forum, UK: Deo, 2006.

Brown, Candy Gunther, ed. *Global Pentecostal Healing*. New York: Oxford University Press, 2011.

Burpee, Florence L. "Hints Regarding Divine Healing." *The Weekly Evangel* 1 (1916) 6.

City of Faith. "City of Faith Offers a Full Range of Services." In *Abundant Life*, September–October 1988, 14–15.

Crouch, John R. "Healing through Prayer and Medicine." *Spiritus: ORU Journal of Theology* 4.2 (2019) 191–203.

Dayton, Donald W. *The Theological Roots of Pentecostalism*. Peabody, MA: Hendrickson, 1987.

Flower, J. Roswell. "Editorial." In *Christian Evangel*, March 1914, 1.

Green, John C. "Appendix Two: Pentecostal Growth and Impact on Latin America, Africa, and Asia." In *Spirit and Power: The Growth and Global Impact of Pentecostalism*, edited by Donald E. Miller et al., 335–37. Oxford: Oxford University Press, 2013.

Harrell, David E., Jr. *Oral Roberts: An American Life*. Bloomington: University of Indiana Press, 1985.

Isgrigg, Daniel D. "'I Tried Poverty': Exploring the Psychological Impact of Poverty and Prosperity in the Life of Oral Roberts." *Spiritus: ORU Journal of Theology* 5.1 (2020). Online. https://digitalshowcase.oru.edu/spiritus/vol5/iss1/4/.

Isgrigg, Daniel D., and Vinson Synan, "An Early Account of Oral Roberts' Healing Testimony." *Spiritus: ORU Journal of Theology* 3.2 (2018) 169–77.

Robeck, Cecil M., Jr. *Azusa Street Mission & Revival: The Birth of the Global Pentecostal Movement*. Nashville: Thomas Nelson, 2006.

Roberts, Oral. *Expect a Miracle: My Life and Ministry*. Nashville: Thomas Nelson, 1995.

———. "God Delights in Supplying the Wants of Men." *Healing Waters*, November 1948, 2, 9.

————. "Healing with the Force of Dynamite." Lecture given at Oral Roberts University, Tulsa, OK, 1964. Audio recording. Online. https://digitalshowcase.oru.edu/oruav/8.

————. "Highlights of Healing." *Healing Waters*, January–February 1948, 1–3.

————. "How God's Healing Power Came to Me." *Healing Waters*, May 1948, 2.

————. "I Believe the Cure for Cancer has a Spiritual Origin." *Abundant Life*, January 1977, 1–2.

————. "I Will Rain Upon Your Desert." *Abundant Life*, October 1977, 5.

————. *Oral Roberts' Life Story as Told by Himself.* Tulsa, OK: Oral Roberts, 1952.

————. "Valley of Tombs." *Healing Waters*, March 1949, 10.

————. "Why I Know God Wants to Heal You!" *Abundant Life*, August 1976, 4.

————. "Winning the War Against Cancer." *Abundant Life*, September 1982, 20–21.

————. "Your Healing in the Roberts' Meetings." *Healing Waters*, September 1948, 2, 9.

Seymour, William J. "The Precious Atonement." *Apostolic Faith*, September 1906, 2.

————. "Salvation and Healing." *Apostolic Faith*, December 1906, 2.

Synan, Vinson. "The Pentecostal Roots of Oral Roberts' Healing Ministry." *Spiritus: ORU Journal of Theology* 3.2 (2018) 293.

Walle, Bernie A. van de. *The Heart of the Gospel: A. B. Simpson, the Fourfold Gospel, and Late Nineteenth-Century Evangelical Theology.* Eugene, OR: Pickwick, 2009.

Williams, Joseph W. *Spirit Cure: A History of Pentecostal Healing.* New York: Oxford, 2013.

Winter, Ralph D. "Editorial Comment." *Mission Frontiers*, January–February, 2009. Online. http://www.missionfrontiers.org/issue/article/editorial-comment2.

Woods, Maggie A. "A Remarkable Healing." *Pentecost*, May 1910, 3.

Yeomans, Lillian B. "Divine Healing." *Pentecostal Evangel*, February 17, 1923, 5.

# 11

# Life from Death

*Illness, Anthropology, and the Christian Faith*

—Giuseppe Cinà

Translated from Italian by Siby Augustine

What sense does the experience of illness have in God's saving plan? And what meaning does it acquire as a result of the redemptive work that the Father has carried out through the incarnation of the only-begotten Son and the gift of the Holy Spirit? Which "word of God" responds to these questions?

## An Anthropology in the Perspective of the "Sick Person"

A simple but attentive reading of an elementary phenomenology of the sick person clearly shows the changes that the human subject undergoes in such conditions.[1] The popular vocabulary expresses it in various ways that correspond to one's culture such as, "falling ill," or "being sick." These are terms that indicate a condition that is not stable, but tentative or temporary. Since human beings are "seekers of meaning" and are open to pursuing life, when illness comes they question, "why," and look for answers.

Kant argued that there are three fundamental questions in life:

- What can I know?

1. Cinà, "Fenomenologia del dolore umano," 87–96.

- What must I do?

- What can I hope for?[2]

Wonder, responsibility, and hope are the existential dynamisms of humankind. These qualities are what lead people to procreate, to understand appropriate behavior, and to enter into a full life. People "project" and stimulate themselves to fulfillment, for example, through marriage or another state of life, perhaps through a mission or a profession. They are thrown into the flurry of life, *projected* toward a desired or dreamed-of future, full of vigor and enthusiasm, like an "exclamation mark."

But what happens to a person if, while carrying out their projects, they are suddenly struck by a serious pathology? Everything changes. Everything is suddenly shrouded in uncertainty and insecurity. That "exclamation mark" (!) becomes twisted and becomes a "question mark" (?). The three Kantian questions are replaced by a series of long and indefinite questions such as:

- Why did this happen to me?

- Why me and now? to

- How can I live my life now?

- Is it really worth living?

Nor can everyone always find adequate answers that bring peace and order in one's inner life. Then one goes in search of someone or something that can help. Competent men and women are called upon in the fields of human and natural sciences and from the religious and theological sciences. Such help can be precious. I do not deal directly with the answers from the human and natural sciences, since it is "theology" that I have to address.

## Responses from Theological-Pastoral Sciences

The term "theology" means "word/discourse about God." So, theology, which is the action of a mind that thinks faith, is the fruit of a "believing" mind. It is a way of reasoning that responds to the word of God. God "speaks"—the revelation—and man responds—the faith.[3] God, in fact, created man to "become partakers of the divine nature" (2 Pet 1:4 RSVCE).

---

2. Alfaro, *Dal problema*, 25–29.
3. Lecuit, "Sur la voie," 81–192.

It is now known that Christian faith does not see illness and death limited to the earthly condition. Every human experience is seen in the perspective of a "beyond." The immanent dimension is open to the transcendence of a personal God, the God of Jesus Christ. But man did not accept God's plan; he closed himself up in his claim to *autonomy*. This is the meaning of "sin": to separate oneself from God in order to manage life *in absolute independence*. But the Lord knows that the "creatures," detached from God, cannot live; they lose the roots of their being.[4] God, however, does not resign himself to this condition, because he loves his creatures. And here is the work of redemption: through the incarnation of the Son and the gift of the Holy Spirit, God restores the relationship. If humans accept, they will live and will live "forever," because they enter into a filial relationship with the Creator and Father.

Christians are ones who open themselves to listening to God, and who live in dialogue with their Creator and Father, a conversation that acquires a dramatic tone in the hour of sorrow. They will therefore have recourse both to the human and natural sciences as well as to the theological sciences. How is contemporary Christian theology moving in this field?[5]

## Dialogic Relationship between the Two Branches of Knowledge: Natural and Theological Sciences

An updated and careful reading of the texts of revelation does not see a clear separation between a purely human anthropology and an anthropology of Christian faith. Rather, there is a continuity that goes from one interpretation to another, moving towards a "beyond" death, which is part of eternal life.[6] Christian spirituality is not detached from the material and corporeal dimension, because spiritual is the body and material is the spirit.[7]

Applying this way of seeing and understanding to Jesus' way of acting in the Gospels, a renowned theologian of our time expresses: "He creates a space of freedom around himself, communicating through his presence a beneficial proximity to all those he meets; he shows a new way of seeing

---

4. John Paul II, "Fides et Ratio"; "Evangelium Vitae" 29–50; Benedict XVI, "Deus Caritas Est" 78–79; Francis, "Laudato Sì" 62–100.

5. John Paul II, "Redemtor Hominis" 8–10; Benedict XVI, "Spe Salvi" 30–31.

6. Heschel, *Chi è l'uomo?*; Lubac, *Sulle vie di Dio*, 13–23.

7. Benedict XVI, "Spe Salvi" 10–12; John Paul II, "Fides et ratio"; Francis, "Lumen Fidei" 29–31; "Evangelii Gaudium" 242–43.

and experiencing the world and how to situate oneself in it."[8] In other words, Jesus broadens the vision of reality. He expands and deepens the knowledge of the *salvific space*, where health opens to salvation, life to new life, time to the eternal, the human to the divine. It is the work of the Spirit of Christ, who renews the face of the Earth.

The faith of a Christian is, in fact, not superimposed on or added to his or her humanity and rationality. A Christian knows not "according to the flesh," but "in accordance with the Spirit" (Rom 8:5), that is, according to a different experience, interior to our sensitivity, more real and profound, animated by the Holy Spirit. The Christian therefore becomes a participant in the divine nature (2 Pet 1:4).[9]

## Illness in Christian Faith

The one who participates in the divine nature can have a realistic perspective, knowing that sickness, suffering, and death are a constant in human life. The apostolic letter, *Salvifici Doloris*, declares: "Sacred Scripture is a great book on suffering."[10] Sickness and death are not an evil in themselves. They are, like any other experience of pain and suffering, a lack of something, a negativity. They are, however, an experience of evil. "Suffering is not directly identifiable with evil (objective), but expresses a situation in which man experiences evil and, by experiencing it, he becomes the subject of suffering. . . . At the center of suffering there is always an experience of evil, because of which he suffers."[11] They must therefore be fought back against. Where possible, sickness and suffering must be eliminated. And if it is not possible to heal, it is necessary to take care of the afflicted person, to strive to soothe them, using both human and natural resources and the contributions that faith offers.[12]

---

8. Albini, "Christoph Theobald"; Theobald, *Trasmettere il Vangelo*; Theobald, *Urgenze pastorali*; Fossion, "Repenser l'évangelization," 583–96; Benedict XVI, "Allargare gli orizzonti."

9. Lecuit, "Sur la voie," 81–192.

10. John Paul II, "Salvifici Doloris" 6.

11. John Paul II, "Salvifici Doloris" 7.

12. John Paul II, "Evangelium Vitae" 39–41, 78–101.

## Illness, Health, and Anthropology

What, then, is sickness according to Christian faith? Sometimes illness is caused by sin—a deliberate claim to autonomy, of separation from the relationship with our ontological roots in God.[13] But this is generally not the case (see Job's experience[14] or John 9:1–3.). "Suffering is a reality that transcends the personal responsibility of the individual and the responsibility of humanity, even if it is also attributable to it."[15] Illness can strike in one or more dimensions, but it is always the unity of the subject who suffers and perceives illness. It is always the "I" in its totality that suffers.[16] Suffering is connected to the very concept of humankind. We are limited and still unfinished creatures who are in the process of moving toward fulfillment. A person is therefore not "perfect" in the sense of being the person God intends. As humans, we are constitutionally fragile beings, from the moment of conception until death. This fragility involves the totality of a person's being in its various dimensions: organic, psychological, relational, and spiritual.

Health, then is the state of well-being in which these four dimensions are in equilibrium with each other, in a condition of harmony. The Christian perspective is clearly readable in the "signs" of healing that Jesus did, as recorded in the Gospels. The evangelist Matthew emphasizes the way in which Jesus healed in quoting from Isaiah 53:4: "He took up our infirmities and bore our diseases" (Matt 8:16–17). Jesus took upon himself the evil of the other. He "assumed" the human condition, marked by sin and finitude, and brought salvation from the evils of our human condition. An axiom of the Catholic faith affirms that "What has not been assumed has not been healed."[17] Therefore, if pain and death have been assumed by Christ, they too have been "healed" or redeemed from their negative aspects. They have become occasions and opportunities to become the way to life, to the point that, according to Christian faith, "life comes from death."[18]

But how does faith interpret this paradox? "Life from death" does not mean that pain and death have become a "good," as if you should pursue them and get them! Jesus never sought death or pain, nor did he demand

13. Congar and Rahner, *Sulla malattia*; Rahner, "L'infermità," 337–45; Balthasar, "La salute," 85–100; Bof, "Malattia," 656–63; Francis, "Evangelii Gaudium," 209–16.

14. Editors' Note: For more on Job's experience, see chapter 15, "A Scientist's Perspective on Disease and Death."

15. Coda, "Dio," 446.

16. Cinà, "L'esperienza," 85–101.

17. Benedict XVI, "Saint Gregory Nazianzus."

18. Balthasar, "Inclusione in Cristo," 215–33; Babini, "L'uomo in Cristo," 157–83.

anything like that from his disciples. He fought against all forms of pain and death. He came to save, to "cut the transcendental roots of evil and death."[19] He came to give us life, and life in abundance (John 10:10). Christians must therefore commit themselves to following their Lord. When sufferings remain in spite of every effort to avoid or contain them, they must be welcomed and be "transformed" by the active and saving presence of the Spirit of Christ who acts in us. Suffering may still remain, but the negative aspects have been cut at the roots and redeemed by the work of the Son. The last word is not death or pain, but life in abundance (John 10:10). That is why we must cooperate in this saving work: "Every man has his own share in redemption. Everyone is also called to participate in that suffering through which redemption has been accomplished."[20]

It is to be asked, then, *how to behave in the face of a serious pathology or any other distress.* It may be helpful to distinguish between diseases of a domestic character and *diseases beyond our capacity to bear.*[21]

## Diseases and Pains That Makes Sense and Those That Do Not

The first category includes numerous situations that can become life lessons, such as the pain of growth and maturation with the education of life. Sometimes the pain has a purifying and correcting function. There is pain which stimulates us to struggle, which resounds like an appeal. It shows life as a task. But there is also a call to, "fill up in my flesh what is still lacking in regard to Christ's afflictions, for the sake of his body, which is the church" (Col 1:24).[22]

This, however, does not affirm that every pain or sorrow has a meaning. Not everyone is always capable of seeing meaning in suffering and accepting it. Perhaps for some it is enough to recall the innocent pain, or the many situations of being humiliated and offended. To this context also belongs the pain caused to oneself and one's loved ones due to the progressive degeneration of life, to the various forms of diminishing of personality, forms of disability, and of insanity—the list is endless and always surprising.

---

19. John Paul II, "Salvifici Doloris," 14.

20. John Paul II, "Salvifici Doloris," 19.

21. We know how much medicine and various psychotherapies can help in multiple situations of suffering. But here the emphasis is on extraordinary suffering, beyond the capacity of individuals or communities to deal with it.

22. See John II, "Christifideles Laici," 53.

Therefore, we must conclude that there are experiences of suffering beyond some humans' capacity to find meaning in them and to endure them. What theology can confront such dramas and tragedies? How can we unravel the paradoxical knot mentioned above, that "life comes from death"?

## Life Comes from Death: A Christian Response

A more or less satisfactory response would require an extensive and in-depth discussion. In the short space of this chapter, I will focus only on two central points, and finally, on resolving the issue. Both arise from the *"Paschal Mystery"* of Christ: the new existence of a Christian, who is a "being-in-Christ," and the meaning of *Christ's experience of human suffering* within the Triune God.

### The "Paschal Mystery": The Christian as a "Being in Christ"

The "Paschal Mystery"[23] is the culminating point of the saving mission of the incarnate Son. It includes the unity of the two dimensions of passion/death and resurrection and outpouring of the Holy Spirit. In this, the relationship of the Paschal event with the experience of human suffering, of sickness and death, finds a solution: human suffering has reached its culmination in the passion of Christ. And at the same time, it has entered into a completely new dimension and into a new order: it has been "linked to love."[24] This has transformed the identity of a Christian into a "being-in-Christ," whose vital dynamism received through baptism is the passing from death to life.

As a "being-in-Christ," our lives are now included in Christ. So our sickness, suffering, and dying, and every other condition of life, take place in our insertion into Christ. This radically transforms the meaning of the experiences of suffering and disease. The most incisive formula is in the letter to the Galatians: "I have been crucified with Christ and I no longer live, but Christ lives in me" (Gal 2:20). Since Christ is risen, the disciple also is risen. "Just as Christ was raised from the dead through the glory of the Father, we too may live a new life" (Rom 6:4). Suffering and dying are the "way to life," to the resurrection. Suffering and dying are the "pains of childbirth" (John 16:21; Rom 8:22–25).

23. Coda, "Pasqua e il Mistero pasquale," 823–29.

24. John Paul II, "Salvifici Doloris," 18. Editors' Note: See also chapter 8, "A Theology of Love in the First Epistle of John."

## Christ's Experience of Human Suffering and the One Triune God

Through Jesus' humanity, the triune God experienced suffering. How did God act? How did the incarnate Son and the Holy Spirit move? At this point we realize that the relationship God has established with humans also has to do with the relationship between the three divine Persons. And here I bypass, so to speak, the intermediate stations of reflection and reach the final point of all the divine work, that is, the "hour" of Jesus, which is the hour of the passage from death to resurrection. It is the moment in which *the tension between Christ and humanity* is manifested in the most radical way.

But it is also necessary to see this from a different angle, that is, in the mystery of the triune God. What do the texts of revelation and Christian tradition tell us? We find words that refer to the tensions that, especially at the hour of suffering and death, explode between God and his creature. They are situated more deeply and paradoxically in the tension revealed in the agony of Gethsemane and the cry of Golgotha, between the freedom of the Father and that of the incarnate Son (Mark 14:36).

Piero Coda, analyzing the prayer in Gethsemane, highlights the tension expressed by the word of Jesus, *"Abba-Padre!"* in Gethsame (which reveals the fatherly and caring face of the Father, experienced and witnessed throughout his life), with the word that Jesus cries out on Golgotha *"Eloì Eloì, lema sabachthani!?"* (Mark 15:34), where Jesus experiences the silence of God. His cry, Coda notes, is "a lacerating question"[25] with respect to the face of the *Abba-Padre* previously invoked; a cry that recapitulates lament and sums up all the "why" of sorrowful humanity.

# The Pathos of Humans in the Pathos of One Triune God[26]

It must therefore be emphasized that in Christian faith the definitive question about disease, suffering, and death must be placed within the relationship between the incarnate Son and God-Abba.[27] This means that, because the incarnate Son has taken upon himself sin, death, and evil, the question, "why?" is within the intimate relationship of *the circular movement between*

---

25. Coda, "Dolore del Padre," 448–50.

26. John Paul II, "Dominum et Vivificantem," 39; Cinà, "Il patos," 209–24.

27. Coda, "Dolore del Padre," 448–50; "Dio e la sofferenza," 346–54; "Pasqua e Mistero pasquale," 823–29.

*the three divine Persons,* that unites them in the unity of divine nature. In that relationship of one to the other there is the *experience of human suffering,* because *"unus de Trinitate passus est"* (one of the Trinity suffered).[28] Now therefore, the pain of a person who is a "being-in-Christ" is in the heart of the trinitarian God, who is the source and fullness of life.

Inevitably, at this point the question arises: what can that suffering mean for the Father and the Holy Spirit? In contemporary theology, it seems to me that it was Balthasar who took up and deepened an intuition of Bulgakov and other Russian theologians on the "ontology of the God-Trinity that is revealed in the Paschal Mystery of Christ."[29]

The Swiss theologian Balthasar, reflecting on the considerations of these thinkers, re-reads the Paschal event of Christ. He sees that in it, Christ brings to completion the revelation of God, of the triune God.[30] In that mystery, each of the divine Persons gives himself to the other so that the other may be. The most explicit reference in this regard, I believe, is the Christological hymn in the well-known passage of the letter to the Philippians (2:5–11). The Apostle invites the members of the community to "have the same mindset as Christ Jesus" (Phil 2:5). The accent is on two significant words about the dedication of the one to the other: *kénosis,* which is the emptying of the self so that the other can assert itself, and *tapéinosis,* which is making oneself small in order to make room for the other.

And this, Balthasar notes, expresses a change in the image of God revealed by Christ. We are thus introduced into the mystery of intra-divine life.[31] The pro-existing attitude of Jesus Christ described in the hymn has its premise in that dynamism of the triune God. If, in fact, Jesus is the revelation of God (John 1:18), the whole life of Christ is a progressive revelation of who God is, a journey that reaches its fullness in his "hour." In that mystery, in fact, it is revealed "to the end" (John 13:1) how much Christ is "love," a pro-existing love, that is, how much love makes him "being-for-the other."[32]

But, since Jesus is "the exact representation of [God's] being" (Heb 1:3), his pro-existence reveals the trinitarian "pro-existence." His hetero-centric attitude reaches the climax in the "Paschal Mystery," in the hour of passion, death, and resurrection. Here the nature of the trinitarian God is revealed: the mutual giving and love among the three divine Persons. In the same way,

28. Coda, "Dolore del Padre," 450.

29. Zàk, "Premessa," 5–25.

30. Balthasar, "La kenosi," 35–47.

31. Balthasar, "La kenosi," 35–47.

32. Benedict XVI, "Deus Caritas Est," 9–11. Editors' Note: Again, see chapter 8, "A Theology of Love in the First Epistle of John."

the human being, "created in the image and likeness of God," is meant to exist for the other, for others, and not for him or herself. This is the "truth" of humankind—being "related" to the other. Since "God is love" (relationship of love, of self-donation), such is also the human person.[33]

## Conclusion

Radical liberation from sin, illness, and death, and from all other negative experiences of life, takes place in the death and resurrection of Christ. For it is in this event that Christ takes upon himself the human condition marked by finitude, and exchanges sin and suffering for a love that is "to the end" (John 13:1). Just as through his suffering and dying, Jesus passed from death to life, so every painful experience of those who are "in Christ" leads the way to the fullness of new life. This is also the decisive place of the revelation of God's identity, who is always at work for the coming of his kingdom. We are called to cooperate in this work, in the certainty that God is always with us (Matt 28:20), in order to grant us the "fullness of divine life"[34] (Rev 22:3–5).

## Bibliography

Albini, Christian. "Christoph Theobald: Un Cristianesimo Capace di Apprendere." June 8, 2010. Online. https://www.ildialogo.org/parola/Approfondimenti_1276009628.htm.

Alfaro, Juan. *Dal problema dell'uomo al problema di Dio*. Translated by A. Rizzi. Biblioteca di Teologia Contemporanea 65. Brescia, Italy: Queriniana, 1991.

Athanasius. *On the Incarnation: The Treatise De incarnatione verbi dei*. London: Mowbray, 1970.

Babini, Ellero. "L'uomo in Cristo." In *L'antropologia teologica di Hans Urs von Balthasar*, by Ellero Babini, 157–83. Milano: Jaca, 1988.

Balthasar, Hans Urs von. "Inclusione in Cristo." In *Le persone del dramma: l'uomo in Cristo*, edited by Hans Urs von Balthasar, 215–33. Teo Drammatica 3. Milano: Jaca, 1993.

———. "La kenosi e la nuova immagine di Dio." In *Teologia dei tre giorni*, by Hans Urs Von Balthasar. Biblioteca di Teologia Contemporanea 61. Brescia, Italy: Queriniana, 1990.

———. "La salute tra scienza e coscienza." In *Homo creatus est*, by Hans Urs von Balthasar, 85–100. Vol. 5 of *Saggi teologici*. Brescia, Italy: Morcelliana.

Benedict XVI. "Allargare gli orizzonti della razionalità." Speech to University Teachers, June 7, 2008. Online. http://www.vatican.va/content/benedict-xvi/it/speeches/2008/june/documents/hf_ben-xvi_spe_20080607_docenti-univ.html.

---

33. Benedict XVI, "Deus Caritas Est," 26–27.

34. Lohfink, *Alla fine il nulla?*

————. "Deus Caritas Est." Encyclical Letter given December 25, 2005. Online. http://
www.vatican.va/content/benedict-xvi/en/encyclicals/documents/hf_ben-xvi_
enc_20051225_deus-caritas-est.html.

————. "Saint Gregory Nazianzus." General Audience, August 22, 2007. Online. http://
www.vatican.va/content/benedict-xvi/en/audiences/2007/documents/hf_ben-
xvi_aud_20070822.html.

————. "Spe Salvi." Encyclical Letter given November 30, 2007. Online. http://
www.vatican.va/content/benedict-xvi/en/encyclicals/documents/hf_ben-xvi_
enc_20071130_spe-salvi.html.

Bof, G. "Malattia." In *Dizionario di Teologia Pastorale Sanitaria*, edited by Giuseppe
Cinà, 656–63. Torino, Italy: Camilliane, 1997.

Bucci, Luca M. *Teologia della malattia. Tentativi dei teologi del '900*. Milano: Glossa,
2018.

Cinà, Giuseppe. "L'esperienza dell'umano soffrire." In *Vita spirituale nel tempo della
sofferenza*, edited by Giuseppe Cinà, 85–101. Rome: Studium Urbis, 2011.

————. "Fenomenologia del dolore umano." In *Vita spirituale nel tempo della sofferenza*,
edited by Giuseppe Cinà, 87–96. Rome: Studium Urbis, 2011.

————. "Il patos dell'uomo nel pathos di Dio." In *Vita spirituale nel tempo della
sofferenza*, edited by Giuseppe Cinà, 209–24. Rome: Studium Urbis, 2011.

Coda, Piero. "Dio e la sofferenza." In *Teologia-Dizionari*, edited by AA.VV., 346–54. San
Paolo, Italy: Edizioni San Paolo.

————. "Dolore del Padre o 'Passione d'amore' del Dio trinitario?" In *Teologia-
Dizionari*, edited by AA.VV., 448–50. San Paolo, Italy: Edizioni San Paolo.

————. "Pasqua e Mistero pasquale." In *Teologia-Dizionari*, edited by AA.VV., 823–29.
San Paolo, Italy: Edizioni San Paolo.

Congar, Yves, and Karl Rahner. *Sulla malattia*. Brescia, Italy: Queriniana, 1976.

Fossion, Andre. "Repenser l'évangelization." *Nouvelle revue théologique* 141.4 (2019)
583–96.

Francis. "Evangelii Gaudium." Apostolic Exhortation given November 24, 2013. Online.
http://www.vatican.va/content/francesco/it/apost_exhortations/documents/
papa-francesco_esortazione-ap_20131124_evangelii-gaudium.html.

————. "Laudato Sì." Encyclical Letter given May 24, 2015. Online. http://www.vatican.
va/content/francesco/en/encyclicals/documents/papa-francesco_20150524_
enciclica-laudato-si.html.

————. "Lumen Fidei." Encyclical Letter given June 29, 2013. Online. http://www.vatican.
va/content/francesco/en/encyclicals/documents/papa-francesco_20130629_
enciclica-lumen-fidei.html.

Heschel, Abraham Joshua. *Chi è l'uomo?* Milano: Rusconi, 1989.

John Paul II. "Christifideles Laici." Apostolic Exhortation. December 30, 1988. Online.
http://www.vatican.va/content/john-paul-ii/en/apost_exhortations/documents/
hf_jp-ii_exh_30121988_christifideles-laici.html.

————. "Dominum et Vivificanteml." Encyclical Letter. May 18, 1986. Online. http://
www.vatican.va/content/john-paul-ii/en/encyclicals/documents/hf_jp-ii_
enc_18051986_dominum-et-vivificantem.html.

————. "Evangelium Vitae." Encyclical Letter. March 25, 1995. Online. http://
www.vatican.va/content/john-paul-ii/en/encyclicals/documents/hf_jp-ii_
enc_25031995_evangelium-vitae.html.

————. "Fides et Ratio." Encyclical Letter. September 14, 1998. Online. http:// www.vatican.va/content/john-paul-ii/en/encyclicals/documents/hf_jp-ii_ enc_14091998_fides-et-ratio.html.

————. "Redemtor Hominis." Encyclical Letter. March 4, 1979. Online. http:// www.vatican.va/content/john-paul-ii/en/encyclicals/documents/hf_jp-ii_ enc_04031979_redemptor-hominis.html.

————. "Salvifici Doloris." Apostolic Letter. February 11, 1984. Online. http://www. vatican.va/content/john-paul-ii/en/apost_letters/1984/documents/hf_jp-ii_ apl_11021984_salvifici-doloris.html.

Lecuit, Jean-Baptiste. "Sur la voie d'une approche dialogale, e Approche dialogale." In *Quand Dieu habite en l'homme,* by Jean-Baptiste Lecuit, 81–192. Paris: Éditions du Cerf, 2010.

Lohfink, Gerhard. *Alla fine il nulla? Sulla risurrezione e la vita eterna.* Biblioteca di Teologia Contemporanea 200. Brescia, Italy: Queriniana, 2020.

Lubac, Henri de. *Sulle vie di Dio.* Rome: Paoline, 1974.

Rahner, Karl. "L'infermità, tempo di prova." In *Nuovi saggi,* edited by Karl Rahner, 337–45. San Paolo, Italy: Edizioni San Paolo, 1968.

Theobald, Christoph. *Trasmettere il Vangelo in libertà.* Bologna: EDB, 2010.

————. *Urgenze pastorali.* Bologna: EDB, 2019

Zàk L'ubomir. "Premessa: verso una ontologia trinitaria." In *Abitando la Trinità: Per un rinnovamento dell'ontologia,* edited by Piero Coda and L'ubomir Zàk, 5–25. Rome: Città Nuova, 1998.

# 12

# Public Health Approaches to Disease from Antiquity to the Current Day

—Stephen Ko

## Introduction

Plagues, pandemics, and chronic diseases have existed from the time of antiquity. The biblical lens focuses on love for the vulnerable, outcast, and minority, yet God does not ignore the well-being and health of the masses. As part of a public health approach to disease, this chapter focuses on natural overlaps between individual health and the sacrifices required for communities to flourish.

## Defining Public Health

Public health is "the science and art of preventing disease, prolonging life, and promoting health through the organized efforts and informed choices of society, organizations, public and private communities, and individuals."[1]

In contrast to the field of medicine, public health focuses on broader societal and community needs rather than individual ones. According to the World Health Organization (WHO), "by definition, public health aims to provide the maximum benefit for the largest number of people."[2] Similarly, the Institute of Medicine (IOM) states the mission of public health as "fulfilling society's interest in assuring conditions in which people can be healthy."[3]

1. Winslow, "Untitled Field of Public Health," 183–91.
2. Violence Prevention Alliance, "Public Health Approach."
3. Walker, "Future of Public Health," 19–31.

At the core lies principle of social justice, providing groups of people the right to be healthy and to live in conditions that ensure their health.

Pandemics are poignant reminders of the significance of public health. From the Greek *pan*, meaning "all" and *demos*, meaning "population," pandemics are epidemics of infectious disease that spread across communities and continents globally. They confront us with not just one sick individual but with millions of ill patients. Pathogens overwhelm both individual immune systems and community healthcare systems. They bankrupt individuals and cripple economies.

While public health professionals detect and respond to diseases of epidemic potential, they also promote healthy lifestyles while researching the determinants of health within populations. They prevent disease through the implementation of educational programs, develop public health guidelines, and provide assistance across communities. They also work to limit health disparities while ensuring equity, quality, and accessibility of programs.

The many facets of public health require partnership and contributions from "public, private, and voluntary entities that contribute to the delivery of essential public health services within a jurisdiction."[4] The Institute of Medicine defines three core functions of public health agencies carried out throughout all levels of government for public health systems to operate effectively: assessment, policy development, and assurance.

Within these core functions, ten essential services are vital for governing bodies, defined by the Centers for Disease Control and Prevention (CDC):[5]

- **Assessment:** Monitor Health, Diagnose and Investigate

- **Policy Development:** Inform, Educate, Empower, Mobilize Community Partnerships, Develop Policies

- **Assurance:** Enforce Laws, Link to/Provide Care, Assure Competent Workforce; Evaluate

Countless models exist, including vaccination of children and adults, to prevent the spread of disease. Education about the risks of smoking, alcohol, and other addictive behaviors benefit susceptible adolescents and teens. Public health agencies develop guidelines to protect workers and establish programs to ensure access to healthy food for school-aged children. Data from the surveillance of diseases and health indicators inform policy decisions.

---

4. "Ten Essential Public Health Services."
5. "Ten Essential Public Health Services."

## Origins of Public Health

Though the term, public health, is a modern one, concepts of community health have existed since antiquity. The Pentateuch is widely regarded as the earliest evidence of public health practices and sanitary guidance.[6] Several of these early books of the Old Testament provide valuable insight into infectious disease transmission and prevention. Leviticus is considered the first recorded health code globally. Levitical law deals with individual and community responsibilities while guiding personal cleanliness, protection against infectious diseases, isolation of lepers, and even guidance for sexual health behaviors.

Infection control and prevention procedures are designed to avert the spread of communicable diseases. They require an understanding of the epidemiology of disease and concomitant risk factors leading to infection. Remarkably, Old Testament authors demonstrated a basic knowledge of the source of infectious agents, susceptible individuals, and transmission dynamics despite the unavailability of modern-day tools.

The laws recorded in Leviticus 15 provide guidance for sexually transmitted infections (STI) that exist even today. In the Septuagint, the Hebrew word for discharge (*zuwb*), was translated as *gonorrhues*.[7] This is the origin of the term, gonorrhea, still commonly diagnosed today. Though details of the incubation period, signs, and symptoms of abnormal discharge are vague, it is nevertheless striking that the clinical syndrome, at-risk population, and transmissibility were considered then. For example, the author of Leviticus carefully defined the means of transmissibility, including contact with the infected person as well as any items they touch, such as clothes, household items, or a bed that might have been contaminated by the infected person's bodily fluids. Susceptible individuals are those who have direct contact with the individual or indirect contact with the infectious agent.

Water, sanitation, and hygiene (WASH) related diseases are timeless, accentuated by socioeconomic disparities in poverty-stricken areas.[8] Access to safe water, adequate sanitation, and proper hygiene are hallmarks of public health programs globally.[9] Though Levitical laws did not include water treatment plants or sewage plans, they considered the safety of drinking water for public consumption. Leviticus chapter 11 recommends against drinking

---

6. Burton, *Microbiology.*

7. Wilkinson, *Bible and Healing,* 49.

8. Cumming et al., "Implications," 173; Wolf, "Faecal Contamination Index," 270–82.

9. "Guidelines on Sanitation and Health."

water polluted with the remains of dead animals (see Lev 11:19–24). There is a conscious realization that any food or water in contact with deceased creatures is potentially associated with contagion.

While waste disposal efforts have evolved over the centuries, the early Israelites embraced sanitation practices that ensured the health of their communities. According to Deuteronomy 23, they were to dispose of waste outside their camp or living quarters. Discarded excrement was to be covered to promote hygiene while preventing illness. Guidance was even provided for clothes with biologic growths. These garments, presumably polluted with mold, were to be burned if fungal eradication was untenable (Lev 13:47–58).

The origin of quarantine comes from the Italian words *quaranta giorni,* meaning forty days.[10] Beginning in the fourteenth century, ships arriving in coastal cities like Venice or Milan were required to anchor at the dock for this period if they departed from ports infected with the bubonic plague. The first quarantine legislation was passed in the Adriatic port city of Ragusa, modern-day Dubrovnik. The law stipulated that "those who come from plague-infested areas shall not enter Dubrovnik or its district unless they previously spend a month on the islet of Mrkan (St. Mark) or in the town of Cavtat, for the purpose of disinfection."[11] Over time, countries would establish systems of governance while attempting to protect their citizens from the risk of contagion. Practices would evolve to include different modes of transportation via air, land, and sea.

While the word quarantine was coined in the fourteenth century, the concepts of quarantine and isolation were practiced several thousand years earlier. Isolation separates sick people with a contagious disease from people who are not ill. Quarantine separates and restricts the movement of people who were exposed to a communicable disease to see if they become sick. Levitical laws took great precautions in dealing with the diagnosis and potential spread of diseases, especially among lepers, within their communities. Unclear diagnoses required individuals to be quarantined for observation until a definitive verdict was available. If a contagious dermatologic condition was diagnosed, the lepers were isolated from the camp while still infectious.

---

10. Crawshaw, "Plague Hospitals," 352.

11. Tomič and Blazina, *Expelling the Plague*, 107.

## The Modern Public Health Approach

The modern public health approach involves four steps:

1. Defining the problem through "surveillance" or the systematic collection of information about the characteristics, magnitude, and scope of the public health issue

2. Establishing the cause through qualitative and quantitative research into risk factors

3. Determining how to prevent or ameliorate the problem by designing, implementing, and evaluating interventions

4. Implementing effective strategies on larger scales while continually assessing their impact.[12]

To implement the public health approach, several core sciences form the foundation for which scientific methods are applied. Public health surveillance monitors public health situations. Epidemiology determines where diseases originate, how and why they move through populations, and to what extent they can be prevented. Laboratories support public health practitioners by performing tests that confirm the diagnosis of a disease or previous infection. Informatics enables the collection, compiling, and presentation of health information and electronic data. Prevention effectiveness examines the effectiveness of public health policy by studying economic data for decision-makers.

As the field of public health matures, schools of public health have proliferated. Within these institutions, five core disciplines form the basis of graduate public health education. These include Biostatistics, Environmental Health Science, Epidemiology, Health Policy and Management, and Social and Behavioral Sciences.[13] In recent years, other important areas have been identified, including global health, maternal and child health, nutrition, occupational health and safety, and laboratory practice.

Ultimately, the goal of the public health approach, core sciences, and fundamental disciplines are to improve the health and well-being of communities. Over time, public health interventions have improved nutritional status, increased access to clean water, and reduced acute infectious diseases. As life expectancy has increased from less than fifty years in 1900 to almost

12. "Introduction to Public Health," 17.
13. Calhoun et al., "Development of a Core Competency Model," 1598–1607.

eighty years today, we can see that interventions have had a prolonged impact on individuals, families, and society.[14]

Traditionally, a four-tier pyramid represented the potential impact of health care interventions. The most significant effect was seen at the base of the pyramid representing population-wide interventions with higher tiers correlating to diminishing impact within primary, secondary, and tertiary care.[15] To better account for non-clinical interventions, other frameworks were created to incorporate the effects of public health interventions. Frieden's five-tier health impact pyramid considers particular interventions and their population impact, which are inversely proportional to the individual effort required to implement them. Socioeconomic determinants of health form the base of the pyramid, indicating interventions with the most significant potential impact. Next are public health interventions that change the context for health, clinical interventions that require limited contact but confer long-term protection, and direct clinical care. At the top of the pyramid are health education and counseling. These behavioral modification techniques require the most individual effort to implement.[16]

## Modern Challenges

Within public health, global health is arguably the most significant social movement of the twenty-first century.[17] Similar to the civil rights movement of the twentieth century and the anti-slavery movement of the nineteenth century, the universal desire for sustainable global health is linked to the interdisciplinary discourse of social justice, human rights, ethical responsibility, and morality.[18] Koplan et al. define global health as "an area for study, research, and practice that places a priority on improving health and achieving health equity for all people worldwide."[19]

The maturation of the field of global health reflects an increasing awareness of the inevitable consequences of globalization, given the extreme disparities in wealth and inequality. At the turn of the century, world leaders came to a consensus on eight Millennium Development Goals for

---

14. DESA, *World Economic and Social Survey.*

15. Gold et al., *For a Healthy Nation.*

16. Frieden, "Framework for Public Health Action," 590–95.

17. Farmer, *Reimaging Global Health.*

18. Brown, "Religion and Global Health," 273–97.

19. Koplan, "Towards a Common Definition."

the international community, each of which relate in some way to promoting health and combating disease:

1. Eradicate extreme poverty and hunger

2. Achieve universal primary education

3. Promote gender equality and empower women

4. Reduce child mortality

5. Improve maternal health

6. Combat HIV/AIDS, malaria, and other diseases

7. Ensure environmental stability

8. Develop a global partnership for development.[20]

These goals expose underlying inequalities between individuals and nations. Following the success of the MDGs, the Sustainable Development Goals (SDG) were designed in 2015 to be a "blueprint to achieve a better and more sustainable future for all."[21] A collection of seventeen global goals to be achieved by 2030, several of the SDGs impact global health issues. These include no poverty, zero hunger, good health and well-being, clean water and sanitation, affordable and clean energy, reducing inequality, sustainable cities and communities, and responsible consumption and production. Pandemics, in particular, such as COVID-19, highlight existing gaps between resource-rich and poor areas. Fundamental inequalities in healthcare systems, access to knowledge, and psychosocial determinants of health play a significant role in differing morbidity and mortality rates during pandemics across communities.

Healthcare systems are affected disproportionately wherever both infrastructure and workforce are strained. Challenges in the scale-up of testing, access to medicines and treatment, distribution of clinical supplies, and utilization of medical care equipment are common during pandemics. These problems are more pronounced when existing healthcare systems are overwhelmed. Where this occurs, there are typically insufficient numbers of healthcare workers, confounding existing needs.

Disparities in access to knowledge are often striking. Healthcare workers, patients, and individuals have significantly diverse access to accurate information, depending on resources in-country. In resource-poor settings, physicians and scientists may lack access to protocols, best practices, and research dissemination. Patients may be unable to participate

20. UN, *Millennium Development Goals.*

21. "Sustainable Development Goals."

in novel studies or drug trials. Resource-constrained settings may have reduced capacity to efficiently and accurately circulate information, exacerbating potential fissures in health literacy, beliefs, and education. This creates a milieu ripe for the spread of myths and incorrect statements, which may further cripple communities.

Inequalities across psychosocial determinants of health, including income, education, housing, stress, racism, and stigma, greatly influence the spread of disease. Communities disproportionately affected by poor socioeconomic factors where poverty is rampant are more likely to succumb to disease. The paucity of housing, use of public transportation, and scarcity of technology in resource-constrained areas can deprive individuals of the ability to protect themselves or family members from infection. Essential workers often experience higher risks for disease, as well as higher levels of stress and anxiety. Racism and stigma may be more pronounced during pandemics than prior, putting more tension on already strained societies.

## Interpreting Pandemics and Public Health Disasters in Light of Scripture

Though the word pandemic is a modern term, plagues and pestilence have existed since ancient times. The Hebrew and Greek words for these occur over one hundred forty times in the Old and New Testaments.[22] They are paradigmatic for the challenges of public health. How do we interpret them?

The earliest philosophers had their theories.[23] Stoicism takes a deterministic view in which pre-existing causes govern all events. According to this philosophy, the path to *eudaimonia* (blessedness) is found in accepting one's plight while not allowing it to control you. In contrast is the Epicurean belief that everything is random and meaningless. Since individuals have no control over their circumstances, they should seek pleasure within all things or at least try to be comfortable. Finally, Platonism posits the reality of different worlds, both concrete and abstract. "Bad things happen here, but we are destined for a different world."[24]

But what do the Scriptures teach? In the Old Testament, plagues and pandemics are expressed as a demonstration of the judgment of God—both personal and communal.[25] Numbers 12 describes the plague of leprosy Mir-

---

22. See "Plague"; "Pestilence."

23. For the following, see Wright, *God and the Pandemic*, 2–3.

24. Wright, *God and the Pandemic*, 2.

25. Editors' Note: Regarding God's "judgment," see the meaning of *tohu wabohu* in

iam experienced after speaking out against Moses. In the book of Exodus, plagues ravage the nation of Egypt when they choose to leave the Israelites in slavery. Later, Ezekiel (5:12) warns Judah that she will be struck with pestilence for her disobedience. With the onset of the Babylonian captivity, fully one-third of the Israelites are condemned to die by plague or famine as a result of displacement under an oppressive regime.

In the New Testament, pestilence and plagues are often signs of the *eschaton* and the final judgment. In both Matthew 24 and Luke 21, famines, pestilence, and earthquakes mark the beginning of the sorrows. At least twelve times in Revelation, God warns of devastating plagues wiping out humanity before the return of Christ. Plagues are accompanied by death, mourning, famine, or fire, according to Revelation 18:8. But in the final two chapters of Revelation, these are reversed with the triumphant return of Christ.

Ironically, God uses pandemics and plagues—which often highlight inequities and disparities—to enact judgment on the sin of individuals and nations. In Matthew 22:37–39, Jesus summarized the law and prophets by saying, "Love the Lord your God with all your heart and with all your soul and with all your mind. . . . Love your neighbor as yourself." According to the prophet Micah, we accomplish this by acting justly, loving mercy, and walking humbly before God (Mic 6:8). We sin when we turn our backs on our neighbors and God.

Time and time again, God shows compassion to the poor, the homeless, the orphans, the oppressed, the foreigner, and the widows (Exod 23:9; Lev 19:33, 34; Ps 68:5; Isa 1:17; Jas 1:27). In Exodus 22:22, Moses cautions the Israelites not to take advantage of widows or orphans. Leviticus 19:10 teaches the Israelites to leave the fallen fruits of the vineyards to the poor and alien. Every three years, they are to bring a tithe of the year's produce and store it in the towns for the Levites, aliens, fatherless, and widows among them (Deut 14:28–29). In the seventh year of the harvest, the land is to lie unplowed and unused so that the poor may harvest food from what is left in it (Exod 23:11).

God's vigorous defense of the marginalized shows how much God despises inequity. Malachi 3:5 warns that God will come for judgment and testify against those who defraud laborers of their wages, who oppress the widows and the fatherless, and deprive aliens of justice. God defends the cause of the poor and needy. Perhaps the fiercest indictment comes from Jesus himself, "Depart from me, you who are cursed. . . . For I was hungry

---

chapter 3, "A Theology of Creation: Order Out of Chaos." People and societies experience the consequences of their choices when they operate contrary to God's intentions for the world.

and you gave me nothing to eat, I was thirsty and you gave me nothing to drink, I was a stranger and you did not invite me in, I needed clothes and you did not clothe me, I was sick and in prison and you did not look after me. . . . Truly I tell you, whatever you did not do for one of the least of these, you did not do for me" (Matt 25:41–43, 45).

While pestilence and plagues symbolize the judgment of God and the manifestation of evil, they also awaken individuals and nations. Second Chronicles 7:13–14 reminds us of this awakening toward transformation of the mind and healing of systems. "When I shut up the heavens so that there is no rain, or command locusts to devour the land or send a plague among my people, if my people, who are called by my name, will humble themselves and pray and seek my face and turn from their wicked ways, then I will hear from heaven, and I will forgive their sin and will heal their land." God uses chaotic conditions, such as pandemics, to awaken Christians and non-Christians from sin and rebellion. It gives an opportunity for repentance and an invitation to a right relationship with God. The process of sanctification results in dying to self and sacrificing for others that they, too, would enter into right relationships with God and others.

## Christian Engagement in Public Health

Plagues, pandemics, and pestilence reveal our insufficiency, frailty, and mortality. They confront our idolatries while forcing us to see the overwhelming needs around us. They expose inequalities that often go unnoticed in the typical rhythms of life. They invite us to repent of self-interest, pride, and self-centeredness. They provide opportunities for communion with God out a deeper felt need for God in the face of risk and fear, and serve as a motivation for outreach to our neighbors.

In her book, *Religion as a Social Determinant of Public Health*, Ellen Idler contends that religious beliefs, practices, and institutions have a direct impact on health through a variety of pathways and indirect effects through their articulation with economic and political determinants.[26] Religion deserves its place with other psychosocial conditions such as poverty, education, income, racism, and discrimination as a determinant of public health. Yet, the church has the unique ability to transform the health of individuals and communities more profoundly. Olav Fykse Tveit, General Secretary of WCC, once said:

26. Idler, *Religion*.

> Hitherto, development actors have generally engaged mostly with the top two levels (policies and practices) and avoided engaging with the foundational level of "beliefs, values, and ideas," even if this is probably the most important level for sustainable change. . . . Because of their fundamental faith commitments to respect human dignity, to serve the community, to protect creation, and to witness to the Divine.[27]

Christian faith is radically different from many societal norms. What sets Christians apart from others is the notion of sacrifice, predicated on the sacrificial life of Jesus. The mark of a believer is a reversal of worldly principles, ideology, and morality—those which are opposed to God's character and purposes. While humanity values strength, power, and comfort, Christ chose strength made perfect in weakness, power through the Holy Spirit, and self-sacrificial love and surrender. According to sociologist Rodney Stark, the explosive growth of Christianity was related to the fact that Christians stayed in urban centers during the epidemics of 165 and 251 CE.[28] By ministering to abandoned infants and plague-infected non-Christians, Christians demonstrated a charity and love which their non-Christians friends and opponents were unwilling to provide. In time, Christianity became the dominant religion in the Roman Empire in part because Christians cared for the ill and the abandoned far better than the pagan religions.

As Christians, we are to love our neighbors as ourselves (Mark 12:31) by embracing the ministry Jesus modeled. This includes a praxis of spiritual healing, but also physical healing—both for sick individuals and for ailing communities. Similar to early Christians, amid the bubonic plague of the 1500s, Martin Luther and his wife Katharina opened up their home as a ward for the infected, while preaching Christ to the dying. To be Christian is to sacrifice for the sick in our midst, providing compassionate and well-informed support to our neighbors, the marginalized, and the poor.

By engaging the field of public health, believers can identify infectious diseases, protect susceptible individuals, and characterize the dynamics of disease transmission as a practice that will bring glory to God. Modern tools of public health allow Christians to engage with vulnerable populations in innovative ways. Surveillance determines the characteristics, magnitude, and scope of public health issues. Risk factors among different people are identified by qualitative and quantitative research, which is a form of truth-telling. The design and implementation of public health interventions align with God's work of healing entire communities.

27. Tveit, *Role of Religion.*

28. Stark, *Rise of Christianity*, xiv.

During pandemics, widespread availability of testing identifies infected cases. Sources of infection are identified during active outbreaks by contact tracing. Epidemiologic studies characterize risk factors for disease while identifying pharmacologic and non-pharmacologic interventions. Quarantine, isolation, and vaccinations protect populations while lowering morbidity and mortality in a collaborative effort to contain infectious agents which are creating havoc globally.

At the base of the health impact pyramid lies socioeconomic determinants of health. The consensus among academics and public health officials is that interventions targeting these factors have the most substantial impact.[29] The World Health Organization's Commission on Social Determinants of Health agreed that "social injustice is killing people on a grand scale."[30] Whether in the context of poverty, homelessness, or relative deprivation, Jesus cares deeply about the marginalized and vulnerable and works through the members of his body to do even greater works than he did while on Earth (John 14:12). Our attitudes and actions towards the hungry, oppressed, widows, foreigners, and orphans should be sacrificially the same following Christ's example of servant leadership (John 13:15). We can advocate for social equity and economic justice the way Christ championed them. During public health crises like pandemics, and at all times in communities throughout the world, we must oppose injustice with relentless determination.

Public health interventions can change the context of health. Society flourishes by making healthy options the default choice regardless of education, income, or societal factors. Clinical interventions like vaccinations confer long-term protection for different populations. By embracing them, there is a rising tide of societal welfare acquired through herd immunity. Common grace is afforded to all communities, regardless of socioeconomic status or existing inequality.

Similarly, mandated quarantine and isolation during acute outbreaks protect the health of communities and nations. Though the behavioral modification techniques used in health education and counseling require considerable effort, they benefit all. Adherence to social distancing and the wearing of facial masks during the respiratory pandemics like COVID-19 protect everyone, especially vulnerable populations.

Holistic ministry was a central tenet of earthly life, both individually and collectively. Throughout his time, Jesus "went through all the towns

29. Marmot, "Social Determinants," 1099–104; Mackenbach, "Socioeconomic Inequalities," 2468–81.

30. CSDH, *Closing the Gap*.

and villages, teaching in their synagogues, proclaiming the good news of the kingdom and healing every disease and sickness. When he saw the crowds, he had compassion on them" (Matt 9:35–36). Through the fidelity of love, he sacrificed his life for one and for all. May we embrace the health of the public, just as we value our own (Matt 12:31). By doing so, we experience the freedom of sacrifice.

## Bibliography

Brown, Peter J. "Religion and Global Health." In *Religion as a Social Determinant of Public Health,* edited by Elle L. Idler, 273–97. New York: Oxford University Press, 2014.

Burton, G. R. *Microbiology for the Health Sciences.* Philadelphia: Lippincott, 1983.

Calhoun, J. G., et al. "Development of a Core Competency Model for the Master of Public Health Degree." *American Journal of Public Health* 98.9 (2008) 1598–1607.

Commission on Social Determinants of Health (CSDH). *Closing the Gap in a Generation: Health Equity through Action on the Social Determinants of Health. Final Report of the Commission on Social Determinants of Health.* Geneva: WHO, 2008. Online. https://apps.who.int/iris/bitstream/handle/10665/43943/9789241563703_eng.pdf;jsessionid=4B0886E3DC5C62A14027BBECBD4BD15F?sequence=1.

Crawshaw, Jane Stevens. "Plague Hospitals: Public Health for the City in Early Modern Venice." *Journal of Public Health* 35.2 (2013) 352.

Cumming, O., et al. "The Implications of Three Major New Trials for the Effect of Water, Sanitation, and Hygiene on Childhood Diarrhea and Stunting: A Consensus Statement." *BMC Medicine* 17.1 (2019) 173.

Department of Economic and Social Affairs (DESA), United Nations. *World Economic and Social Survey 2007: Development in an Ageing World.* New York: United Nations, 2007. Online. https://www.un.org/en/development/desa/policy/wess/wess_archive/2007wess.pdf.

Farmer, Paul, et al. *Reimaging Global Health: An Introduction.* Berkeley: University of California Press, 2013.

Frieden, Thomas R. "A Framework for Public Health Action: The Health Impact Pyramid." *American Journal of Public Health* 100.4 (2010) 590–95.

Gold, Marthe, et al. *For a Healthy Nation: Return on Investments in Public Health.* Hyattsville, MD: US Department of Health and Human Services, 1994.

"Guidelines on Sanitation and Health." *World Health Organization,* October 1, 2018. Online. https://www.who.int/water_sanitation_health/sanitation-waste/sanitation/sanitation-guidelines/en.

Idler, Ellen L. *Religion as a Social Determinant of Public Health.* New York: Oxford University Press, 2014.

"Introduction to Public Health." *Centers for Disease Control and Prevention,* n.d. Online. https://www.cdc.gov/publichealth101/documents/introduction-to-public-health.pdf.

Koplan, Jeffrey P., et al. "Towards a Common Definition of Global Health." *The Lancet* 373.9679 (2009) 1993–5.

Mackenbach, Johan P., et al. "Socioeconomic Inequalities in Health in 22 European Countries." *New England Journal of Medicine* 358.23 (2008) 2468–81. Online. https://www.nejm.org/doi/full/10.1056/nejmsa0707519.

Marmot, Michael. "Social Determinants of Health Inequalities." *The Lancet* 365.9464 (2005) 1099–1104. Online. https://www.thelancet.com/journals/lancet/article/PIIS0140-6736(05)71146-6/ppt.

"Pestilence." *Blue Letter Bible*. Online. https://www.blueletterbible.org/search/search.cfm?Criteria=pestilence&t=KJV#s=s_primary_0_1.

"Plague." *Blue Letter Bible*. Online. https://www.blueletterbible.org/search/search.cfm?Criteria=plague&t=KJV#s=s_primary_0_1.

Stark, Rodney. *The Rise of Christianity: How the Obscure, Marginal Jesus Movement became the Dominant Religious Force in the Western World in a Few Centuries*. San Francisco: HarperCollins, 1997.

"Sustainable Development Goals." *United Nations*, n.d. Online. https://www.un.org/sustainabledevelopment/sustainable-development-goals.

"Ten Essential Public Health Services." *Centers for Disease Control and Prevention*. Online. https://www.cdc.gov/publichealthgateway/publichealthservices/essentialhealthservices.html.

Tomić, Zlata B., and Vesna Blanzina. *Expelling the Plague: The Health Office and Implementation of Quarantine in Dubrovnik, 1377–1533*. Montreal, Quebec: McGill-Queen's University Press, 2015.

Tveit, Olav Fykse. "The Role of Religion in Sustainable Development and Peace." Speech given at Partners for Change: Religions and the 2030 Agenda for Sustainable Development, Berlin, Germany, February 17–18, 2016. Online. https://www.oikoumene.org/en/resources/documents/general-secretary/speeches/the-role-of-religion-in-sustainable-development-and-peace/@@download/file/TheRoleofReligioninSustainableDevelopmentandPeace.pdf.

United Nations. *The Millennium Development Goals Report 2013*. New York: United Nations, 2013. Online. https://www.un.org/millenniumgoals/pdf/report-2013/mdg-report-2013-english.pdf.

Violence Prevention Alliance. "The Public Health Approach." n.d. Online. https://www.who.int/violenceprevention/approach/public_health/en.

Walker, Bailus, Jr. "The Future of Public Health: The Institute of Medicine's 1988 Report." *Journal of Public Health Policy* 10.1 (1989) 19–31.

Wilkinson, John. *The Bible and Healing: A Medical and Theological Commentary*. Grand Rapids: Eerdmans, 1998.

Winslow, C. E. A. "The Untitled Field of Public Health." *Modern Medicine* 2 (1920) 183–91.

Wolf, J., et al. "A Faecal Contamination Index for Interpreting Heterogeneous Diarrhoea Impacts of Water, Sanitation and Hygiene Interventions and Overall, Regional and Country Estimates of Community Sanitation Coverage with a Focus on Low- and Middle-income Countries." *International Journal of Hygiene and Environmental Health* 222.2 (2019) 270–82.

Wright, N. T. *God and the Pandemic: A Christian Reflection on the Coronavirus and Its Aftermath*. Grand Rapids: Zondervan, 2020.

13 _____

# A West African Perspective on God and Disease

—Kalemba Mwambazambi

Traditional West Africans' perception of God, evil powers, and disease is a controversial and misunderstood concept. Various Western scholars' erroneous claims about African religious beliefs have been a factor in this controversy, although African scholars like John S. Mbiti have refuted some of these claims.[1]

This chapter will describe cultural background and beliefs lying behind traditional African thinking about God and evil powers, how this relates to disease, and how traditional Africans believe the evil of disease can be overcome. We will then look at how this traditional understanding relates to the HIV/AIDS crisis and conclude with reflections on the church's responsibility and role in addressing HIV/AIDS issues in West Africa.

## Traditional Views of God

The knowledge of God as Supreme Being has been part of African culture from time immemorial. Before missionaries arrived, significant numbers of traditional West African people believed in God as the creator of the universe who also sustains it.[2] Due to human limitations and powerlessness in the face of death and calamities, including inability to control mighty rivers and thunderstorms, Africans have historically believed there must be

1. Ekeke and Ekeopara, "God, Divinities, and Spirits," 209.
2. Mbiti, *African Religions*, 40.

a Supreme Being who is superior to these powers, and whose assistance they can turn to in their limitations and powerlessness.[3]

Traditional beliefs and understandings of God can be found in songs, proverbs, recitals, liturgies, and the names people give him. For example, the Akan of Ghana say, *Onyame ma wo yadee a oma wo aduro*: "If God gives you disease he gives you medicine."[4] In Sierra-Leone, people call the Supreme God, *Ngewo*, which means the eternal one who rules from above. The Yoruba of Nigeria call God *Olodumare*, meaning the King or Chief, the one who wields authority, unchanging and reliable. The Yoruba also use the name, *Olorun*, meaning the Lord of heaven, "the author of all things both visible and invisible."[5] In Ghana, the Akan perception is that the Supreme Being (*Onyame*) is the "provider for human needs, the sustainer of life."[6]

## Traditional Views of Spirits

The majority of West African people believe that God is above all and is at work through ancestral spirits and diviners.[7] God is a real personal entity whose help can be sought in times of trouble such as HIV/AIDS, Ebola, and Coronavirus pandemics. But this help is sought through intermediate beings[8] known by different names such as divinities, gods, demigods, or nature spirits.[9] In addition, ancestor veneration is generally regarded as the central practice of African traditional religion, as the ancestors are invoked more often than the gods or spirits. Thus, ancestors may wield power for good such as giving children, ensuring a good harvest, and increasing wealth. Or these same ancestors may cause drought, flood, famine, plague, diseases, and other natural disasters in the lives of their descendants.[10]

Many West African people have a strong sense of evil spirits. Evil is presumed to be the result of hostile forces which have power to influence people's lives and circumstances, including inflicting damage on people, their communities, or their property. These spirits demand worship and are said to possess supernatural powers with which they punish or reward their

---

3. Kalemba, *Le VIH/AIDS*, 22.

4. Opong, "Comparative Study," 175.

5. Ekeke and Ekeopara, "God, Divinities, and Spirits," 211.

6. Opong, "Comparative Study," 82.

7. Obinna, *Life Is Superior to Wealth?*, 135.

8. Idowu, *African Traditional Religion*, 170.

9. Asare and Danquah, "African Belief System," 1.

10. Westerlund, *African Indigenous Religions*, 94.

worshippers.[11] Ekeke and Ekeopara write that evil spirits may cause terrible harm to humans through causing "madness or epilepsy, and other terrible sickness."[12] We could add HIV/AIDS, Ebola, and COVID-19 to that list. It is also believed that human beings have the power to manipulate the forces of nature by ritual means to cause harm to their enemies.[13]

## Traditional Understandings of Evil and Disease

Malicious individuals causing sickness (through witchcraft) is one of the three ways Westerlund observed that many traditional Africans view the origins of disease. The other sources of disease are supra-human (ancestors, spirits, and divinities), and natural or physical causes.[14] When the ancestors are not treated with respect, according to tradition, they may punish people with disease.[15] An example of a physical cause, from a Western perspective, is that someone who breaks sexual taboos may contract HIV/AIDS or venereal diseases.

But for both traditional and modern Africans, families are unlikely to link the spread of HIV/AIDS to sexual acts. Because sex is a taboo subject, parents as well as church leaders face a huge challenge when they must talk about sexuality with their children and/or church members. Many feel ashamed about sexual teachings. The downside of this is harmful to young boys and girls who discover the reality of sex by curiosity, media influence, or friends, unprepared by their families or church. Consequently, young West Africans are often exposed to HIV/AIDS contamination due to ignorance, prostitution, adultery, sex outside marriage, etc.[16] When the connection between the action and its consequences is not obvious to many traditional Africans, it is easy for them to believe that an individual or family who suffers ill health, accident, or other mishap, has been the victim of malevolent witches[17] or of evil spirits.

11. Sarpong, *People Differ*, 95.

12. Ekeke and Ekeopara, "God, Divinities, and Spirits," 217.

13. Farrington, *Youth Crime*, 17.

14. Westerlund, *African Indigenous Religions*, 6.

15. Westerlund, *African Indigenous Religions*, 93–94.

16. Kalemba, *Le HIV/AIDS*, 174.

17. Ekeke and Ekeopara, "God, Divinities, and Spirits," 209.

# Traditional Understandings of Healing as Overcoming Evil

To ward off evil, traditional African people use a series of superstitious practices, including certain taboos of speech or behavior and amulets worn for protection. They believe they can avoid evil by performing the correct magico-religious act, which will give them control over the malicious spirit or force. When disruptions of life occur or trouble comes to an individual or community, traditional Africans find it necessary to call on an expert to divine the cause and prescribe a remedy. Usually the same person acts as both diviner and traditional healer. It is interesting that people will often seek help from the very people who are believed to have caused the misfortune in the first place, since it is generally believed that the same powerful force may act for good or evil in different circumstances and for different people.[18] Remedies may include a sacrifice, a ritual, or medicines to be taken.[19]

Since evil is understood in West Africa primarily as powerlessness, healing is understood as the overcoming of evil powers acting on a person's body or mind. Healing is not based only on physical conditions, but also on spiritual, psychological, cultural, and socio-economic aspects of individuals, families, and communities.[20] The non-Christian African has a ready-made formula for dealing with his difficulties. He presumes witchcraft or a spirit (ancestral or demonic), and performs the appropriate religious rites which restores his self-confidence, and all is well again.[21] Being restored to health is not just about the proper functioning of bodily organs, but it consists of mental, physical, spiritual, and emotional stability of oneself, family members, and community. Good health, in other words, involves good relationships with one's ancestors and the community,[22] maintaining a balance between the visible and invisible worlds. The maintenance of good relationships with God, ancestors, and community is thought to be humanity's greatest ethical obligation and determines the quality of life.[23]

When relationships deteriorate, socially disruptive forces often originate from human jealousy and ambition. The persons with such evil intentions are called witches and sorcerers. Many traditional African communities and African theologians are of the view that some illnesses which defy Western

---

18. Adeyemo, *Salvation*, 33.

19. Thorpe, *African Traditional Religions*, 116.

20. Obinna, *Life Is Superior to Wealth?*, 135.

21. Ekeke and Ekeopara, "God, Divinities, and Spirits," 217.

22. Omonzejele, "African Concepts of Health," 120.

23. Kalemba, *Le VIH/AIDS*, 173.

medicine have been transmitted through witchcraft and unseen forces.[24] If a person dies prematurely or without leaving offspring, this is usually attributed to witchcraft, and a person who dies of unnatural causes in this way is considered dangerous, and is more likely to become an evil spirit, rather than an ancestor who brings blessing and protection to his descendants and their community. So, health amongst traditional Africans is not based merely on how it affects the living, because it is of paramount importance that the ancestors stay healthy so that they can protect the living.

## The Church's Role in Addressing Disease and the HIV/AIDS Crisis in West Africa

Fear of ancestors and sorcery has persisted in the Christian community. Physician Daniel O'Neill comments that if Christian faith-based approaches do not address "the underlying spiritual beliefs and realities that interface with physical illness, those who are seeking healing will consult traditional healers whose cosmology leads to fear and misplaced trust."[25]

A case study by Harjula shows that in some communities Christian workers have been able to replace the role of the traditional healer by discerning spiritual roots that may be causing a disease.[26] Onyinah emphasized Jesus as the source of fullness for life as "Proto-Ancestor" and "Proto-Initiator" who gives life force to the sick, especially for those who participate in the new clan or tribal community of faith.[27] Igenoza from Nigeria sees these Christian leaders enable traditional Africans to reject the practices of divination, magic, or ancestral sacrifices, yet complement traditional herbal remedies with the gifts of scientific biomedical services (such as anti-retroviral therapy) and the church's role in healing the whole person in community—placing their trust in the Living God.[28] Some churches are beginning to close the gap between biblical and indigenous practices to "express the faith in ways that are sensible in their contexts."[29] Bevans gives an example of the renewed creation-centered interest in African churches of the use of herbs for healing, something that was rejected by early Western

24. Obinna, *Life Is Superior to Wealth?*, 137.
25. O'Neill, "Toward a Fuller View."
26. Harjula, "Human Responsibility," 12–13.
27. Onyinah, "Akan Witchcraft," 87–88.
28. Igenoza, "Medicine and Healing."
29. Asamoah-Gyadu, "Mission to Set the Captives Free."

missionaries as fetishism, but is being seen as God's gift in creation, but not at the exclusion of bio-medicine.[30]

The church must stand in contrast to traditional African beliefs that diseases such as HIV/AIDS come from evil spirits or witchcraft. Instead, the people of God must demonstrate God's loving character and the fruits of his Holy Spirit for healing. One way to do this is in how the church responds to the HIV/AIDS crisis. People living with HIV/AIDS are generally in dire need of spiritual, moral, psychological, social, material, and financial support. However, many ecclesiastical communities and churches in West Africa remain uncommitted to the fight against HIV/AIDS. Some West African Christians consider HIV/AIDS as God's punishment for immoral people.[31]

While this disease can be attributed in part to sinful behavior, other factors are also responsible for spreading it to innocent people, such as poverty, irresponsible actions, and a lack of appropriate means of prevention. Worried by such church attitudes and behaviors, Ludolff advises: "Churches have not been very involved in the struggle against AIDS, while the church should have the solutions to the world's problems. Now is the time to make a real difference."[32]

Fortunately, many African Christians have started to understand the enormous consequences of HIV/AIDS and its causes so that they are able to handle the problem more comprehensively. The HIV/AIDS pandemic provides the opportunity for the church to contribute positively in reducing the spread of HIV/AIDS and to strengthen its holistic mission.[33] Through educating its people to follow biblical principles such as abstinence before marriage, selfless sharing of resources, reducing stigma, caring for the sick, etc., the church can help develop ethical individuals and communities who can both stop HIV/AIDS and carefully support persons who are living with the disease.[34]

Persistent pressure to educate West African families, church leaders, and community members has started to bear fruit. Reporting on HIV/AIDS support work by African Pentecostals, Adogame has demonstrated that the project empowers individuals and families to prevent HIV/AIDS by using peer education, interpersonal communication, counseling, drama, and HIV/AIDS education modules in the church's Bible college curriculum. For individuals, the church offers peer education and counseling to promote risk-reduction behaviors. For families, the church emphasizes parent-child communication and conducts seminars to empower parents

30. Bevans, "Mission of the Spirit," 31.

31. Dill and Porte, *Choose Life*, 23.

32. Ludolff, "Training Youth, 110.

33. Kalemba, "Role of the Church."

34. Dill and Porte, *Choose Life*, 1; Adogame, "HIV/AIDS Support," 481.

to discuss sexuality issues frankly in the context of their faith and the growing epidemic.[35]

There is a need to mobilize all West African forces to fight the HIV/ AIDS pandemic by promoting positive transformation that includes mental and behavioral change. It is therefore important to encourage and motivate families, churches, and public health institutions to promote sex education, without complacency or shame, in accordance with God's Word. Church leaders should promote community support groups for all ages to form the basis of emotional and psychological support for all affected and infected people. Churches can educate their young people with moral and hygienic principles from the word of God, with application to such topics as evil spirits, disease, and HIV/AIDS prevention.

It is essential that the church facilitate and revitalize Christian families in the fight against HIV/AIDS. The task of the government, community, healthcare providers, church, and family are to encourage each member to get tested and to know their status in relation to HIV/AIDS. Church leaders and trained public health agents must provide spiritual, moral, material, and psychological encouragement to every person living with HIV/AIDS. These people need support that is medically compliant, that includes taking care of the individual, and that promotes neighborly love in the community. The church can act as a catalyst regarding conflict and misunderstandings and contribute toward sexual ethics and education to help West African people choose to walk in God's will for a better life. That will be pleasing to God who is above all, creator and sustainer of the universe, eternal, and immortal.

## Bibliography

Adogame, Afe. "HIV/AIDS Support and African Pentecostalism: The Case of the Redeemed Christ Church of God (RCCG)." *Journal of Health Psychology* 12.3 (2007) 475–84. Online. http://hpq.sagepub.com/content/12/3/475.refs.html.

Asamoah-Gyadu, J. Kwabena. "Mission to Set the Captives Free: Healing, Deliverance, and Generational Curses in Ghanaian Pentecostalism." *International Review of Mission* 93.370/371 (2004) 389–406.

Asare, Mavis, and Samuel A. Danquah. "The African Belief System and the Patient's Choice of Treatment from Existing Health Models: The Case of Ghana." *Acta Psychologica* 3.4.49 (2017) 1–4.

Bevans, Stephen. "Mission of the Spirit." *International Review of Mission* 103.1 (2014) 30–33.

Dill, Johan, and Andre de la Porte. "A Value Based Response to HIV and AIDS." In *Choose Life: A Value Based Response to HIV and AIDS*, edited by Andre de la Porte, 1–14. Pretoria: C. B. Powell Bible Centre, 2006.

35. Adogame, "HIV/AIDS Support," 478.

Ekeke, Emeka C., and Chike A. Ekeopara. "God, Divinities, and Spirits in African Traditional Religious Ontology." *American Journal of Social and Management Sciences* 1.2 (2010) 209–18. Online. https://scihub.org/AJSMS/PDF/2010/2/AJSMS-1-2-209-218.pdf.

Farrington, David P. "Youth Crime and Antisocial Behavior." In *The Social Child*, edited by A. Campbell and S. Muncer, 353–92. Hove, UK: Psychology, 1998.

Harjula, Raimo. "The Human Responsibility in the Practice of the Traditional East-African Healer: A Case Study." *Scandinavian Journal of Social Medicine. Supplementum* 31 (1982) 12–18.

Idowu, E. Bolaji. *African Traditional Religion: A Definition.* London: SCM, 1973.

Igenoza, Andrew Olu. "Medicine and Healing in African Christianity: A Biblical Critique." *African Ecclesial Review* 41 (1999) 145–63.

Joint United Nations Programme on HIV/AIDS (UNAIDS). *Global Report: UNAIDS Report on the Global AIDS Epidemic 2013.* New York: United Nations, 2013. Online. https://www.unaids.org/sites/default/files/media_asset/UNAIDS_Global_Report_2013_en_1.pdf.

Joint United Nations Programme on HIV/AIDS (UNAIDS) and the United Nations Children's Fund (UNICEF). *Children on the Brink 2004: A Joint Report of New Orphan Estimates and a Framework for Action.* 4th ed. New York: United Nations, 2004. Online. http://data.unaids.org/publications/external-documents/unicef_childrenonthebrink2004_en.pdf.

Kalemba, Mwambazambi. *Le VIH/AIDS, Analyse, Développement et Implications.* Milton, UK: Langham, 2017.

———. "The Role of the Church and Other Public Health Providers in the Fight against HIV/AIDS in Sub-Saharan Africa." *WCIU Journal*, February 7, 2020. Online. https://wciujournal.wciu.edu/health-and-disease/2020/2/7/the-role-of-the-church-and-other-public-health-providers-in-the-fight-against-hivaids-in-sub-saharan-africa.

Ludollf, Abel. "Training Youth Leaders for an HIV and AIDS Youth Programme." In *Choose Life: A Value Based Response to HIV and AIDS*, edited by Andre de la Porte, 1–9. Pretoria: CB Powell Bible Centre, 2006.

Mbiti, John S. *African Religions and Philosophy.* London: Heinemann SPCK, 1975.

Obinna, Elijah. "Life Is Superior to Wealth?: Indigenous Healers in an African Community, Amasiri, Nigeria." In *African Traditions in the Study of Religion in Africa*, edited by Abe Adogame et al., 135–48. Farnham, UK: Ashgate, 2012.

Omonzejele, Peter F. "African Concepts of Health, Disease, and Treatment: An Ethical Inquiry." *Explore* 4.2 (2008) 120–23.

O'Neill, Daniel W. "Toward a Fuller View: The Effect of Globalized Theology on an Understanding of Health and Healing." *Missiology: An International Review* 2 (2017) 204–14. Online. https://doi.org/10.1177/0091829616684863.

Onyinah, Opoku. "Akan Witchcraft and the Concept of Exorcism in the Church of Pentecost." PhD diss., University of Birmingham, 2002.

Opong, Andrew Kwasi. "A Comparative Study of the Concept of the Divine in African Traditional Religions in Ghana and Lesoto." DLitt et Phil diss., University of South Africa, 2002.

Sarpong, Peter K. *People Differ: An Approach to Inculturation in Evangelisation.* Accra: Sub-Sahara, 2002.

Westerlund, David. *African Indigenous Religions and Disease Causation.* Leiden: Brill, 2006.

# 14

## An East African Perspective on God and Disease

—Jim Harries

Westerners struggle with the apparent biblical link between sin and illness. The impression given, that God likes clobbering sinners, runs contrary to their understandings of his graciousness. Of course, some sins, such as excesses of drunkenness and sexual immorality, clearly cause diseases like liver problems and STDs. Yet many "bad" people also live long healthy lives.

Western scholarship finds "secular" solutions to the problem of illness and disease. But the assumption that the West can legitimately represent mankind as a whole is, I suggest, grossly overplayed. For example, the secular notion that micro-organisms are responsible for much human disease is foreign to traditional African thinking. Educated African people (and it is only the educated who have the command of European languages that gives them a voice in the West) would not deny knowing what "germs" are. But at the same time, the way many African people live, what they say in informal contexts, how they behave and the beliefs they demonstrate by their actions, seem to be in practice largely incompatible with faith in secular explanations for disease.

Many indigenous people's thinking does not distinguish the "natural" from the "spiritual." In an African worldview, what has corrupted creation is likely to be understood as being people's envy of one another.[1] Rene Girard would consider this to be mimetic rivalry.[2] In the absence of a material

1. Harries, "Witchcraft, Envy," 129–39.
2. Girard, *I See Satan*, 11.

source for misfortune, people look elsewhere for a cause, which tends to confirm innate suspicions that problems are caused by people who have some reason to not like us. Typically these are people we suspect of being envious of us, or to use Girard's terms again, who are dissatisfied with the process of imitation, which dissatisfaction leads to scandal that can result in violence.[3] Given this perception, the way forward is not to "analyze our world" as Fountain suggests in chapter 7.[4] It is more likely to be to protect ourselves from the impact of the envy of others.

The above mentioned author, Girard, realized that for ancient Greeks, as in Africa today, terms that are the equivalent to the English word disease (such as the term, plague) can be a type of social unrest.[5] Robert Parker, in his book, *Miasma: Pollution and Purification in Early Greek Religion*, explores the concept of "pollution" in ancient Greece. He finds that countering this, and not modern "science," underlies the healthcare system.[6] Girard's writings reveal that people's innate tendency to imitate one another pushes them towards conflict with others who have what they want, a conflictual orientation that seems to generate a parallel to the ancient Greek pollution. For Girard this is resolved through a murder, or a substitutionary sacrifice in lieu of a murder.[7] Something very similar is still very widespread in Africa, shown through the prominence of witch accusation.[8] Girard makes a clear case for use of the Bible as a means to healing.[9]

In the massive spread of Pentecostalism around Africa today, many Pentecostals believe that healing is achieved through expulsion of what is "bad" (from above, pollution), through prayer (i.e., exorcism). In African thinking (which can only be learned through immersion in African languages) the link between sickness and sin related to envy can be shown more explicitly by identifying "ill-health" as being associated with social tensions or stress (to use English terms). Very literally, a widespread term used in Swahili for healing, *kupona*, is "to cool." Healing, in African languages, is like cooling of interpersonal tensions. These often arise from imbalances in gift-giving, a perception that others are getting advantage

---

3. Girard, *I See Satan*, 24.

4. Assuming that Fountain's reference is to the physical world, as perceived in the West.

5. Girard, *I See Satan*, 53.

6. Parker, *Miasma*, 1.

7. Girard, *I See Satan*, 82.

8. Asamoah-Gyadu, "Witchcraft Accusations"; Iwenwanne, "Pentecostal Pastors."

9. Girard, *I See Satan*, 106.

at one's own cost, which brings us back to envy as a perceived cause of misfortune, including illness.

A point made by Ralph Winter, that God is not the cause of sickness, is quite unnecessary in the parts of the majority world known to me. In traditional East African culture, God is not blamed for sicknesses. Rather, driving out evil spirits through exorcism is a common remedy for maladies.

This raises the question of just what ought then to be the way forward in and for today's globalizing world, specifically when it comes to healthcare and dealing with disease?[10] I propose, admittedly as a simplification, that it might be to enable African and other majority-world people to have a greater grasp of secularism than they have to date. I make that suggestion on the basis of my understanding that secularism emerges from Christianity, and can even be considered a form of Christianity.[11] Therefore, encouraging a greater degree of understanding of secularism requires teaching theology—imparting an understanding of truth about God.

A helpful place to start before considering what might be needed in theology for Africa is to explore the widespread pre-existing understanding of the nature of God found on the continent. Many African people's innate understanding of God, as demonstrated in their languages,[12] is that he is the provider. Provision for prospering was an important acknowledged role for God before African people came to learn more about God from missionaries.[13] The wide spread of the prosperity gospel over Africa also demonstrates clearly (I think!) that something of the same order was already present before missionaries brought the gospel.

Westerners have given this faith in God as provider, a major boost. Due to their activities, African people have in recent centuries enjoyed levels of "material development" that were previously unheard of. African people nowadays have shoes, clothing, metal and plastic kitchen utensils, buckets, phones, radios, TVs, wheels, wheelbarrows, cars, buses (this list could just go on and on and on) that were previously totally absent. Hence, faith in God the provider may well be currently at an all-time high!

10. In my use of the term "disease" here, I assume a Western view of disease, as a biomedical malfunction of some kind. Yet, it is difficult, in an article that considers African understandings of disease, to be entirely clear on what is being referred to when the latter is so different from the former yet the same term is used for both.

11. Taylor, "Western Secularity," 38. My citing of Taylor is just an example of someone who demonstrates the widespread comprehension that secularism is a peculiar product of Christian belief.

12. Such as *Mungu, Lesa, Nyasaye, Zambi*, and so on.

13. Moore, "Africa, Animism."

A feature of this innate (some would say pre-colonial) understanding that I want to consider here is clearly demonstrated by the widely spread practice of the prosperity gospel today. Western missionaries have not had to go out of their way to teach African people to acquire the prosperity gospel. They have acquired it anyway. One route by which they have acquired it is by observing Western missionaries who while strongly advocating the name of Jesus, have lived and currently live at a level of prosperity that is way beyond reach for many African people. (The same, missionaries and other Westerners, commonly advise African people that they too can achieve such levels of prosperity, and provide guidance on how to achieve it.) It should not take a genius to realize that the correlation between faith in Jesus and worldly wealth is noticed. In the absence of other clear indication as to why Westerners tend to prosper financially, faith in Jesus can be given the credit for it.

Missionaries and other Westerners being imitated may well be speaking in a way that seeks to be other than the prosperity gospel. In the West today, after all, material prosperity is seen as arising largely as a result of a rational profit-maximizing means of engaging with the physical world. Westerners would prefer African people to learn to follow the same, that they see as a rational means, to raising one's standard of living. African holism, however, is such that such engagement with the material world can remain invisible, leaving African people to interpret wealth as arising from prayer, i.e., through the prosperity gospel.[14]

If African people who (like all of us) are desirous to prosper, understand God as providing prosperity, and if at the same time Westerners are providing prosperity for them, this easily results in an idolatry in which the Westerner takes the place of God. Biblically speaking, I take idolatry as being a serious crime; it clearly contravenes the Ten Commandments. It is widely recognized that this current transformation of the perceived identity of God in Africa, related to the prosperity gospel, is problematic. Despite many Westerners' profuse efforts, a solution is proving difficult to find. I suggest that this is because the behavior of Westerners tends itself to build on or confirm rather than to question or undermine the prosperity gospel.

My reader will recognize that having people follow required prescriptions originating in the West in order to eradicate disease, will be to further endorse and not challenge the already innate widespread African conception that the god who is a great provider is a white man. Western missionaries will acknowledge that ultimately the "healer" is God, yet their need to control medical circumstances so as to fulfil requirements to achieve

14. Reese, *Roots and Remedies*, 63.

healing often requires them to be in charge to dictate prescriptions that may make little sense to not-secular African people.

To transform innate perceptions of God in Africa does not require proving, yet again, how capable are Westerners, so that they take on in many ways the identity of whatever it is in African languages that translates the English term, God. To see one's way around this deception from within the West is increasingly difficult. I recognize my own overcoming of the deception as having only been enabled by my living in African community using African languages for thirty-one years.

Biblically speaking, all of humankind needs to pay constant attention to God so that wrong understandings of him are transformed. This is why learning from the Bible is a central and constant part of Christian living. The question then, is how can an incorrect understanding of God, such that he is a Westerner, be transformed? How can credit for healing, for example, be deflected from Westerners to God?

Contrary to a dominant view which says that the most important thing that the West has to offer the rest of the world is its capital, science, and technology, I suggest that the most important properties that it must seek to share with others are qualities such as faith, hope, love, trust, endurance, faithfulness, long-suffering, peace, and joy in the Lord. These are seen by many as being biblical qualities.

Let us take just one of these, trust. Trust creates capital. Creation of credit by modern banks is effective only because of trust. Should there ever be a "run on the bank," banks are forced to close their doors. They do not have all the cash in hand to pay everyone should all their customers decide to withdraw their savings! They may have only a fraction of it. Banks loan more money than they receive. They can do so because people trust that on the rare occasion that they want cash, that they will get it. It is this kind of trust in the system that enables banks to radically raise the money supply to an economy. Without trust, such generation of capital could not occur.

If indeed, as I suggest may be the case, lack of trust is a feature of many African communities today, then empowering African communities to engage their own capitalism instead of depending on that of others (to be able to create their own credit), is not to give them money or even medicines, but to empower them to trust one another.

Possession of the above qualities comes to those who accept the good news of Jesus Christ. The key means by which Westerners may be able to begin to be involved in sharing some of the above listed qualities, is to share that good news. To do so requires what we commonly refer to as "vulnerable mission."[15] This involves service by an outsider from the West to majority world people in which key relationships are built entirely on resources and languages indigenous to the local people. Only thus can majority world people be enabled to be honest to the West, instead of bending the truth they communicate so as to maximize their income from donors. Only thus, by grasping indigenous categories of thought, can Western people acquire a sufficiently deep grasp of the way of life of majority world people as to engage with them intelligently and effectively. The alternative I am proposing to global-wide disease eradication as far as the West is concerned, is presentation of the gospel of Christ to the majority world by vulnerable Westerners.

African people can thus be empowered through divine truth to begin to grasp aspects of secularism that the West currently uses to its own benefit. This requires beginning with pre-colonial African theology, often expressed today as the prosperity gospel, as well as perception of other areas of African life recently concealed as a result of attempts at achieving global secular hegemony. The gifts of the Spirit being found to be of more immediate pertinence to Africa than technology and science, suggests that Christian mission should emphasize the gospel over and above what is sometimes known as "secular development," including biomedicine.

## Bibliography

Asamoah-Gyadu, J. Kwabena. "Witchcraft Accusations and Christianity in Africa." *International Bulletin of Missionary Research*, January 1, 2015. Online. https://journals.sagepub.com/doi/10.1177/239693931503900107.

Boggs, James P. "The Culture Concept as Theory, in Context." *Current Anthropology* 45.2 (2004) 187–209.

Calhoun, Craig, et al. "Introduction." In *Rethinking Secularism*, edited by Craig Calhoun et al., 3–30. Oxford: Oxford University Press, 2011.

Cavanaugh, William T. *The Myth of Religious Violence: Secular Ideology and the Roots of Modern Conflict*. Oxford: Oxford University Press, 2009.

Girard, Rene. *I See Satan Fall Like Lightening*. Translated by James G. Williams. Maryknoll: Orbis, 2001.

Harries, Jim. *Anti-Racism Exposed: How Secularism Kills Africa*. Forthcoming.

———. *Materiality and "Religion": Explaining Deliverance Ministry in Africa*. Forthcoming.

———. "Witchcraft, Envy, Development, and Christian Mission in Africa." *Missiology: An International Review* 40.2 (2012) 129–39.

Iwenwanne, Valentine. "Pentecostal Pastors Continue to Brand Children as Witches in Nigeria." *TRTWorld*, December 7, 2018. Online. https://www.trtworld.com/magazine/pentecostal-pastors-continue-to-brand-children-as-witches-in-nigeria-22281.

15. See http://www.vulnerablemission.org.

Jindra, Michael. "The Dilemma of Equality and Diversity." *Current Anthropology* 55.3 (2014) 316–34.

Jones, Ben. "The Making of Meaning: Churches, Development Projects, and Violence in Eastern Uganda." *Journal of Religion in Africa* 43 (2013) 74–95.

Manuel, Paul Christopher, and Miguel Glatzer. "'Use Words Only If Necessary': The Strategic Silence of Organized Religion in Contemporary Europe." In *Faith Based Organizations and Social Welfare: Associational Life and Religion in Contemporary Western Europe*, edited by Paul Christopher Manuel and Miguel Glatzer, 1–8. Palgrave Studies in Religion, Politics, and Philosophy. Basingstoke: Palgrave MacMillan, 2019.

Moore, Nick. "Africa, Animism, and the Dangers of the Prosperity Gospel." *imb*, October 26, 2018. Online. https://www.imb.org/2018/10/26/africa-animism-prosperity-gospel.

Parker, Robert. *Miasma: Pollution and Purification in Early Greek Religion*. Oxford: Clarendon, 1983.

Pinker, Steven. *The Blank Slate: The Modern Denial of Human Nature*. London: Penguin, 2002.

Reese, Robert. *Roots and Remedies of the Dependency Syndrome in World Missions*. Pasadena, CA: William Carey Library, 2010.

Smith, Linda Tuhiwayi. *Decolonizing Methodologies: Research and Indigenous Peoples*. London: Zed, 1999.

Taylor, Charles. "Western Secularity." In *Rethinking Secularism*, edited by Craig Calhoun et al., 31–53. Oxford: Oxford University Press, 2011.

Tijimes, Peter. "Desire, Technology, and Politics." *Contagion* 6 (1999) 85–89.

15 _____

# A Scientist's Perspective on Disease and Death[1]

—Richard S. Gunasekera

## Introduction

Scientific evidence and genetic information discovered in the past few decades, particularly from molecular biology and genomics, have provided a surprising amount of support for biblical beliefs. There is much knowledge and evidence that can be gained in support of the biblical record through the proper use of the modern scientific method. The main goal of this chapter therefore, is to bring together scientific and biblical material bearing on the origins of disease and death, to offer mechanisms and evidence that we propose can be understood theologically as the "works of the devil" (1 John 3:8). Thus, in addition to the biblical record, a genomics and *scientific* perspective on the origin of disease and death is now available for the post-modernist.

In this chapter we describe how infectious agents insert DNA segments into the cells of living things, in some instances even into the nucleus of the cell and the very genome of a person, causing suffering, pain, and disease passed to the progeny of the host through many consecutive generations. These kinds of diseases lead to certain premature death. This is the opposite of what Jesus came to bring: "I have come that they may have life" (John 10:10). According to the Scriptures, Christ healed the sick of diseases, raised the dead, drove out demons, and alleviated suffering (Mark 1:31–34) throughout his ministry.

1. This chapter is adapted from the author's book, *Origins: Perspectives on the Origins of Man, Disease, and Death*. Used by permission.

Here, we investigate and attempt to offer a scientific theory at the molecular level as to the origins of disease *via* biological and genetic mechanisms including the activity of external agents—which distort God's original good creation—from an analysis of the genetic and DNA data revealed in the Human Genome Project and from microbiological research. For these purposes the word "genome" is defined as all genetic material found in a representative cell of a particular species. Genetic material—which is mainly comprised of DNA—is considered the blueprint of life. The genetic code—which is the coded expression of the blue print in DNA—is the basis of life through which all physiological and metabolic form and function of life is governed (more on this is found below in a section titled "Genetics 101.") However, basic genetic studies have shown that genetic material is susceptible to mutations by external agents leading to disease and death. We therefore postulate that genetic and infectious diseases, caused by the mutations of DNA or the transmission of mutated genes, or caused by viral, bacterial, and other infectious agents inserting foreign DNA into very genome of humans, can be considered part of the "works of the devil" as described in 1 John 3:8, which is what the Son of God came to destroy.

## Integrating Science and the Biblical Cosmic Battle

Scripture states that the Edenic creation was perfect and good (Gen 1–2). Furthermore, the original Edenic environment does not describe death, diseases, or suffering. At the DNA ("genomic") level, this could mean that the first humans had a genome with correct DNA sequences without mutations such as deletions or insertions with foreign DNA sequences. And this genome would not have had the susceptibility to random mutations and corruption, as is found in all creatures since the fall of man. The first human genome would have had the correct DNA sequences that would express functional proteins and not truncated proteins that cause disease (e.g., sickle cell anemia), often leading to death. In fact, DNA without erroneous sequences (discussed below) could be considered to be immutable, and thus life in the original creation would have been without disease and death.

However, very early in the Bible, a demonic entity appears, bent on causing destruction and death in God's creation.[2] In addition to the Genesis 3 account of Satan's work causing the fall of humankind, one of the early books of the Bible, the book of Job, also begins by relating the

---

2. Editors' Note: On the plausibility of spirit-agents corrupting God's good creation, see chapter 19, "Why Creation Groans: Responding to Objections to the Corruption of Nature (CON) Hypothesis."

destructive nature of Satan's actions, including causing disease and death. In Job 1:7 and 2:2 we see Satan roaming back and forth throughout the Earth. As part of an attempt to scorn Job's devotion to God, Satan asked for and received permission to harm Job. Immediately "Satan went out from the presence of the LORD and afflicted Job with painful sores from the soles of his feet to the crown of his head" (Job 2:7). According to this passage, Satan has the power to inflict disease. Although we don't know the means or mechanisms by which he caused Job to have sores all over his body, it is not hard to imagine that disease might be one of the weapons in his arsenal fitted to inflict suffering and death throughout history.

Unfortunately, in today's post-modern world, particularly in the West, attributing evil to Satan and the demonic world is no longer acceptable and fashionable.[3] The worldview which ignores the spiritual world's influence on the material world is called the "excluded middle" by missiologists.[4] A spiritual kingdom that is controlled by satanic forces is clearly mentioned in Ephesians 6:12: "Our struggle is not against flesh and blood, but against the rulers, against the authorities, against the powers of this dark world and against the spiritual forces of evil in the heavenly realms." The suffering of satanically or demonically affected people leading to death and suicide, is recorded in the lives of Judas (Matt 27:5), King Saul (1 Sam 31:4–6), and others. These Scriptures, and many others, evidence worldwide spiritual opposition to the person, work, and glory of God in history.

## Scientific Theories of the Origins of Disease and Death

If indeed humans were created originally to live without death, the question that begs to be examined by theologians and scientists is: did sin have a physiological as well as a spiritual effect on man? If the act of sin brought about death as we know it, then we can investigate the mechanisms by which this death might have been brought about at the molecular level.

Two fundamental scientific theories for the etiologies of disease—infections and genetic disorders—overlap with one another. Genetic and infectious causes together cover many of the diseases that lead to impairment, suffering, disease, and death. These sources of disease raise a theological

3. Editors' Note: In chapter 19, "Why Creation Groans: Responding to Objections to the Corruption of Nature (CON) Hypothesis," Gregory Boyd argues, "It is apparent that the current 'climate of opinion' regarding the disbelief in spirit-agents is nothing more than an assumption shared by a relatively small cadre of Western scholars."

4. Hiebert, "Flaw of the Excluded Middle," 414–21.

question: Is Satan involved in corrupting life at the microbiological, molecular, and nuclear level? It is beyond dispute that all of humankind is now destined to aging and disease, ending ultimately in physical death. Disease is a response to either environmental factors, infections, or inherited factors. After some background information, we will look at genetic and infectious disease theories, and how satanic influence might be involved.

## Genetics 101

### The Human Genome Project (HGP)

The Human Genome Project was an international collaboration of mapping the genetic material (DNA) found in human cells. This mapping involved the sequencing of 3.2 billion nucleotides. If stretched out, a DNA molecule would form a very thin thread, about six feet long. The total length of the combined DNA molecules in one adult human is equivalent to nearly seventy trips from the Earth to the sun and back.[5] DNA is thought of as the "blueprint" molecule of life. It directs the transmission of specific traits from one generation to its progeny through different genes. These direct the cell to express the various types of proteins of the body according to the genetic code (Figure 1).

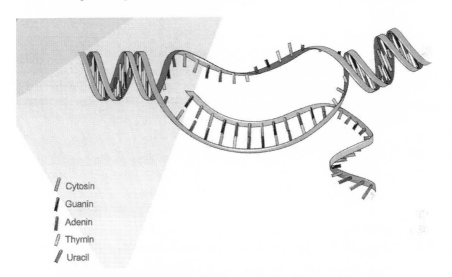

Cytosin
Guanin
Adenin
Thymin
Uracil

**Figure 1.** The DNA double stranded molecule transcribes its specified code to form an RNA single strand, which forms the

5. Chen, "Length of a Human DNA Molecule."

various types of proteins. The small units are the nucleotides
with the abbreviations, CGAT.[6]

In each and every one of these cells is a nucleus (except in red blood
cells). In every nucleus is a full set of chromosomes. Humans have forty-six
chromosomes in their genome: twenty-three from the mother and twenty-
three from the father. Every chromosome is a singular strand of tightly
coiled DNA. On every strand of DNA are segments that code for proteins.
These protein coding segments—known as genes—do the physiological
and biochemical work to build the physical and anatomical structure and
function of every living thing.

Interestingly, the whole DNA strand is not made up of a continuous
sequence of genes. A surprising finding regarding the human genome is
that only 1.5 percent of the total DNA, with its more than three billion units
(nucleotides), is actually used to form the proteins that build the physical
and anatomical structures of humans, and other living things, and which do
the physiological and biochemical work necessary for life.

## "Junk DNA" and Mutations

What is 98.5 percent of DNA doing if it doesn't code for proteins? Even before the human genome-mapping project, scientists called this "Junk DNA."
This "dark side" of the genome consisting of the so-called "Junk DNA"
contains "intron" sequences (non-coding regions of the genome) including
mobile DNA ("jumping genes" or "transposable elements") that are found
interspersed in the genome. "Junk DNA" also includes "pseudo genes" resulting from random deletions and insertions of DNA in chromosomes,
which are two major mechanisms of DNA mutation.

A triggering event can activate the transposable or "jumping" genes.
In an experiment with corn stalks and unusual changes in their appearance,
geneticist and Nobel Prize winner Barbara McClintock pointed out that the
transposable elements switched locations on the DNA strand due to the corn
stalk being stressed by drought. That was the triggering event.[7]

The ENCODE project[8] studied the functional nature of these non-
coding portions of the genome. As the scientific journal, *Nature,* reports:

6. Servier Medical Art by Servier is licensed under a Creative Commons Attribution 3.0 Unported License. See https://creativecommons.org/licenses/by/3.0.

7. McClintock, "Origin and Behavior," 344–55.

8. ENCODE: The Encyclopedia of DNA Elements is a public research project,
which aims to identify functional elements in the human genome.

> One of the more remarkable findings . . . is that 80 percent of
> the genome contains elements linked to biochemical functions,
> dispatching the widely held view that the human genome is
> mostly "Junk DNA." Of note, these results show that many DNA
> variants previously correlated with certain diseases lie within or
> very near non-coding functional DNA elements, providing new
> leads for linking genetic variation and disease.[9]

There are various mechanisms by which the DNA can become mutated.
One mechanism is "frameshift mutation." This is caused by an insertion or
deletion in a DNA sequence that shifts the way the sequence is read. Frame-
shifts account for a significant percentage of errors in DNA. Several diseases
have frameshift mutations as part of their cause such as Crohn's disease,
cystic fibrosis, or colorectal cancer.

## Genetic Diseases

In considering genetic diseases, there are two major types of genetics to
understand: classical and molecular.

### Classical Genetics

This is what most people are aware of when they think about genetics. Sickle
Cell Anemia, Phenylketonuria (PKU), and Hemophilia are usually inherited genetic diseases. Inherited traits can come through a dominant gene
(only one parent may contribute the gene and it will still express itself, as
with the trait of brown eyes); a recessive gene (in which the person must
inherit the gene from both parents, as is the case with blue eyes); X-linked
traits (coming from the mother), and other variants of these.

In the case of X-linked diseases, the carrier may not show the disease
at all, while their progeny may have it full blown. A good example of this is
hemophilia. One can look at the pedigree of the European families related
to Queen Victoria to see how it was passed down either as a carrier gene or
as a full-blown disease. No one in the previous generations had the disease
so that means a genetic (mutation) event occurred in the Queen's genes and
was passed down through her germ line cells. Only males are affected while
females are the carrier of the gene. So Alexis Romanov, a great grandson
of Queen Victoria, had full-blown hemophilia, but his mother, the Queen's

---

9. Ecker et al., "Genomics," 52–54.

granddaughter, did not have the disease, but was instead the carrier of the mutated (X-linked) gene.

Another aspect to consider is genetic predisposition. This is a "minor mutation" that may be found in the genome of a person but may not show up as a full-blown disease unless they are exposed to other factors (such as environmental factors). A good example of a genetic predisposition is the mutation in BRCA genes for breast cancer. We know that the carriers have an increased chance of getting the disease although some may carry the BRCA I or II gene mutations but will never get the disease.

## Molecular Genetics

Molecular genetics has to do mainly with studies at the molecular level such as with DNA studies in genetic-related disease. A good example is cancer. Many people know that cancer is a "genetic" disease but the truth is, less than 10 percent of cancers are inherited. So why do we call the disease genetic if more than 90 percent of cancers are not inherited? Cancer is usually an adult disease that is due to external factors causing mutation in otherwise healthy DNA. Some mutations give rise to cancers. Most melanomas, for example are a result of DNA mutating in skin cells due to deleterious UV rays from the sun. This genetic mutation is a result of environmental factors, not something that a person can blame his/her parents for, nor can they pass it on to their progeny.

Scientists, including the author, have done genetic, nutrition, cancer, and epidemiological research and have postulated that some cancers, particularly hormone-related cancers such as those of the prostate and breast, are often due to environmental and diet-related factors.[10] The mutation caused by often-unknown external factors gives rise to uncontrolled cell growth, leading to tumors and possible metastasis. Finally, in the vast number of cases, the uncontrolled disease leads to death.

## Infections and Germ Theory

In addition to genetic diseases, infection is a leading cause of disease—by various pathogens including bacteria and viruses. Viruses usually inject their foreign DNA (or RNA) into the cells of their host. These foreign

---

10. Gunasekera et al., "Activity of Citrus Pectin"; "Differential Anti-Proliferative Activity"; "Lycopene and Lutein"; Gunasekera and Hyland, "In Vivo Regulation"; Liu et al., "Citrus Pectin"; Somasundaram et al., "Differential Phosphorylations of NFkB"; "Enhancement of Chemotherapeutic Activity."

pieces of DNA can then go into the nucleus and possibly incorporate into the chromosome of a cell.

## Bacteria

Bacteria infectious agents are tiny, single cell creatures able to infect and kill highly sophisticated multi-cellular humans by causing diseases such as pneumonia and tuberculosis. Some of these bacteria, such as *Klebsialla pneumonia*, have morphed into "superbugs" through the mechanism of mutations, and have become resistant to the very medicines scientists have synthesized to fight disease. To address this problem, the author, together with fellow scientists, is using a "nanomolecular" approach to kill these superbugs.[11] The author, very recently, has used light activated molecular nanomachines as a medical application to drill into and kill antibiotic re-sistant bacteria. The designers of the first of these rotary nano molecules received the Nobel Prize for chemistry in 2016. These biomedical applica-tions are the first of such being made with nanomedicine by the author and his group at Rice University and Biola University.

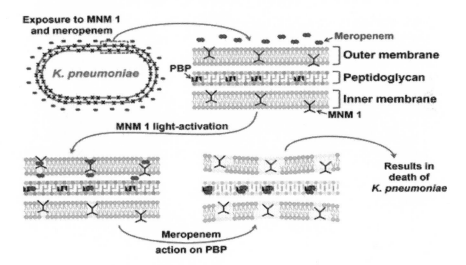

**Figure 2:** K. pneumoniae exposure to molecular nanoma-chines, meropenum, and light.[12]

---

11. Galbadage et al., "Molecular Nanomachines Disrupt Bacterial Cell Wall"; Gu-nasekera et al., "Molecular Nanomachines Can Destroy Tissue."

12. Galbadage et al., "Molecular Nanomachines Disrupt Bacterial Cell Wall."

Another dangerous bacterium is *Yersinia pestis,* which causes the bubonic plague. It is very much alive and well, even today, and is seen in animal populations. In the fourteenth century, almost half of the European population was wiped out by this bacterium which had become extremely virulent. This is similar to what is happening at the present time with the COVID-19 pandemic. A relevant question is, what mechanism caused this bubonic plague to become so virulent in the past and not now?

## Viruses

Viruses are not considered life forms, but machine-like "particles" that co-opt the cellular functions of their hosts to replicate themselves, causing damage to the host organism. Viral infections are caused by viral particles injecting DNA or RNA (both classified as nucleic acids or genetic material) into the host cell, resulting in infection (Figure 3). These viral nucleic acids use the amino acids and machinery of the host cell to make proteins and other molecules needed to propagate themselves. Some viruses incorporate their DNA or RNA into the chromosome DNA of the host cell permanently, thus corrupting the original genome DNA of the host. This inserted DNA or RNA will then henceforth be copied every time the cell divides and potentially could be passed on to future generations.

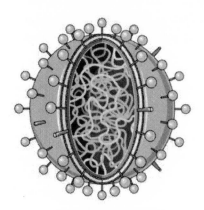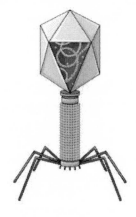

**Figure 3:** Examples of viruses (DNA is in the middle of the protein envelope).[13]

13. Servier Medical Art by Servier is licensed under a Creative Commons Attribution 3.0 Unported License. See https://creativecommons.org/licenses/by/3.0.

The coronavirus family is a family of viruses that usually causes upper respiratory tract infections. The common cold is one kind of infection these viruses can cause. A much more fatal disease, severe acute respiratory syndrome (SARS), caused by SARS-CoV-1, is a disease that broke out in 2002. Its genetic cousin, SARS-CoV-2 causes the current widespread COVID-19 pandemic. What is interesting is that their genetic origins lie in two animals.[14] This has been concluded by genetic studies done on corona viruses that inhabit bats and a scaly-skinned mammal called a pangolin.[15] Genomic studies done on the SARS CoV-2 that infect humans show that the coronavirus species that infect bats have 96 percent genetic homology (similarity). However the coronavirus that is found in the pangolin has in addition to the similar genomic homology, a physical homology of the spike protein that is very similar to the one that infects humans. This implies functional similarity between Pangolin-CoV and SARS-CoV-2.[16]

The interesting question here is, how did these animal coronaviruses begin to infect humans? The answer presumably lies in the mutations that have taken place that have made these relatively harmless viruses to become extremely virulent to humans.

## Satan's Role in Disease?

Are these deadly bacteria and viruses of satanic origin? Are they original creations by a benevolent creator which have been distorted to cause disease by an agent of intelligent evil? Drug-resistant bacteria and viral corruption mechanisms of DNA could be considered two examples of the "wiles of the devil" striking at the heart of God's creation by distorting, counterfeiting, and masquerading as healthy DNA. What better way to corrupt God's creation of life than by distorting the very blueprint of the intelligently designed molecule of life (DNA)—the core of the human being and the heart of the cell?

One scientific hypothesis as to the origins of disease via the activity of Satan, proposed here, comes from the analysis of the genetic and DNA data revealed by the Human Genome Project. The findings of the ENCODE Project show that the non-coding regions of the genome play a particularly important role in the causation and/or prevention of disease. Genetic disease

14. Editors' Note: For more detail on the interface between animal and human populations in spreading disease, and human moral responsibility in this regard, see chapter 7, "A Theology of Ecology."

15. Zhang et al., "Probable Pangolin Origin," 1346–51.

16. Zhang et al., "Probable Pangolin Origin," 1346–51.

could be explained as satanically-caused (or influenced) mutations that take place in the "good" 1.5 percent of the genome that codes for the proteins that make up the physical body. Such mutations can be as small as a point mutation. In Krouzon's syndrome, for example, only one pair out of 3.2 billion nucleotides are involved, but it results in horrible genetic defects and a short life. Other deletions, insertions, and similar DNA corruptions can occur at the chromosomal level, including trisomies such as Downs, Patua, Edwards's syndrome, or Trisomy-9, etc. (The last three syndromes usually result in death before or shortly after birth.) Random mutations and genetic rearrangements almost always lead to disease, suffering, and death. Could this be part of Satan's spiritual warfare against humanity, and/or a manifestation of the curse on the "ground" brought about by original sin?

What is most interesting in the case of cancer is, a) DNA corruption in otherwise good DNA sequences and b) the elusive nature of the cause of the carcinogenesis. In the case of viral infections, the virus injects its DNA or RNA into the hosts after hijacking the cells of the host. This foreign viral DNA (or RNA) could eventually get incorporated into the genome and cause havoc. These mutations of the otherwise good DNA provide an explanation for why cancer (Figure 4), which attacks the very core of the blueprint of life in any cell, could be considered the direct work of the destroyer (Rev 9:11). Scripture informs us that the evil one destroys by distorting, counterfeiting, and masquerading.[17] Disinformation (false teaching) and deception are clearly the works of the enemy and Scripture records that Satan is well known for deceiving people (Col 2:8; 1 Tim 4:1; Gen 3). Perhaps cancer and genetic mutations are his ultimate weapons, caused by distorting the "truth" of the healthy DNA sequences. Could this be a form of an intelligent agent of evil?

17. Stedman, *Spiritual Warfare.*

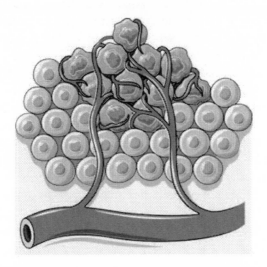

**Figure 4:** A Cancer[18]

How and why do such mutations occur? Where did these external agents come from? If genetic mutations leading to disease and death are not the work of a benevolent creator, is this the work of the devil? (1 John 3:8b). If Satan is indirectly responsible for causing distortions of DNA in our genome, how can that be understood scientifically? Were transposable elements originally built into the genome? It is well known that transitional elements are an extensive source of mutations and genetic polymorphisms.[19]

How did Adam's perfect genome turn into a genome that has large amounts of repetitive transposable elements and genomic "junk" sequences with DNA variants that cause disease?

One possible mechanism is through retroviruses, which provide a link between infectious and genetic diseases. Scientists hypothesize that transposable elements could have come from an ancient infection, perhaps a retrovirus, that infected the genome.[20]

If speaking in evolutionary terms, this ancient retrovirus infection would have occurred ten to sixty million years ago. We postulate that demonic agents could be the source of a retrovirus through which a transposable element is introduced. Transposable elements and other similar

18. Servier Medical Art by Servier is licensed under a Creative Commons Attribution 3.0 Unported License. See https://creativecommons.org/licenses/by/3.0.

19. Bourque et al., "Ten Things."

20. Broecker and Moelling, "Evolution of Immune Systems."

mechanisms dramatically distort genetic content by causing mutations, rearrangements, insertions, deletions, chromosomal malformations, and duplication errors in the DNA. All these things are genetics errors that lead to disease, sterility, and/or death.

As mentioned above, McClintock's experiments showed that stress causes genes in corn to "jump" or transpose. Transposable elements may offer some mechanistic evidence that infirmities and violence in nature that characterize the early record of life are the result of nature being corrupted by fallen powers who had been given authority over various aspects of creation.[21] If Satan and his demons can distort genes (DNA) to become transposable elements that jump around the genome, by causing anxiety, fear, worry, or temptation toward sloth, gluttony, lack of rest, environmental pollution, etc., they could be responsible for disease and even death. And when the genome is changed before a person procreates, this could cause these deleterious mutations to be passed on to the next generation.

Is it possible that the traumatic event that caused the original human retrovirus infection was the result of two things: (1) the extreme stress caused by disobeying God and suddenly getting caught, and thus having a weakening of natural immunity, and (2) God withdrawing his hand of protection, which allowed Satan to influence the genetics of humans? We see the effect of human disobedience to God in the Edenic narration. Similarly we see the effects of satanic activity leading to temptation today. Harmful effects can result when humans succumb to temptation both as recorded in Scripture and in our daily lives. Fear, anxiety, and worry follow sin and disobedience, which in turn cause depression and stress, some to extreme levels that can cause various medical conditions, diseases, and death. (See Figure 5.)

21. Editors' Note: See chapter 4, "Early Church Perspectives on the Cosmic Conflict," regarding the early church's affirmation that fallen powers had authority over aspects of creation.

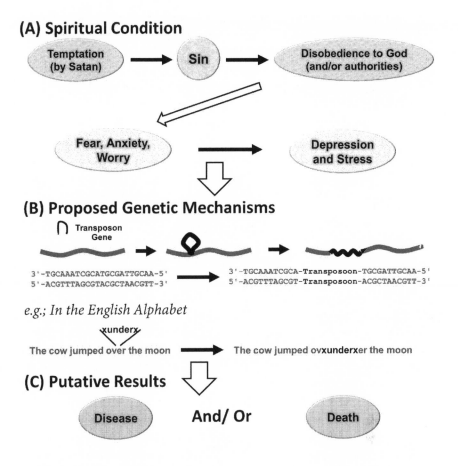

## (A) Spiritual Condition

## (B) Proposed Genetic Mechanisms

*e.g.; In the English Alphabet*

## (C) Putative Results

## Conclusion: Corrupted Life Is a "Work of the Devil"

Scripture states that God's Edenic creation was very good (*meod*, Gen 1:31). At the genomic level this could mean a putative human genome without mutation and error. However, as the Genesis narrative records, evil came into this world when Satan marred God's kingdom by enticing humans to rebel against God, which caused death to come into the world—the consequence God had warned the first humans about. This death now seems to be programmed into the very DNA of humans and other living things.

DNA in all creatures is now degenerate—in plants, animals, fungi, protozoans, viruses, etc.—leading all of life, including the entire human race, to experience disease and death. The ENCODE Project ascertains that a larger percentage of non-coding DNA regions have DNA elements which are responsible for causality for disease, which may suggest corruption of the genome by the deceiver. Hence, the causality of genetic diseases (from inherited genes or from random mutations) or from infectious agents such as retroviruses which insert their DNA into the very genome of other organisms, causing suffering, pain, and death, could be, in turn, attributed to the "works of the devil."

## Bibliography

Bourque, Guillaume, et al. "Ten Things You Should Know about Transposable Elements." *Genome Biology* 19.199 (2018). Online. https://genomebiology.biomedcentral.com/articles/10.1186/s13059-018-1577-z.

Broecker, Felix, and Karin Moelling. "Evolution of Immune Systems From Viruses and Transposable Elements." *Frontiers in Microbiology* 10.51 (2019). Online. https://www.frontiersin.org/articles/10.3389/fmicb.2019.00051/full.

Chen, Steven. "Length of a Human DNA Molecule." In *The Physics Factbook: An Encyclopedia of Scientific Essays,* edited by Glenn Elert. 1998. Online. https://hypertextbook.com/facts/1998/StevenChen.shtml.

Ecker, J. R., et al. "Genomics: ENCODE Explained." *Nature* 489 (2012) 52–54.

Galbadage, T., et al. "Molecular Nanomachines Disrupt Bacterial Cell Wall, Increasing Sensitivity of Extensively Drug-Resistant Klebsiella Pneumonia to Meropenem." *ACS Nano* 13.12 (2019) 14377–87. Online. https://www.ncbi.nlm.nih.gov/pubmed/31815423.

Garcia-Lopez, Victor, et al. "Molecular Machines Open Cell Membranes." *Nature,* August 31, 2017. Online. https://www.nature.com/articles/nature23657.

Gunasekera, Richard S. *Origins: Perspectives on the Origins of Man, Disease and Death—with DNA Evidence from the Human Genome.* Pasadena, CA: William Carey International University Press, 2014.

Gunasekera, Richard S., et al. "Activity of Citrus Pectin and Other Heparan Sulfate Mimetics at the FGF Signal Transduction Complex." *Journal of Nutrition* 131 (2001) 3127S–50S.

———. "Bioactive Molecules from Fruits and Vegetables Significantly Potentiate Traditional Chemotherapy." *Acta Horticulturae* 841 (2009) 55–60.

———. "Differential Anti-Proliferative Activity of Carotenoids on Prostate Cancer Cells and Studies of PSA Expression in Prostate Biopsies." *Journal of Nutrition* 134.12 (2005) 3521S.

———. "Lutein Inhibits Growth of Human Prostate Cancer Cells and Potentiates Capsaicin, Curcumin, and the Traditional Chemotherapy Agent, Camptothecin." *Current Topics in Phytochemistry* 12 (2014) 1–9.

———. "Lycopene and Lutein Inhibit Proliferation in Rat Prostate Carcinoma Cells." *International Journal of Nutrition and Cancer* 58.2 (2007) 171–77.

———. "Molecular Nanomachines Can Destroy Tissue or Kill Multicellular Eukaryotes." *ACS Applied Materials & Interfaces* 12.12 (2020) 13657–70.

———. "Phyto-Bioactive Food Pyramid: A Healthy Dietary Plan for Preventing Certain Common Cancers." *WCIU Journal,* October 2014. Online. https://wciujournal.

wciu.edu/health-and-disease/2018/10/8/phyto-bioactive-food-pyramid-a-healthy-dietary-plan-for-preventing-certain-common-cancers?rq=gunasekera.

Gunasekera, Richard S., and K. Hyland. "In Vivo Regulation of Phenylalanine Hydroxylase in the Genetic Mutant hph-1 Mouse Model." *Molecular Genetics and Metabolism* 98 (2009) 264–72.

Hiebert, Paul G. "The Flaw of the Excluded Middle." In *Perspectives on the World Christian Movement: A Reader*, edited by Ralph D. Winter and Steven C. Hawthorne, 414–21. 4th ed. Pasadena, CA: William Carey Library, 1999.

Hopper, Judith. "A New Germ Theory." *Atlantic*, February 1999. Online. https://www.theatlantic.com/magazine/archive/1999/02/a-new-germ-theory/377430.

Liu, D., et al. "Near-Infrared Light Activates Molecular Nanomachines to Drill into and Kill Cells." *ACS Nano* 13.6 (2019) 6813–23.

Liu, Y., et al. "Citrus Pectin: Characterization and Inhibitory Effect on Fibroblast Growth Factor-receptor Interaction." *Journal of Agricultural Food Chemistry* 49 (2001) 3051–57.

McClintock, Barbara. "The Origin and Behavior of Mutable Loci in Maize." *Proceedings of the National Academy of Sciences USA* 36.6 (1950) 344–55. Online. https://www.ncbi.nlm.nih.gov/pmc/articles/PMC1063197.

Somasundaram, G., et al. "Differential Phosphorylations of NFkB and Cell Growth of MDA-MB 231 Human Breast Cancer Cell Line by Limonins." *Acta Horticulturae* 841 (2009) 151–54.

———. "Enhancement of Chemotherapeutic Activity of Curcumin and Capsaicin by Bioflavone α* on Human Prostate Cancer Cells." *Journal of Nutrition* 134.12 (2005) 3521S.

Stedman, Ray C. *Spiritual Warfare: Winning the Daily Battle with Satan*. Portland, OR: Multnomah, 1975.

Winter, Ralph D. "The Works of the Devil?" Lecture given at the Presbyterians for Renewal Breakfast at General Assembly, Fort Worth, TX, 1999. Online. https://static1.squarespace.com/static/5b3157f3b40b9d21a8096625/t/6054beb181d9e76c8f4a0d47/1616166586016/works+of+the+devil-+rdw.pdf.

Zhang, Tao, et al. "Probable Pangolin Origin of SARS-CoV-2 Associated with the COVID-19 Outbreak." *Current Biology* 30 (2020) 1346–51. Online. https://www.cell.com/current-biology/pdf/S0960-9822(20)30360-2.pdf.

16 _____

# A Practical Missiology Regarding Disease and Healing

—Daniel W. O'Neill

How do we apply the spiritual, social, and material realities of disease with a view toward healing? In reflecting on the problem of disease, disability, and death in my practice of community hospital-based family medicine, coupled with theological and biblical reflections in seminary studies, and global service in under-resourced countries, a practical globalized theology is emerging. I present this with no illusion that it plumbs the depths of the mystery of the heavenly or earthly realities. Nor does it present an exhaustive pan-cultural solution. Yet effective, contextualized approaches need to begin to be developed for a more full-orbed response in a globalized world at the level of community.

## Pathology

Pathology is the study of disordered states of being—a study of suffering. It describes what is at variance with normal, and affects both structure and function. Diseases can be categorized as infectious, or from deficiencies, trauma, hereditary conditions, mental disorders, or physiologic conditions. The human immune system is designed to keeps the body pure, free of invasive species or cellular mutations from within, but it can turn on itself in autoimmune diseases. DNA codes are messages for proper function, but are subject to corruption through insertions or deletions of base pairs.[1] This is similar to the insertion of "not" by the serpent in the garden

1. Editors' Note: For more detail, see chapter 15, "A Scientist's Perspective on

to the Creator's message to humanity "you will *not* certainly die" (Gen 3:4). Insertions and deletions in the DNA code also serve as a metaphor for the dire dangers of adding to or subtracting from the revealed word of God (Deut 4:2; Rev 22:18–19). Environmental toxins and ionizing radiation as well as retroviruses affect genes, and human behaviors and emotions are strongly associated with disease. In the emerging field of behavioral epigenetics, it is thought that learned behaviors (eg., those contrary to God's best intentions for us) may become expressed through methylation of DNA which can be passed along in the flesh of subsequent generations, often compounded and magnified.[2]

Paul Tillich wrote that the concept of health cannot be defined without relation to its opposite—disease. Jesus as Savior (*soter*) can also be thought of as Healer, Tillich notes, and there would be no conflict but the most "intimate relation" between the religious and medical. "Health is disease conquered."[3] The search for up-stream causes of disease is vital for human flourishing. How early human life is treated, especially in the first one thousand days from conception, has profound effects on human health and human capital development in nations.[4] Once these multi-faceted etiologies can be identified, a host of means can be deployed to prevent, contain, or eradicate that which demeans or destroys life. Mission history professor, Wilbert Shenk, writes, "All the forces and powers that touch human life come under scrutiny. Those that oppress the poor and destroy life are to be exposed and denounced. Good news means that men and women can be set free from life-destroying powers."[5]

## Presence

Jesus was the perfect model for how to live (Heb 1:3) and what to do and teach (Acts 1:1), seamlessly combining character, practice, and instruction. In his incarnation, he fully identified with the corporeality of human life with ground-level service. He expressed compassion toward the crowds, because they were harassed and helpless, like lost sheep without a shepherd (Matt 9:36). Instead of being paralyzed with disappointment or mired in sentimentality, Jesus was motivated to set people free, to heal, and to teach

---

Disease and Death."

2. Powledge, "Behavioral Epigenetics," 588–92.

3. Tillich, *Meaning of Health*, 59–60.

4. De Angulo and Losada, "Emerging Health Paradigm," 113–28.

5. Shenk, "Recasting Theology of Mission," 105.

them as the Good Shepherd and Rabbi that he was. Lament and compassion are necessary but insufficient reactions to those affected by evil. Efforts toward healing the material or meta-physical intermediaries are a pro-active response to disease, a praxis toward liberation, which might come at great cost. In addition, a full-orbed response to disease includes teaching divine connections in order for the oppressed to enter into lasting relationship with the living God who heals, makes whole (*holoklēros*, 1 Thess 5:23; James 1:4), and sets free, "to open their eyes and turn them from darkness to light, and from the power of Satan to God" (Acts 26:18).

Jesus fulfilled Isaiah 61:1–2 which he read in the synagogue in his hometown Nazareth (Luke 4:14–21). His presence healed, demons fled, and good news was shared with the poor. His life both fulfilled and overcame the law of sin and death, and then broke the prophetic trifecta of sin's consequences of sword, famine, and plague by *being* the Prince of Peace (by disarming the sword), the Bread of Life (by satiating hunger), and the Healer—casting out demons and healing disease (by dispelling plagues). It was a clear glimpse of the kingdom of God and the defeat of the prince of this world being driven out (*ekblethesetai*) (John 12:31). His followers likewise were called out to preach the truth, heal diseases, and cast out (*ekballete*) demons in Jesus' name (Matt 10:8; Mark 6:13). Jesus gave his body over to a bloody and violent death, completing his identification with the human race embedded in affliction and subjected to death. By his death, he disarmed the devil, who holds the power of death, in order to "free those who all their lives were held in slavery by their fear of death" (Heb 2:15). James Bruckner developed the idea of good and bad dominion as a major theme of the Bible, highlighting the command for Genesis 1:28 to properly subdue, "any chaos that would disturb or destroy human life."[6]

Apart from, and in addition to, efforts to eradicate disease individually, regionally, and globally, the crucible of illness is a place where comforters, companions, physicians, nurses, therapists, pastors, technicians, chaplains, priests, and counsellors can *dwell* in order to help the afflicted frame their illness in light of God's ultimate healing intentions and actions. God's people give honor to his name by attributing all healing to God, living lives of caring and compassion, speaking the truth in love, identifying and naming (diagnosing), casting out (eradicating), rebuking evil, and comforting the afflicted. A comprehensive, ground level, collaborative, and integrated approach is a truly biblical approach.

6. Bruckner, *Healthy Human Life*, 15.

## Praxis with Patience

However, we must caution against a utopian view and a modernist super-optimism in which all the works of the opposers and oppressors can be completely vanquished prior to the *eschaton*. We can retain a realistic but not fatalistic resignation that the current epoch of history will continue to have what Winter called "physical distortions and intellectual delusions"[7] (the "tares" of Matt 13:24–30) until the Day of the Lord and the renewal of all things. Allen Verhey, by highlighting the lament in Job 3, eschews a spiritual or medical triumphalism which views righteousness being an antidote to sickness or sadness, and medical wizardry a cure for all diseases. Although his terminology de-emphasizes the role or even reality of the Satan, and he uses a more pastoral approach instead of an interventionalist approach, he makes an important emphasis on the value of lament.[8] Despite the humbling limitations of healing, the present reality empowers our purpose, requires perseverance for this labor of love, and makes us long for something better. We pray for God's kingdom to come on Earth as it is in heaven, and work toward a degree of that unfolding and future reality among all the people groups of the world. Many are languishing apart from a healing relationship with the living God, so we are called to move beyond lament toward liberation and align more completely with God's redeeming will in all of creation.

## Partnerships

While adversarial relationships have existed in heaven and Earth, there are collaborative alignments which can advance God's best intentions for the world. Christians must rise above their often insular beginnings and "not limit the field of cooperators."[9] Secular-minded people of good will who seek to tackle the powers that inhibit human flourishing are unwittingly doing the will of God to an extent. People of Christian faith can align themselves with these efforts to identify and eliminate causes, with elevated levels of conscientiousness, as an act of Christian service. This can be seen as both serving God's purposes of healing and expressing loving kindness toward our global neighbors. Not only does this enhance witness to the

---

7. Winter, "Unfinished Epic," 323.

8. Verhey, *Reading the Bible*, 120–21.

9. Gettman, *Do you Really Want to Be Healed?*, 13.

power of Christ in pluralistic contexts, but it can become deeply motivating and lead to sustainable engagement.

In contrast to the destruction wrought by organisms vying for survival at the expense of the host or prey, there are well-known symbiotic relationships in biology, which confer mutual advantage. This is evident in the burgeoning study of the health-promoting human microbiome—what we might call the "good" bacteria and viruses in the gut, skin, and soil, which confer significant health advantages. This symbiosis is an example of the delicate balance of the created order, which, as an important part of planetary ecological balance, can be easily disrupted. Inordinate or inappropriate use of antibiotics, increasing metabolic disorders such as diabetes mellitus, dietary indiscretions, mental illness, environmental toxins, depleted soil, etc. can disrupt this delicate balance leading to susceptibility to disease.

We must not lose sight of human culpability for disease causation, as well as human responsibility for its management, control, and eradication. Disease mitigation and healing efficacy require synergy with those called according to God's purposes (Rom 8:28), cooperation with God's Spirit, assistance by angelic beings, and agreement among God's co-workers across denominational and organizational boundaries. In addition, those people of good will of any faith, secular organizations, and health systems, can be used by God for alignment toward his ultimate purposes, despite the corruptions resident in each of them.

## Purging

Like human beings and nation-states, creatures and microorganisms vie for space, control, and advantage for their species. This material, social, and ecological battleground may reflect the spiritual battleground to which the Scriptures testify as a present reality. The concept of peace (Hebrew, *shalom*) is instructive here as a divine intention for right relationships. This state of wholeness is expressed in three epochs:

1. In the primordial Edenic state

2. In examples of a faithful, called-out, covenant-keeping community (however imperfect)

3. In the prophetic images portrayed of the new heavens and Earth.

These are all marked by intimacy, trust, symbiosis, harmony, and human and planetary flourishing. *Realizing* these states of being is the driving desire and purpose of the Creator, who is worthy of adoration from every fiber of a liberated creation, reoriented toward harmony and abundant life. Anything opposed to the trajectory of this perfect will, self-destructs and constrains this kingdom objective and the life-giving presence of God. Brenda Colijn writes that "salvation is rescue and healing, room to thrive, safety and well-being. It is present whenever people receive forgiveness of sins through Jesus Christ, but also whenever people experience deliverance from danger or oppression or physical or emotional healing."[10]

Invasive and destructive species, multi-drug resistant strains of tuberculosis, and other pathogenic bacteria, parasites, and viruses are examples of the corruption of natural selection or, in Ralph Winter's hypothesis, the result of intentional malevolent powers. These, he hypothesized, affect creation at the material and biological level in order to maximize human illness and early death, and to resist or evade eradication.[11] The developing world has received much value by Christian efforts to manifest truth in the fabric of life by using modern medicine and public health to "name the powers," and "cast them out" when possible, as a display of God's presence and love. This takes an iterative process of discernment, innovation, advocacy, and dominion to purge tainted areas of life and restore harmony. However, caution is needed to counter a triumphalist bravado regarding disease, sin, and death. Modernist efforts to escape the drudgery of traditional primal societies by harnessing nature to create a better world has tended to overreach and even alienate in a globalized world permeated by intractable evils.[12]

## Proclamation

When Israel entered the promised land, they were instructed to proclaim curses on mount Ebal and blessings on mount Gerizim. God sets before us, intentionally, the choice of both blessings and curses (Deut 11:26–29). The juxtaposition of bad news and good news highlights the reality of both. He desires that we chose life (Deut 30:19) and takes no pleasure in the death of anyone (Ezek 18:32). Both the Spirit and the Word work together to promote and sustain life. "The Spirit gives life; the flesh counts for nothing. The words I have spoken to you—they are full of the Spirit and life" (John 6:63). Words matter as an explanation of a disease process or to engender hope and confidence. "Good news gives health to the bones" (Prov 15:30). Words also matter as the identity and worth of Jesus of Nazareth is

10. Colijn, *Images of Salvation in the New Testament*, 142–43.

11. Editors' Note: For a scientific hypothesis on how malevolent powers might bring about disease, see chapter 15, "A Scientist's Perspective on Disease and Death."

12. Ott and Netland, *Globalizing Theology*, 10.

proclaimed as healer and redeemer, "and by his wounds we are healed" (Isa 53:5). Howard Snyder expressed what Ralph Winter noted about the mission of God being bigger than we might have thought: "The gospel is good news about personal, social, ecological, and cosmic healing and reconciliation. It is good news to the whole creation—to the whole earth and in fact to the whole cosmos."[13] This would, of course, include all other created beings as well as every tribe, tongue, and nation.

## Power until *Parousia*

Working toward health and wholeness of body and mind is not to labor in vain, because any work to restore or redeem the fallen creation is to cooperate with God's intention for the creation upon Jesus' return (1 Cor 15:58). It is an effort to reconcile what was fractured, to mend what was corrupted. Bruckner agrees: "Healing transcends biomedical categories because it addresses more than the disease . . . it restores relationships."[14] N. T. Wright develops this clearly: "All we do in faith, hope, and love in the present, in obedience to our ascended Lord and in the power of his Spirit, will be enhanced and transformed at his appearing."[15] The hope of the resurrection of the bodies of the redeemed supports, and does not undermine, work toward physical wholeness. Caird writes, "Any achievement of man in the old order, however imperfect, provided it has value in the sight of God, will find its place in the healed and transfigured life of the New Jerusalem."[16] We cooperate with our Creator in his movement to purge and restore a harmonious world in the area of human and ecological health, whether it is on a large or small scale. Christopher Wright notes that "All of our work now contributes to the content of the new creation."[17] Christ's resurrection was the beginning of the new creation, and when Christ returns to make all things new (Rev 21:5), suggests Stearns, "it will be to complete the work that we, his followers, have begun in his name."[18]

---

13. Snyder, *Global Good News*, 244.

14. Bruckner, *Healthy Human Life*, 213.

15. Wright, *Surprised by Hope*, 143.

16. Caird, *Commentary on the Revelation*, 300.

17. Wright, *God I Don't Understand*, 219–20.

18. Stearns, *Hole in Our Gospel*, 69.

## Conclusion

The blind spot that Ralph Winter sensed in Western theology is being filled by increasingly globalized theological reflection, ecological conscientiousness, emerging scientific evidence, and a realistic, pro-active application of the living word to ground-level complex problems. The praxis of actively disrupting complex relationships with the dark principalities and powers, facing the challenges of the corrupted material world, and seeking to restore right relationships with the Creator and the groaning creation longing for redemption, is what Daniel Fountain called "the most exciting adventures of life."[19] Calling the exegetes of Scripture, the exegetes of the material world, and the exegetes of humans together in a full-orbed response to disease is a long overdue convergence for the *missio Dei*.

## Bibliography

Angulo, Jose M. de, and Luz S. Losada. "The Emerging Health Paradigm in the Twenty-First Century: The Formative First One Thousand Days of Life." *Christian Journal for Global Health* 3.2 (2016) 113–28. Online. https://doi.org/10.15566/cjgh.v3i2.38.

Bruckner, James K. *Healthy Human Life: A Biblical Witness.* Eugene, OR: Cascade, 2012.

Caird, George B. *A Commentary on the Revelation of St. John the Divine.* Harper's New Testament Commentaries. New York: Harper and Row, 1966.

Chan, Simon. *Grassroots Asian Theology: Thinking the Faith from the Ground Up.* Downers Grove, IL: InterVarsity Academic, 2014.

Colijn, Brenda B. *Images of Salvation in the New Testament.* Downers Grove, IL: InterVarsity Academic, 2010.

Gettman, Larry R. *Do you Really Want to Be Healed?: A Compelling Chronicle of Medical Missionary Work in India.* Pittsburg: Rose Dog, 2005.

Ott, Craig, and Harold A. Netland, eds. *Globalizing Theology: Belief and Practice in an Era of World Christianity.* Grand Rapids: Baker Academic, 2006.

Powledge, Tabitha M. "Behavioral Epigenetics: How Nurture Shapes Nature." *BioScience* 61.8 (2011) 588–92. Online. https://academic.oup.com/bioscience/article/61/8/588/336969.

Shenk, Wilbert R. "Recasting Theology of Mission: Impulses from the Non-Western World." *International Bulletin of Missionary Research* 25.3 (2001) 98–107. Online. https://doi.org/10.1177/239693930102500301.

Snyder, Howard A., ed. *Global Good News.* Nashville: Abingdon, 2001.

Stearns, Richard. *The Hole in Our Gospel: What Does God Expect of Us?.* Nashville: Thomas Nelson, 2010.

Tillich, Paul. *The Meaning of Health: The Relation of Religion and Health.* Richmond, CA: Richmond, 1981.

Verhey, Allen. *Reading the Bible in the Strange World of Medicine.* Grand Rapids: Eerdmans, 2003.

19. Fountain, *God, Medicine, and Miracles,* 70

Winter, Ralph D. "The Unfinished Epic." In *Frontiers in Mission: Discovering and Surmounting Barriers to the Missio Dei*, edited by Ralph D. Winter, 317–26. 4th ed. Pasadena, CA: William Carey International University Press, 2008.

Wright, Christopher J. H. *The God I Don't Understand*. Grand Rapids: Zondervan, 2008.

Wright, N. T. *Surprised by Hope*. New York: Harper One, 2008.

# 17

## A Missiology That Includes
## Fighting Disease[1]

—Ralph D. Winter with Beth Snodderly

The responsibility of humans for restoring the reputation of God (who, according to many confused people, is the cause of suffering and sickness) is now much larger than ever before. That responsibility is also more logical and urgent than ever before. The evil working of the adversary is right before our eyes picking off believer after believer, long before natural death.[2] When will we arise to work with God to destroy the works of the devil?

## A Summary of the Biblical Theme of Cosmic Battle

A missiology of disease recognizes that fighting disease, even to the point of eradication, is part of a cosmic battle against the works of the devil that God has invited believers to join alongside the Son of God. The Bible consists of a single drama: the entrance of the kingdom, the power, and the glory of the living God in this enemy-occupied territory. From Genesis 12 to the end of the Bible, and indeed until the end of time, there unfolds the single, coherent drama of "the kingdom strikes back." This would make a good title for the Bible itself were it to be printed in modern dress (with Gen 1–11 as the introduction to the whole Bible). In this unfolding

1. This article consists of excerpts from the Winter writings listed in the Bibliography. Used by permission.

2. Editors' Note: Although Winter wrote this paragraph in 2003, it has special meaning for the world currently in crisis with the COVID-19 pandemic.

drama we see the gradual but irresistible power of God reconquering and redeeming his fallen creation through the giving of his own Son at the very center of the four thousand-year period ending in 2000 CE. This is tersely summed up: "The reason the Son of God appeared was to destroy the works of the devil" (1 John 3:8 ESV).

This counterattack against the evil one clearly does not await the appearance of the good Person in the center of the story. Indeed, there would seem to be five identifiable epochs of advance prior to the appearance of Christ as well as five after that event. The theme that links all ten epochs is the grace of God intervening in a world which "lies in the power of the evil one" (1 John 5:19 ESV), contesting an enemy who temporarily is "the god of this world" (2 Cor 4:4 ESV) so that the nations will praise God's name. His plan for doing this is to reach all peoples by conferring an unusual "blessing" on Abraham and Abraham's seed (Abraham's children-by-faith), even as we pray, "Thy kingdom come."

By contrast, the evil one's plan is to bring reproach on the name of God. The evil one stirs up hate, perhaps distorts even DNA sequences, and authors suffering and destruction of God's good creation. Satan's devices may very well include devising virulent germs in order to tear down confidence in God's loving character. All over the Earth people are dying prematurely in suffering and pain due to an onslaught from the microbiological world that we are only beginning to understand and that has not been understood theologically.

Today our God is being blamed for all kinds of evil. When people get sick, they commonly assume "God did it" for some unknown reason. That misunderstanding does not glorify God. We need to recognize the very radical and significant decision of God to create beings, angelic and human, with true free will and to work through both the angelic and human intermediaries. Christ has called us not merely to witness but to be salt and light in a world of evil, corruption, and disease.

## Misunderstandings about Disease, the Bible, God's Will, and God's Character

In this mandate to glorify God by representing God's character we must consider these questions:

- Does God send disease or does God want to do away with it?
- How does attributing disease to God affect God's reputation?

- Will people want to follow a God they believe punishes them with disease?

- How do we reconcile the differing Old and New Testament viewpoints?

It is a very perplexing question of how the New Testament is different from the Old Testament. Misunderstandings about God's character and God's will can arise from misunderstanding the nature of biblical revelation. Some may point to accounts in the Old Testament that indicate the people of Israel believed God sent disease as punishment for wrongdoing. For example, in Genesis 12:17, "the LORD inflicted serious diseases on Pharaoh and his household because of Abram's wife Sarai." However, very few people today understand the Bible to be a continuous story of developing insight on the part of a people God was teaching. It took two thousand years for some ideas to become relevant. I feel it is important to acknowledge that our Christian Bibles reveal many evidences of having incorporated perspectives from outside the Abrahamic genetic lineage. God did not just wave a wand and take his people from four thousand years ago into the present without any transitional periods in between. If we believe that, we are unfair to the Bible itself. The Bible—as it stands—is an inerrant record that portrays the progressive impact on a given nation (Israel) of God's will. And we can't read just one part of the Bible—that's just one part of the story. We need to see the whole story, and where it's going. And the fact is, that while in the Old Testament Satan is only referred to a few times, in the New Testament Satan/the devil/the evil one is mentioned about one hundred times.

Once Satan is in the picture (if we believe he is), no amount or kind of harsh or heartless evil should be unexpected in any quarter. "The devil . . . was a murderer from the beginning" (John 8:44). "Do not be like Cain, who belonged to the evil one and murdered his brother" (1 John 3:12). Right from the beginning of his ministry Jesus engaged in the cosmic battle with the devil and amazed people with the authority he had over demonic behavior, including disease: "Jesus healed many who had various diseases. He also drove out many demons, but he would not let the demons speak because they knew who he was" (Mark 1:34; also see Matt 4:23–24; Luke 4:40–41). In the New Testament, deliverance from disease is a sign of the "good news" of the kingdom of God. "Jesus went throughout Galilee, teaching in their synagogues, proclaiming the good news of the kingdom, and healing every disease and sickness among the people" (Matt 4:23). Luke reports that as the crowds followed Jesus, he "welcomed them and spoke to them about the kingdom of God, and healed those who needed healing" (Luke 9:11). This is what God's will and loving character looks like.

The seeming contradictions between the Old and New Testament views are resolved when we take into account that Jesus is the full representation of God's character. He is the complete revelation of God's will, which is diametrically opposed to the murderous character of God's adversary. "The Son is the radiance of God's glory and the exact representation of his being" (Heb 1:3).

## The Devil's and Demons' Role in Disease

The Old Testament view of attributing disease caused by microbiological evils (such as boils, leprosy, or plague) to God's punishment for sin, sounds a lot like some contemporary Christian views of disease, and for the same reason: there is no Satan in the picture. Both views put the blame on the person who is suffering or on God, because they do not recognize the devil and demons as the source of illness. Our current theological literature, to my knowledge, does not seriously consider disease pathogens from a theological point of view—that is, are they the work of God or Satan? Much less does this literature ask the question: does God mandate us to eliminate pathogens? I am aware that only in recent history have humans recognized that much sickness is due to ingenious, invisible, deadly forms of intelligent life. Our forefathers who were the caretakers and creators of our theology—our Calvins and Luthers, Augustines and Aquinases—were unaware of the microscopic world. Therefore, they had no opportunity to decide whether germs brought a great shadow on the glory of God, or, thus, whether fighting those destructive entities would be a significant means of glorifying God. But what if all disease pathogens as well as all violent forms of life are the work of Satan? What would Jesus have said about fighting germs had the people of his time known about germs? How would that amplify and refocus our global mission?

To me the most profound issue facing missions today is the absence of a concept of an adversary in our theology of church life and mission.[3] The "works of the devil" would seem to include the perversion of the very structure of life at DNA levels. The discovery of thousands of defective genes in the human genome is possibly evidence of demonic activity at the DNA

---

3. Editors' Note: This concern of Ralph Winter's has been addressed in this book, particularly in these chapters: chapter 2, "A Theology of Creation: Order Out of Chaos"; chapter 4, "Early Church Perspectives on the Cosmic Conflict"; chapter 18, "An Enemy Did This: A Cosmic Conflict Understanding of 'Natural' Evil"; and chapter 19, "Why Creation Groans: Responding to Objections to the Corruption of Nature (CON) Hypothesis."

level.[4] Even the violent traits of animals and man may exhibit the same kind of distorting influence at that level.

My pastor used to say that "Satan's greatest achievement is to cover his tracks." That, surely, is why we get out of practice speaking of him or recognizing his works or even recognizing his existence. Yet, when we reinstate his existence as an evil intelligence loose in God's creation, only then do a lot of things become clear and reasonable. Otherwise God gets blamed for all kinds of evil: "God took my wife," etc. I find it difficult, after making this switch, not to conclude that Satan's angels are the source of life-destroying forms of life, vicious animals, bacteria, viruses. Not that demonic beings created them but that they tampered with their DNA to distort them.

## Fighting Disease Is Part of the Mandate to Care for Creation and to Take It Back from the Rulership of the Devil

To "destroy the works of the devil" means thus to take it as part of our efforts, our mission to glorify God, to restore, with God's help, what Satan has distorted. The Genesis mandate to man to care for life and creation (Gen 1:28) would seem to include serious human efforts in collaboration with God to restore (to redeem) all perversions of disease or violence in the various forms of life. All creation groans and strains according to Romans 8, waiting for its redemption. But if we talk about redemption we have to talk about restoration of creation. You can't just talk about a ticket to heaven in the pocket of human beings. It is as though some people think to escape this world is more important than to restore God's glory through the conquest of the destructive and distorting elements of satanic fury against God. Getting human beings redeemed is not the end, it's the beginning. The advance of God's kingdom consists not merely of the rescue of humans but includes the restoration of a corrupted creation and the defeat of the evil one. Once restored in repentance and faith, in the blessing of God, redeemed man is now expected to resume his original purpose, to work with God for the restoration of all creation, and in the process make crystal clear that Satan, and not God, is the initiator of evil and depravity.

But for most evangelicals there is a massive "disconnect." We can clearly see a monstrous, pervasive distortion in creation, but we don't realize how illogical it is to blame all that on God, as some do. We need a closer study of the Book of Creation to discern the difference between the beauty

4. Editors' Note: See chapter 15, "A Scientist's Perspective on Disease and Death."

God put there and the violence and gruesome cruelty Satan has put there. Our disconnect from the reality of Satan's work blinds us to the theological significance of the corruption of all creation. By corruption of creation we must recognize genetic damage (not just "defects") both before and after conception, terribly hostile pathogens, viruses, bacteria, parasites, wild animals, as well as warlike and genocidal humans. The corruption of creation by intelligent evil has turned the story of our planet into the story of a battle. Unfortunately, there is a widespread blindness to the corruption of all creation and our responsibility to restore it.

The divine response to this corruption was a plan to defeat the evil one, restore creation, and reclaim all the peoples of the Earth. A principal means for this is the redemption of man through a chosen nation, on the basis of "the lamb slain from the foundations of the world" (Rev 13:8 KJV). As Abraham's children, we have inherited the family responsibility of God's concerns and purposes which are to become our concerns and purposes. The Abrahamic "blessing" is a key concept. It returns "families," that is, *nations,* to his household, to the kingdom of God, so that the nations will "declare his glory" (Ps 96:3). But the nations are being prevented from declaring God's glory by the scarcity of evidence of God's ability to cope with evil. If the Son of God appeared to destroy the works of the devil, then what are the followers and "joint heirs" of the Son of God supposed to do to bring honor to his name?

## Missiological Implications: Fighting Disease Helps Glorify God by Displaying God's Character and Rectifying God's Damaged Reputation

We will have a much-empowered gospel if we accept our mandate to restore creation. It crucially enlarges our understanding of the devastation of Satan's ongoing activities in distorting creation and thus tearing down God's glory. It therefore requires a larger presentation of the gospel to unreached peoples. It defines a larger mission of not just getting people out of this world safely into heaven, but that of getting redeemed people to turn around and fight along with God against the evil one.

We should speak of four levels of strategy and purpose:

1. Getting people "saved"

2. Winning them to the lordship of Christ and into his family

3. Glorifying God

4. Distinguishing evil from God and fighting "the works of the devil" as a means of glorifying God, that is, understanding the lordship of Christ as involving us in an all-out war against evil, disease, corruption—a war in which we can expect suffering, hardship, and death.

The assumption of some people seems to be that the advance of God's kingdom consists merely of the rescue of humans, not the restoration of a corrupted creation and the defeat of the evil one. But getting people delivered from Satan isn't the main point. Rather, the point is getting creation delivered from Satan. Saving human beings is only part of the restoration of creation. It is a very important part, if for no other reason than both good angels and redeemed people are part of the process of beating down the gates of hell. The principal concern of the Bible is God and his name. The destruction of God's will is the problem.

Some will say, "What in the world could microbes have to do with the kingdom of God or global evangelism?" The answer is simple. Distorted microbes war against the kingdom of God. Distorted genes make animals violent and destructive. Destructive parasites kill off many varieties of plant and animal life. The malarial parasite alone kills over one million people each year, most of them children.[5] All this massive damage to the purposes of the kingdom of God amounts to noise so loud that people can't hear what we are preaching to them.

If we are to glorify God, is it not essential to free him from the accusation that he, not Satan, is the author of evil? How attractive is our invitation to people to return to and yield to their Father in heaven if they continue to believe that he is the one who deliberately contrives for most everyone to die in suffering? Unless Satan is in the picture and we are known to be fighting his deadly works, we are allowing God's glory to be marred and torn down.[6]

We have a mandate to restore God's reputation among all peoples by more adequately representing God's character. While Christians are noted for being kind to people who are already sick, curiously and ominously, to this day, Christians are not well known for fighting the viruses, the

---

5. UNICEF, "Reality of Malaria."

6. Editors' Note: God's justice requires judgment against sin, often in the form of God allowing humanity to experience the consequences God warns us about. This includes sometimes allowing Satan to inflict disease (as expressed in the Job narrative). So, in one sense, God is responsible for these diseases by permissive will. At times, these are permitted by him for our own spiritual good (e.g., Paul's thorn in the flesh, "a messenger of Satan" [2 Cor 12:7]). God makes "beauty instead of ashes" (Isa 61:3), but we cannot say with biblical integrity that God does not allow those ashes to awaken us to his beauty.

bacteria, and the tiny parasites that cause illness.[7] The fact that Jesus did not talk about germs does not mean that he wants us to be silent on that subject today. It is common today among many evangelicals to be content with the first-century understanding of nature. But the challenge for us today is to discover what Jesus would have said had the people then known what we know today about germs.

## Conclusion

Jesus challenged every kind of evil. Today, there is a large array of diseases from smallpox to SARS to Guinea worm to river blindness to tuberculosis to dengue fever which we have to go out and slay.[8] Once we remove our religious glasses that seem to see everything in terms of how we can have our sins forgiven and get to heaven, we can begin to glimpse an almost entirely new scene in which the issue is not so much salvation as service, that is, what we do after we get forgiven. In fact, Jesus actually said, "Whoever tries to keep their life will lose it, and whoever loses their life will preserve it" (Luke 17:33).

If someone on the mission field who has never heard of the Bible were to read the Gospels for the first time, they would clearly get the idea that the kingdom of God (or the kingdom of heaven) is the main subject—not in the sense of "how to get to heaven" but how the power, the rule, the authority of God—of heaven—can get to Earth, how God's will can come on Earth as it is in heaven. We misrepresent God if we talk only about getting to heaven. We must also reveal by our actions his concern for the conquest of evil and disease.

It would seem embarrassing that Jimmy Carter, a Sunday School teacher, not a theologian, nor a mission executive, nor a missiologist, has actually done more than anyone else in arousing world opinion to the need to eradicate diseases, not just extend health care after people get sick. Apparently that kind of vision is not, at this stage of history, something that can be credited either to Christian theology or to missiology, but rather to the energy and intuitive theology of a past president of the USA who happened to be well known on a world level.

7. Editors' Note: Winter did not live long enough to know of Richard Gunasekera's recent work, described in chapter 15, "A Scientist's Perspective on Disease and Death." Dr. Gunasekera is actively engaged in fighting deadly bacteria and viruses (including the coronavirus) using "nanomachines." He does this as an intentional means of fighting "the works of the devil" in the realm of disease and for the glory of God. Winter, however, had invited Gunasekera to collaborate with him and co-author an article on this topic in the early 1990s when they discussed the molecular biology of death and disease.

8. Editors' Note: In 2020 we need to add COVID-19 to this list.

In all of our commendable haste to get to the ends of the Earth and to the last group which has never heard the gospel, we may be overlooking the fact that the vast bulk of the Western world no longer believes in the Bible and no longer follows our faith—partly because people have not noticed believers at the forefront of efforts to defeat the evils of this present world. Does that mean our immense overseas achievements are going to be only temporary? Are we preaching a "relapsing" Christianity?

When souls are saved they are not merely supposed to be survivors singing of their salvation, but soldiers deliberately choosing to enter into the dangerous, sacrificial, arduous task of restoring the glory of God for all to see. "Let your light shine before others, that they may see your good deeds and glorify your Father in heaven" (Matt 5:16). I do not think that the world is going to get better and better until Jesus comes to congratulate us on our accomplishments, but I do think he expects us to work toward that end, whether it is attainable or not, as a means of glorifying his name and empowering our evangelism. What rings in my ears is the phrase in the parable, "occupy till I come" (Luke 19:13 KJV).

If we can properly re-contextualize our faith at this time, we will no longer need simply to trust that in God's sovereign purposes there are good things even when things go wrong. We can both recognize the truth of that and also work against the causes of evil and suffering. In that case we are free to understand that God is expecting us to join in that effort. Jesus said, "As the Father has sent me, I am sending you" (John 20:21).

To destroy the works of the devil is one major way in which our testimony of word and deed can glorify the true nature of our living God, our loving Heavenly Father. It is not an alternative to evangelism, it will make our evangelism more credible. *It is to rectify our God's damaged reputation.* It is to avoid extending the implicit and embarrassing policy of almost constantly misrepresenting him in our mission work around the world. Attacking the roots of disease is part and parcel of our basic mandate to glorify God in all the Earth.

## Bibliography

Boyd, Gregory A. "Evolution as Cosmic Warfare: A Biblical Perspective on Satan and 'Natural' Evil." In *Creation Made Free: Open Theology Engaging Science*, edited by Thomas J. Oord, 125–45. Eugene, OR: Pickwick, 2009.
———. "A War-Torn Creation." In *Evangelical and Frontier Mission Perspectives on the Global Progress of the Gospel*, edited by Beth Snodderly and A. Scott Moreau, 286–93. Oxford: Regnum, 2011.

Snodderly, Beth. "The Story of the Battle for Our Planet: Declaring God's Glory among All Peoples." In *Foundations of the World Christian Movement: A Larger Perspective,* edited by Beth Snodderly and Ralph D. Winter, 25–31. Pasadena, CA: Institute of International Studies, 2009.

United Nations International Children's Emergency Fund (UNICEF). "The Reality of Malaria." *UNICEF,* n.d. Online. https://www.unicef.org/media/files/malariafactsheetafrica.pdf.

Winter, Ralph D. "Basic Concepts." In *Frontiers in Mission: Discovering and Surmounting Barriers to the Missio Dei,* edited by Ralph D. Winter, 26–27. 4th ed. Pasadena, CA: William Carey International University Press, 2008.

———. "Beyond Transformation." In *Frontiers in Mission: Discovering and Surmounting Barriers to the Missio Dei,* edited by Ralph D. Winter, 279–85. 4th ed. Pasadena, CA: William Carey International University Press, 2008.

———. "A Blindspot in Western Christianity?" In *Foundations of the World Christian Movement: A Larger Perspective,* edited by Beth Snodderly and Ralph D. Winter, 319–22. Online. https://static1.squarespace.com/static/5b3157f3b40b9d21a8096625/t/5ed13d18cfba127f3c41f09d/1590770998243/foundations+reader.pdf.

———. "Editorial." *International Journal of Frontier Missiology* 19.2 (2002) 4. Online. http://www.ijfm.org/PDFs_IJFM/19_2_PDFs/02%2004%20Editorial_19_2.pdf.

———. "The Future of Evangelicals in Mission." *Mission Frontiers,* September 1, 2007. Online. http://www.missionfrontiers.org/issue/article/the-future-of-evangelicals-in-mission.

———. "The Greatest Mistake in Missions." In *Frontiers in Mission: Discovering and Surmounting Barriers to the Missio Dei,* edited by Ralph D. Winter, 164–66. 4th ed. Pasadena, CA: William Carey International University Press, 2008.

———. "In Pursuit of the Full Gospel." In *Frontiers in Mission: Discovering and Surmounting Barriers to the Missio Dei,* edited by Ralph D. Winter, 167. 4th ed. Pasadena, CA: William Carey International University Press, 2008.

———. "Lecture 7. The Gospels and Christ: A Global Perspective." 2009. Online. http://www.foundationscourse.org/uploads/documents/intros/7_lecture.pdf.

———. "Lecture 18. Indicators of the Future." 2009. Online. http://www.foundationscourse.org/uploads/documents/intros/18_lecture.pdf.

———. "Let's Be Fair to the Bible." Unpublished paper, April 29, 2009. Online. https://static1.squarespace.com/static/5b3157f3b40b9d21a8096625/t/5eadf5ecc49d1044cff38e03/1588458988502/Let%27s+Be+Fair+to+the+Bible.pdf.

———. "The Most Precarious Frontier." In *Frontiers in Mission: Discovering and Surmounting Barriers to the Missio Dei,* edited by Ralph D. Winter, 48–56. 4th ed. Pasadena, CA: William Carey International University Press, 2008.

———. "One in Love Address." Lecture given at One in Love (OIL) Conference, Binghamton, NY, January 5, 2005.

———. "Roberta Winter Institute." In *Frontiers in Mission: Discovering and Surmounting Barriers to the Missio Dei,* edited by Ralph D. Winter, 177–80. 4th ed. Pasadena, CA: William Carey International University Press, 2008.

———. "Seizing the Future." Lecture given at the US Center for World Mission Seminar, Pasadena, CA, 2006.

———. "The Story of Our Planet." In *Frontiers in Mission: Discovering and Surmounting Barriers to the Missio Dei,* edited by Ralph D. Winter, 249–70. 4th ed. Pasadena, CA: William Carey International University Press, 2008.

―――. "A Summary of Ralph D. Winter's Warfare Missiology." In *Foundations of the World Christian Movement: A Larger Perspective*, edited by Beth Snodderly and Ralph D. Winter, 33–36. Pasadena, CA: Institute of International Studies, 2009. Online. https://static1.squarespace.com/static/5b3157f3b40b9d21a8096625/t/5e d13d18cfba127f3c41f09d/1590770998243/foundations+reader.pdf.

―――. "Theologizing the Microbial World." In *Frontiers in Mission: Discovering and Surmounting Barriers to the Missio Dei*, edited by Ralph D. Winter, 203–5. 4th ed. Pasadena, CA: William Carey International University Press, 2008.

―――. "Twelve Frontiers of Perspective." In *Frontiers in Mission: Discovering and Surmounting Barriers to the Missio Dei*, edited by Ralph D. Winter, 28–39. 4th ed. Pasadena, CA: William Carey International University Press, 2008.

―――. "Unfinished Epic." In *Frontiers in Mission: Discovering and Surmounting Barriers to the Missio Dei*, edited by Ralph D. Winter, 317–26. 4th ed. Pasadena, CA: William Carey International University Press, 2008.

# 18

# An Enemy Did This

*A Cosmic Conflict Understanding of "Natural" Evil*[1]

—GREGORY A. BOYD

The kingdom of heaven is like a man who sowed good seed in his field. But while everyone was sleeping, his enemy came and sowed weeds among the wheat, and went away. When the wheat sprouted and formed heads, then the weeds also appeared. The owner's servants came to him and said, "Sir, didn't you sow good seed in your field? Where then did the weeds come from?" "An enemy did this," he replied. (Matt 13:24–28)

MY TWO DAUGHTERS WERE eight- and ten-years-old when our next door neighbor invited them over to look at a nest of three adorable newly born bunnies tucked away on the side of his house. My daughters were spellbound. My neighbor told them they were free to check on the bunnies as often as they liked, though they had to promise not to touch them or the nest.

For the next week or so my daughters would occasionally visit this nest and would return home excited to report how the cute little bunnies were doing. On this one day, however, my daughters returned from their bunny-nest expedition in a state of hysteria. It turned out that our neighbor's two Springer Spaniels had somehow escaped out of their gated back yard earlier in the day. My neighbor estimates they were loose for ten to twenty minutes before he discovered they'd gone missing. However long it was, it was long enough for his carnivorous pets to discover a free snack.

1. I place scare quotes around "natural" whenever speaking about "natural" evil to indicate that, in my perspective, there is actually nothing *natural* about so-called "natural" evil.

Unfortunately, my young daughters witnessed the gory left-overs. To say they were traumatized is an understatement.

As we continued to process this macabre event that evening, my ten-year-old asked: "Why didn't God protect those poor little bunnies?" I was struggling to formulate an answer when my eight-year-old followed it up with an even tougher one: "Why would God create mean dogs that like to eat little bunnies in the first place!?" Why indeed.

Without realizing it, my daughters had just expressed one of the most challenging philosophical problems that all who believe in an all-loving and all-powerful Creator must wrestle with. The problem is enshrined in Tennyson's immortal poem, "In Memorium A. H. H." He notes that "Man," who is nature's "last work,"

> trusted God was love indeed
>
> And love Creation's final law—
>
> Tho' Nature, red in tooth and claw
>
> With ravine, shriek'd against his creed.

How can we believe the Creator is "love indeed" and "love Creation's final law" when nature, "red in tooth and claw," screeches against this "creed"?

The nearly uniform acceptance of the theory of evolution within the scientific community has significantly exacerbated this problem, for now we Christians must acknowledge that nature has been "red in tooth and claw" since around the time of the Cambrian explosion five hundred sixty million years ago, which is when we first find evidence of predation. Marguerite Shuster summarizes the challenge evolution poses when she writes:

> The evidence virtually compels assent to the assumption that death and the suffering that goes with it have been a reality since the beginning of the drama of life in this world. Nature has always been red in tooth and claw—sometimes in fantastically brutal ways that mock the very thought of a loving or even benign divine hand designing it thus.[2]

The compelling evidence Shuster speaks of obviously undermines the traditional apologetic that placed the blame for nature's savagery on the fall of the first humans.[3] And this forces the question: If nature's violent streak can't be

---

2. Shuster, *Fall and Sin*, 74.

3. Some have attempted to salvage the traditional position by suggesting that God cursed nature millions of years before Adam and Eve were created on the basis of God's foreknowledge of Adam and Eve's rebellion. See, e.g., Brunner, *Christian Doctrine of Creation and Redemption*, 131. Among other significant challenges, I fail to see the

blamed on human free will, how can we avoid concluding that this streak is the result of the Creator's intentional design?

It's worth noting that this problem played no small role in Darwin's own loss of faith. Though he once considered becoming a minister, he was appalled at "the clumsy, wasteful, blundering, low, and horribly cruel works of nature" that he discovered while working out his original theory of evolution.[4] In a letter to his colleague, Asa Gray, Darwin states:

> There seems to me too much misery in the world. I cannot persuade myself that a beneficent & omnipotent God would have designedly created the Ichneumonidae with the express intention of their feeding within the living bodies of caterpillars, or that a cat should play with mice.[5]

Darwin concluded that if there was an intelligent design going on through the evolutionary process, it would have to be the design of "the devil's chaplain."[6] The Ichneumonidae that Darwin mentioned is an interesting case in point. This wasp-like insect plants its eggs inside caterpillars. The eggs soon hatch, and the Ichneumon larva nourish themselves by devouring the insides of its host over a two-week period of time, ingeniously avoiding damage to any vital organs so as to keep the caterpillar alive until they are ready to make their escape.[7]

Granted, in this instance we're only talking about caterpillars, but my daughters' question, and Darwin's question, nevertheless remains: Why would a "beneficent and all-powerful God" "designedly create" a horrific "natural" arrangement such as we find between the Ichneumonidae and their unfortunate hosts? We could ask the same question of thousands of other misery-inflicting insects, parasites, viruses, and animals. What good purpose could the Creator have had in mind when God created viruses like those responsible for COVID-19, Ebola, and AIDS? And why would a benevolent Creator arrange things such that "most of the creatures on this planet live in constant and justified fear of the rest, or pay their way as slowly dying hosts to unthinkable lodgers"[8]?

---

justice of subjecting innocent animals to millions and millions of years of suffering on the basis of a sin that humans would eventually commit.

4. Darwin, "Letter 49."

5. "Darwin, "Letter 2814." On Darwin's theologizing, see Hunter, *Darwin's God.*

6. In 1856, Darwin wrote to his friend Joseph Hooker the following classic lines: "What a book a Devil's Chaplain might write on the clumsy, wasteful, blundering, low, and horridly cruel works of nature!" (Darwin, "Letter 49").

7. Shaw, "Ichneumonidae."

8. Watson, *Dark Nature*, 249. For interested readers, this book provides an eye-opening sampling of some of the most horrific examples of nature's cruelties.

# Attempts to Address the Problem of Animal Suffering

Christian theologians, philosophers, and scientists have attempted to address this problem in a variety of different ways.

## 1. Is Animal Suffering Evil?

First, some have argued that animal suffering doesn't constitute an evil that needs to be reconciled with the benevolent character of God.[9] Animals obviously experience something like pain, this view argues, but we anthropomorphize them if we project onto them the human experience of suffering, for animals lack self-consciousness. An animal thus experiences painful sensations, but there is no "self" that is aware that it is experiencing these sensations. In this view, an animal's reaction to pain should be understood as analogous to how a human responds to a painful prick when under anesthesia. The body flinches in pain, but there is no corresponding mental awareness of it. Hence, animal pain need not be considered an evil that we need to try to get God off the hook for.

While this view was once dominant in Western culture, increasing numbers today consider it problematic. For starters, all psychologically healthy people intuitively feel that it is morally wrong for humans to inflict pain on animals unnecessarily. But this conviction presupposes that animal suffering is analogous to human suffering, to one degree or another. Moreover, human infants also lack self-consciousness and thus do not experience suffering the same way adults do, yet we instinctively assume that infant suffering is sufficiently analogous to adult suffering to consider their suffering a wrong that needs to be rectified as soon as possible. I know of no compelling reason why we should not extend a similar line of analogous reasoning toward animals, especially toward those that are our closest cousins.

On top of this, there is an increasing amount of scientific evidence suggesting that the gulf between humans and animals, and especially between humans and their nearest cousins, is not nearly as great as was once imagined. Yes, our higher reasoning and language capacities are much greater than our closest cousins, but all indications are that our capacity to *experience emotions* is surprisingly similar.[10] And finally, I would argue

9. See Murray, *Red in Tooth and Claw*, 41–72. Editors' Note: For an additional perspective on animal suffering and human responsibility, see chapter 7, "A Theology of Ecology: Earth Care and Health."

10. See discussions by Suchocki, *End of Evil*; Tattersall, *Becoming Human*; Waal,

that animal suffering ought to be considered an evil if for no other reason than because Scripture consistently depicts God expressing concern for the welfare of animals and as treating animal cruelty as an injustice.[11] For good reason, therefore, the number of Christians who defend this once dominant position is relatively small and still dwindling.

## 2. Process Philosophy

A second way of dealing with the problem of animal suffering that seems to be gaining in popularity in Christian academic circles has been to adopt the perspective of process philosophy, or something closely akin to it.[12] In essence, this view (sometimes referred as "panentheism") holds that God and the world are two co-eternal, mutually dependent, mutually influential realities. In this view, the world is ultimately comprised of countless momentary centers of experience, called actual occasions. At every moment God influences each actual occasion in the best possible direction, but each actual occasion possesses a measure freedom or creativity as to how it will respond to God's influence. In this view, all disharmonies in creation, including all animal and human suffering, are the result of the manner in which actual occasions respond to God's influence, not the fault of God. We might think of process philosophy as applying the free will defense for the problem of evil at the level of actual occasions, not merely at the level of humans.

Process philosophy effectively exonerates God of any complicity with suffering, but it does so at a high price, at least from an orthodox Christian perspective.[13] For one thing, because it denies the traditional doctrine of *creation ex nihilo*, the God of process thought is a significantly constrained deity. God isn't free to choose to create a world or not, for example, let alone to decide what kind of world God would want to create. Indeed, in classic process thought, God and the world are bound by the same set of metaphysical

---

*Our Inner Ape.* For an excellent summary of the evidence concerning the emotional lives of animals, see Scully, *Dominion*, 197–246.

11. See, e.g., Gen 1:29–30; 8:1; Exod 23:4–5, 12; Deut 22:4–7; 25:4; Ps 36:6; 50:11; 104:14; 147:9; Prov 12:10; 27:23; Jonah 4:11; Hos 2:18; Hab 2:17; Matt 6:26–30; Luke 12:22–24. Also see Linzey, *Animal Gospel*.

12. For an excellent introduction, see Cobb and Griffin, *Process Theology.* For several process theodicies, see Griffin, *God, Power, and Evil*; Whitney, *Evil and the Process God.*

13. For several critical appraisals of process thought, see Boyd, *Trinity and Process*; Davaney, *Divine Power*; Gruenler, *Inexhaustible God*; Basinger, *Divine Power in Process Theism.*

principles. In the words of Alfred North Whitehead, in process thought, "God is not to be treated as an exception to all metaphysical principles. . . . He is their chief exemplification."[14] It is hard to see how such a metaphysically constrained God is consistent with the biblical depictions of God acting in new and surprising ways, such as when God performs miracles, becomes incarnate, sends forth his Spirit into the hearts of believers, answers prayer, and reconciles creation with Godself on the cross.

Similarly, it is difficult to see how the God of process thought could ever promise that suffering will someday be eliminated from the cosmos (Isa 11:6–9; Rev 21:1–4). For these and other reasons, I don't consider the process theologians' way of accounting for nature's violent streak to be viable for people who are committed to the authority of Scripture and to Jesus as the definitive revelation of God.

## 3. Argument that Violence is Inevitable

A third major way many Christian thinkers have attempted to give an account of the violent streak in nature is to argue that this violence is inevitable, if not necessary, given God's over-all objectives for creation, which include the eventual evolution of beings who possess free will and who are therefore capable of self-sacrificial love. Different thinkers work this out in different, though not necessarily mutually exclusive, ways.

For example, Chris Southgate has argued that evolution could not have produced morally responsible agents apart from the painful process of "selving," including pain "caused to organisms by disease," which the evolutionary process provides.[15] Sarah Coakley has similarly argued that the evolutionary process required suffering if it was to arrive at human beings who are capable of altruistic love.[16] And Jürgen Moltmann, Nancy Murphy, George Ellis, and others have argued that the manner in which life feeds on life throughout nature reflects the cruciform character of God and was necessary given God's cruciform goals for creation.[17]

14. Whitehead, *Process and Reality*, 343.

15. Southgate, *Groaning of Creation*, 65.

16. Coakley, *Sacrifice Regained*.

17. Moltmann, *Science and Wisdom*; Murphy and Ellis, *On the Moral Nature of the Universe*; Rolston, "Does Nature Need to Be Redeemed?," 205–29; "Kenosis and Nature," 43–65. Scholars who argue along these lines frequently emphasize that God had to in a sense withdraw Godself (*kenosis*) to make space for the creation of a semi-autonomous non-divine world, which is why God seems absent in creation and why creation itself has a cruciform quality to it. See, for example, the collection of essays in Polkinghorne, *Work of Love*.

Still others have argued that, for God to arrive at agents who are capable of making morally responsible choices between possible courses of action, nature itself had to be indeterminate, free to explore possibilities, which is what we see unfolding in the evolutionary process.[18] These thinkers sometimes appeal to the fact that the first Genesis creation account ascribes a degree of autonomy and agency to the Earth: "let *the earth* put forth" (Gen 1:11–12, 24 KJV). On the other hand, a number of thinkers have argued that nature does not yet reflect the benevolent character of God simply because it is a work in process. They thus lay stress on the eschatological fulfillment of creation, when nature will finally reflect that *shalom* of God.[19]

Then there are some who have argued that, whatever merits other proposals may have, the horrors that permeate nature are such that we must accept that there is something in the cosmos that is opposing God in the evolutionary process. For example, William Messer builds on Barth's concept of *Das Nichtige* ("Nothingness"), which gives creation a "shadow side" to account for nature's horrors.[20] Along similar lines, Celia Deane-Drummond has argued that, while the wisdom (*sophia*) of God permeates creation and was embodied in Christ, we must also accept that there is a "shadow Sophia" at work in creation.[21] And drawing on Jesus' parable of the wheat and tares, with which I began my essay, Nicola Creegan has argued that we live in "a wheat and tares universe," though she believes that concepts of "Satan" or "the evil one . . . do not serve us well today" in that they are no longer plausible.[22]

## A Critique of These Theological Views

Each of these authors grant that there is something amiss with creation, though they each treat this as a mystery that cannot be penetrated, which of course means that their work does not constitute a theodicy that relieves the Creator of the responsibility for the suffering God's creation brings about.

It lies outside the purview of this essay to review the various arguments that could be marshalled for and against each of these positions. A few brief observations must suffice. First, it is not clear how those who hold that the violence and suffering that permeates nature is necessary or

---

18. See Russell, "Groaning of Creation," 120–42.

19. For example, see Haught, *Deeper Than Darwin*.

20. Messer, "Natural Evil after Darwin," 139–54.

21. Deane-Drummond, *Christ and Evolution*.

22. Creegan, *Animal Suffering*, 7, 93. For various perspectives regarding the application of Jesus' parable to creation, see Creegan, *Animal Suffering*, 82–96.

inevitable can also believe that nature will someday be completely free of violence. If Springer Spaniels won't be devouring little bunnies when God's kingdom comes in fullness, why must it be natural to them to devour them now? John Haught and others rightly celebrate the eschatological libera- tion of nature and the animal kingdom, but what is left unanswered is why Springer Spaniels were created with the "natural" instinct to devour bunnies in the first place.

Second, I find it hard to interpret the manner in which many creatures survive only by stealing the life of other creatures to be a reflection of the cruciform character of the Creator. While the cross reveals a God of *self- sacrificial* love, predators *force* their prey to be sacrificed.

Even more importantly, with the exception of the last one, none of these theories can make plausible sense of the biblical teaching that *some- thing has gone terribly wrong* with our cosmos. Stated in the language of the church tradition, the cosmos is "fallen." According to Paul, the creation we currently live in has been "subjected to frustration" and longs to be "liber- ated from its bondage to decay" (Rom 8:20–21). So too, the New Testa- ment consistently depicts the entire cosmos as needing redemption, which is why God's work on the cross is not just considered Good News for hu- mans: it's Good News *for the whole creation*, including the animal kingdom (Rom 8:18–25; Eph 1:10; Col 1:15–20).[23]

Finally, while scientists today could in principle explain all the in- firmities that Jesus healed during his ministry as natural by-products of the laws of physics, Jesus and the Gospel authors nevertheless consistently diagnose these sorts of infirmities as things that *God does not will* and that *ought not be there*. To the contrary, Jesus consistently reveals the all-loving character and will of his heavenly Father by delivering people from these infirmities. In fact, throughout the New Testament, death itself is depicted as an alien intruder that is contrary to the Creator's good design (1 Cor 15:54–57; Heb 2:14; Rev 21:4).

In light of considerations such as these, I have a hard time accept- ing that the suffering that animals and people experience at the hands of nature is simply the inevitable natural by-product of the good world God created. And as I've already said, while the last proposal we explored rightly acknowledges that the horrors that permeate nature indicate that something is significantly off with our cosmos, they do not go further to offer explana- tions as to why the all-powerful and benevolent Creator would not, or could not, prevent this.

---

23. See Linzey, *Animal Gospel.*

## The Corruption of Nature Hypothesis: A Fourth and Final Explanation for Nature "Red in Tooth and Claw"

This fourth and final way Christian thinkers have attempted to explain why nature is "red in tooth and claw" goes beyond acknowledging that something has gone wrong with the cosmos to venturing *an explanation* for what went so wrong. The remainder of this essay will be a defense of this position.

C. S. Lewis captures the heart of this fourth approach when he notes that Jesus, together with the authors of the New Testament and most orthodox Christian theologians prior to modern times, believed "the story that man was not the first creature to rebel against the Creator, but that some older and mightier being long since became apostate and is now the emperor of darkness and (significantly) Lord of this world." In Lewis's view, this "mighty created power had already been at work for ill on the material universe . . . before ever man came on the scene." Hence, he proposes, this power "may well have corrupted the animal creation before man appeared," which is why we find throughout nature that "some animals live by destroying each other."[24] As Lewis notes, this "mighty power" is identified in the New Testament as Satan or the devil, and the New Testament ascribes a truly remarkable degree of authority to this nefarious cosmic agent.

Before discussing the New Testament's view of Satan, however, I think it is important to realize that the Bible reflects an awareness that something is askew in God's good creation long before the New Testament came on the scene. Consider, for example, the first Genesis creation account as it recounts God's original instruction to humans.

> I give you every seed-bearing plant on the face of the whole earth and every tree that has fruit with seed in it. They will be yours for food. And to all the beasts of the earth and all the birds in the sky and all the creatures that move along the ground—everything that has the breath of life in it—*I give every green plant for food*. (Gen 1:29–30)

Whatever else we make of this intriguing passage, its author clearly did not understand predation to be a natural part of God's plan. Neither was nature originally intended to be so difficult for humans to exercise dominion over (Gen 3:17–19).

Related to this, conservative Old Testament scholars frequently argue that, while all other ancient Near Eastern creation accounts depict the creation as coming about by one deity vanquishing one or more opposing

---

24. Lewis, *Problem of Pain*, 134–35.

deities, the two creation accounts in Genesis are completely free of cosmic conflict. In scholarly jargon, these accounts are supposedly free of the *chaoskampf* (conflict-with-chaos) motif that permeates other ancient Near Eastern literature. Not all scholars agree with this assessment, however.[25] For example, some reputable scholars have argued that the "deep"(*tehom*) in Genesis 1:2 retains some of the menacing quality it has throughout the ancient Near East, which is presumably why God's Spirit must hover over it.[26] Others note that the original humans were commanded not only to exercise loving dominion over the Earth and animal kingdom, but to also "subdue" (*kābash*) whatever needed to be subdued (Gen 1:28). The word *kābash* has the connotation of conquering something (see, e.g., Num 32:22, 29; Josh 18:1). Fretheim argues that in Genesis it has the more specific connotation of "to bring order out of continuing disorder."[27] This suggests that, even before the human fall, there were aspects of creation that remained resistant to the loving dominion of humans and therefore opposed to the will of the Creator.

As a final example in Genesis, we read in Genesis 2 that God instructed the original human to guard (*shamar*) the Garden (Gen 2:15). Translations typically translate *shamar* as "keep" or "care for," which gives the impression that the primary thing Adam had to protect the Garden from were weeds. Interestingly enough, however, troublesome vegetation like weeds don't make their appearance in this narrative until after the human rebellion (Gen 3:17–19). Moreover, the Genesis author uses *shamar* again in Genesis 3:24, where the cherubim and flaming sword are said to "guard the way to the tree of life" once Adam and Eve were expelled from the Garden. I thus contend that it would in this context be more appropriate to translate *shamar* as "guard," in the mandate of Genesis 2:15, and I submit that we learn in Genesis chapter 3 what the original human was supposed to protect the Garden from, when the crafty serpent makes his appearance.

Even more significantly, in my mind, is that fact that the two creation accounts that we find in Genesis are not the Bible's only creation accounts. Indeed, there are a half dozen or more other creation passages in the Old Testament, and, interestingly enough, each of these passages borrows

25. On this biblical motif and scholarly discussions surrounding it, see Boyd, *God at War*, 73–113. The classic work on this theme is Gunkel, *Schöpfung und Chaos*. Other helpful sources are Levenson, *Creation and the Persistence of Evil*; Wakeman, *God's Battle with the Monster*; Cross, *Canaanite Myth and Hebrew Epic*; Görg, *Mythos und Mythologie*, 97–155; Forsyth, *Old Enemy*. Editors' Note: Also see the discussion of "*tohu wabohu*" in chapter 3, "A Theology of Creation: Order Out of Chaos."

26. See, e.g., König, *New and Greater Things*, 15–18; Barth, *Church Dogmatics*, 3/1:102–3; Levenson, *Creation and the Persistence of Evil*, 5, 121–23.

27. See Fretheim, *Creation Untamed*, 14; cf. 33–34.

heavily from their ancient Near Eastern neighbors as they depict Yahweh battling hostile waters and/or cosmic beasts (e.g., Leviathan, Rahab, Yamm) as God works to create and protect the world.[28]

While the language of Yahweh battling hostile waters and cosmic monsters is obviously mythic and reflects God stooping to accommodate the fallen and culturally conditioned minds of God's people at the time, I submit that the reality to which this mythic language points is not mythic. As we are about to see, the truth that the Creator faces opposition as God seeks to carry out God's redemptive purposes receives strong confirmation in the New Testament.[29] Both Old and New Testament authors are uniformly confident that Yahweh can ultimately handle these cosmic foes. Yet, God's victory is considered praiseworthy precisely because these foes are considered *real* and *formidable*.[30]

For a variety of reasons, the Jewish understanding of the cosmic forces that oppose God grew considerably more intense in the two centuries leading up to the first century. A significant number of Jews embraced "the apocalyptic worldview" in which (among other things) the world is conceived of as a battlefield between God, God's righteous angels, and God's people, on the one side, and malevolent angels and human foes of God, on the other.[31] And while Satan is a relatively minor figure in the Old Testament, he (or some similar figure, e.g., Mastema, Beelzebul) begins to appear increasingly mighty and malevolent in the apocalyptic writings of the time.

Yet, the apocalyptic depictions of a supremely evil cosmic agent are relatively tame compared to the way Satan is depicted in the New Testament. For starters, Jesus three times referred to Satan as "the prince of this world" (John 12:31; 14:30; 16:11). The word *archōn* ("prince," "ruler") was used in political contexts to denote "the highest official in a city or a region in the Greco-Roman world."[32] Hence, while Jesus certainly believed that God the Father governs the creation as a whole, he was nevertheless insistent that Satan is the highest ruling authority over our "world."

In this light, it's hardly surprising that Jesus didn't dispute Satan's claim to own all the authority of the kingdoms of the world and to be able

---

28. See, for example, Ps 29:3–4; 104:3–9; 74:13–17; 89:9–11; Prov 8:27–29; Job 9:13; 38:6–11; Hab 3:8–15. I cannot here address the question of how these *chaoskampf* creation accounts can be integrated with the accounts in Genesis, but see Boyd, "Evolution as Spiritual Warfare," 125–45.

29. So argues Wright, "Place of Myth," 18–30.

30. A point emphasized by Levenson, *Creation and the Persistence of Evil*, 18–19. See also König, *New and Greater Things*, 46.

31. See Boyd, *God at War*, 72–80.

32. Arnold, *Powers of Darkness*, 81.

to give them to whomever he wanted (Luke 4:5–6). The book of Revelation reinforces this view as it depicts all worldly government as "Babylon," the political wing of Satan's empire which he uses to deceive the world.[33] Along the same lines, the apostle Paul referred to Satan as "the god of this age" (2 Cor 4:4) and "the ruler of the kingdom of the air" (Eph 2:2). According to the cosmological thinking of the time, the realm of "the air" referred to the domain of spiritual authority directly over the Earth. The author of Ephesians was thus essentially reiterating Jesus' teaching that Satan is the "ruler of this world." The Johannine literature makes the point even more forcefully when it teaches that "the whole world is under the control of the evil one" (1 John 5:19) and that Satan "leads the whole world astray" (Rev 12:9; cf. 20:3, 8). Short of embracing a Manichean-type dualism, it is hard to see how New Testament authors could have ascribed more authority to Satan than they actually did.

The remarkable stature of Satan is similarly reflected in the New Testament's teaching that the primary reason the Son of God came to Earth was to destroy the devil and his works (1 John 3:8; cf. Col 2:14–15; Heb 2:14). In the Gospel of John, Jesus claims that he came to drive out the ruler of this world, which he in principle accomplished on the cross (John 12:31; cf. 16:11). Closely related to this, the dominant theme of John's dualistic-tending Gospel is that Jesus—the one who is "light" and is "from above"—came to confront and overcome Satan—who is "darkness" and "from below."[34]

Along similar lines, the authors of the Synoptic Gospels view the healing and deliverance ministry of Jesus and his disciples as a sustained assault on Satan's empire (e.g., Luke 10:17; Acts 10:38). Peter makes the point well when he summarizes Jesus' ministry by saying, "he went around doing good and *healing all who were under the power of the devil*" (Acts 10:38).[35] The assumption is that all who are afflicted are directly or indirectly suffering "under the power of the devil," and Jesus freed them from their oppression by healing them. In fact, the word that the Synoptic authors sometimes use for "affliction" is *mastix*, which literally means "flogging,"[36] In their view, people who suffer afflictions were being beaten up by God's cosmic foes.

33. See Rev 13; 14:8; 17:5; 18. Also see Gwyther, "New Jerusalem versus Babylon"; Ellul, *Apocalypse*.

34. For example, John 1:4–5, 9; 8:23, 44; 14:17, 27; 15:18–19; 16:33; 17:9. On the strong, quasi-dualistic, warfare motif in John, see Boyd, *God at War*, 227–31; Kovacs, "Now Shall the Ruler of This World," 227–47; Coetzee, "Christ and the Prince," 104–21.

35. For a full treatment of the connection between Jesus' healing ministry and spiritual warfare, see Boyd, *God at War*, 192–214.

36. For example, see Mark 3:10; 5:29, 34; Luke 7:21. Compare the use of *mastix* in, e.g., Acts 22:24; Heb 11:36, where its castigatory meaning ("scourging") is more

Reiterating a similar motif, the New Testament describes human salvation as freedom from Satan's bondage. For example, in the process of recounting his conversion before King Agrippa, Paul noted that Jesus told him he was sending him to open the eyes of Gentiles to "turn them from darkness to light, and from the power of Satan to God, so that they may receive forgiveness of sins and a place among those who are sanctified by faith in [him]" (Acts 26:18). So too, Paul reminded the Colossians that their salvation consists of the fact that God, "has rescued us from the dominion of darkness and brought us into the kingdom of the Son he loves" (Col 1:13). Salvation in the New Testament is at its heart the process of being delivered from the hopeless misery of Satan's imprisonment and being allowed to share in the life, harmony, and joy of the kingdom of God's beloved Son.

The stunning authority ascribed to Satan in the New Testament is further reflected in the many activities ascribed to him. For example, in the book of Hebrews Satan is said to hold the power of death (Heb 2:14) and in Revelation he is portrayed as having a certain amount of authority to control natural phenomena (Rev 13:13; 19:20; cf. Job 1:12, 16, 18–19; 2:7). Satan is also depicted as continually tempting people to fall (Luke 4:2; 2 Cor 2:9–11; 1 Thess 3:5; 1 Tim 3:7). Indeed, Jesus went so far as to claim that every single duplicitous word that a person is tempted to utter "comes from the evil one" (Matt 5:37).

Peter captures the ever-present threat that Satan poses when he depicts him as an ever-present prowling lion seeking to devour people (1 Pet 5:8). So too, Jesus refers to Satan as "the enemy" who attempts to ruin the faith of new disciples and who plants weeds among the good wheat field of God's kingdom (Matt 13:24–40). Paul similarly teaches that Satan blinds the minds of all who refuse to believe the gospel (2 Cor 4:4) and describes the Christian life as one sustained battled against forces of darkness (2 Cor 2:9–11; 10:3–5; Eph 4:26–27; 6:10–17).

One simply can't read the New Testament seriously and fail to get the impression that Satan is a ubiquitous force of destruction in our world, and that he is persistently working to undermine God's good designs for people and for creation. C. S. Lewis is hardly overstating the matter when he sums up the New Testament's perspective by claiming; "There is no neutral ground in the universe: every square inch, every split second, is claimed by God and counterclaimed by Satan."[37]

---

obvious. See also John 19:1, "Then Pilate took Jesus and had him flogged," *mastigoō*, from the root word, *mastix*.

37. Lewis, *Christian Reflections*, 41.

Satan is by no means the only hostile cosmic power known to New Testament authors, however. In keeping with the apocalyptic worldview of their day, the New Testament also refers to other classes of fallen powers that are part of Satan's regime. We find references to "rulers," "principalities," "powers," and "authorities" (Rom 8:38; 13:1; 1 Cor 2:6, 8; 15:24; Eph 1:21; 2:2; 3:10; 6:12; Col 1:16: 2:10, 15), along with "dominions" (Eph 1:21), "powers" (Eph 6:12; Col 1:16), "thrones" (Col 1:16), "spiritual forces" (Eph 6:12), "elemental spiritual forces" (Col 2:8, 20; Gal 4:3), "gods" (1 Cor 8:5; 2 Cor 4:4), and a number of other spiritual entities.[38] In the first-century apocalyptic worldview, these various titles refer to different levels of powerful spirit-agents or forces that exercise an oppressive and destructive influence over particular aspects of creation, society, and human-made institutions.[39] I will henceforth refer to these agents simply as "the powers."

Given the remarkable power, status, and pervasive influence that is ascribed to Satan and other cosmic-level powers in the New Testament, I am frankly surprised how rarely Christian thinkers appeal to these opposing powers as they attempt to make sense of the horrors found in the evolutionary process and throughout nature today. If Satan or the powers are directly or indirectly behind the "natural" infirmities that Jesus healed, how could we *not* suspect they exercise some corrupting influence on nature?

This question becomes all the more forceful when we consider Jesus' "nature miracles," for a plausible case can be made that these miracles directly connected the corrupting work of the powers with natural phenomena.[40] Consider the Gospels' account of Jesus and his disciples being caught in a fierce storm while crossing the Sea of Galilee (Mark 4:36–41). With their boat about to capsize the disciples woke Jesus from his sleep and implored him to save them. Jesus promptly "rebuked the wind and said to the waves, 'Quiet! Be still!'" (Mark 4:39). The wind and waves immediate obeyed and Jesus chastised his disciples for lacking faith (Mark 4:40).

The description of Jesus rebuking (*epitimaō*) the storm and commanding the waves to be silent (or "choked," *phimoō*) fits the descriptions of Jesus elsewhere rebuking and silencing demons (e.g., Mark 1:25; Luke 4:35). This suggests that the Gospel authors understood Jesus to be confronting a

38. For example, it is likely Paul is referring to demonic entities in Romans 8:39. See Dunn, *Romans 1–8*, 513.

39. For a thorough treatment and application of the New Testament's language about the powers, see Wink, *Naming the Powers*; *Ummasking the Powers*; *Engaging the Powers*. See also O'Brien, "Principalities and Powers," 353–84; Berkhof, *Christ and the Powers*.

40. For the following, see Boyd, *God at War*, 205–14.

demonic power when he rebuked and choked the storm.[41] The fact that the apocalyptic worldview of Jesus' day included the belief that aspects of nature were under the abusive power of demonic forces strengthens this conviction, as does the fact that this account is immediately followed in the synoptic Gospels by the episode of Jesus casting out "Legion" (Mark 5:1–13).

What strengthens this interpretation still further is that, according to many scholars, the narrative of Jesus rebuking this threatening storm builds on the Old Testament theme of Yahweh "rebuking" the "raging waters" that all ancient Near Eastern people believed encompassed and threatened the Earth (e.g., Ps 18:15; 104:7; 106:9). This narrative thus associates a potential "natural" disaster with the cosmic foes Yahweh has been battling throughout history. This of course doesn't imply that there is a specific demonic power behind every life-threatening storm. But it does suggest that life-threatening "natural" disasters were not part of God's original design for creation.

Closely related to the storm-choking narrative is a curious episode in which Jesus cursed a fig tree because it had not produced any figs (Mark 11:12–14; Matt 21:18–19). What is particularly puzzling about this episode, which contains Jesus' only destructive miracle, is that Mark explains that the reason the fig tree had no figs was because *it wasn't the season for figs* (Mark 11:13). At first glance, it might appear that Jesus simply lost his temper and used his supernatural power to punish a poor tree whose only crime was being in the wrong place during the wrong season. If we understand this episode against the background of the apocalyptic thought of Jesus' day, however, we see something quite different going on.

Famine was widely believed to be the work of the devil in apocalyptic thought, and barren or infected fig trees were widely regarded as symbols of this fact (Mark 13:8; Rom 8:35).[42] What is more, many Jews of this time believed the Messiah would free nature from Satan's grip, thus putting an end to things like famines and diseases. When we interpret Jesus' cursing of the fig tree in this light, it seems likely he was proclaiming that he was the Messiah by "cursing the curse." Jesus was in effect presenting himself as the long awaited deliverer who would "destroy the devil's work" (1 John 3:8) and eventually restore all creation. This episode thus presupposes the

41. In the words of James Kallas, "If language means anything at all, it appears that Jesus looked upon this ordinary storm at sea, this ordinary event of nature, as a demonic force, and he strangled it" (Kallas, *Synoptic Miracles*, 65).

42. On the barren fig tree being a symbol of the curse, see Davies, *Paul and Rabbinic Judaism*, 39; Kallas, *Synoptic Miracles*, 95. On the fruitful fig tree as a symbol of restored creation, see Heirs, "Not the Season for Figs," 394–400; Derrett, "Fig Trees in the New Testament," 249–65.

apocalyptic view that the corrupting influence of Satan and other demonic powers are behind "natural" disasters.

What makes "natural" evil so much more challenging to explain than suffering that results from human decisions is that in the latter case we can appeal to the free will of created agents and thus need not blame God. But whose free will, other than God's, is there to appeal to in order to account for the massive carnage and waste that characterized the evolutionary process and permeates creation today? There is none, *unless we take the Bible's depiction of Satan and demonic powers seriously*. Once we accept this, it becomes apparent that there is no categorical difference between "natural" evil and moral evil. In *both* cases we can appeal to the free will of created agents. It's just that in the latter case, our appeal is to *human* agents, while in former, our appeal must be to *spirit*-agents.[43]

As mentioned earlier, this was the uniform perspective of the post-apostolic fathers.[44] These early Christian thinkers believed that God gave spirit-agents free will and placed them in authority over aspects of creation, just as God did with humans over the Earth and animal kingdom (Gen 1:26–28). For example, a second-century theologian named Athenagoras argued that "the Maker and Framer of the world distributed and appointed . . . a multitude of angels and ministers . . . to occupy themselves about the elements, and the heavens, and the world, and the things in it, and the godly ordering of them all."[45] Similarly, Origen held that every aspect of nature was under the care of "invisible husbandmen and guardians."[46] St. Gregory at a later date reiterates the prevailing view of the early church when he said; "In this visible world . . . nothing can be achieved except through invisible forces."[47]

At the same time, these theologians also unanimously affirmed that the Creator had endowed these cosmic level spirit-agents with free will, just as God did humans. "Just as with men, who have freedom of choice as to both virtue and vice," Athenagorus wrote, "so is it among the angels."[48] "Natural"

43. It is sometimes objected that the free will defense fails as a theodicy so long as God has the power to revoke free will any time he chooses. I will respond to this objection in chapter 19, "Why Creation Groans: Responding to Objections to the Corruption of Nature (CON) Hypothesis."

44. On the central role of Satan, the powers, and demons in the early church's approach to the problem of evil, see Boyd, *Satan*, 39–49; Russell, *Satan*; Ferguson, *Demonology*; Gokey, *Terminology*. Editors' Note: Also see chapter 4, "Early Church Perspectives on the Cosmic Conflict."

45. Athenagoras, *Plea for the Christians*, 2, 142.

46. Origen, *Against Celsus* 8.31.

47. Gregory, *Dialogues* 4.5 (199).

48. Athenagorus, *Plea for the Christians*, 2, 142.

evil was thus consistently explained in the early church as the result of spirit-agents rebelling against God and thus using their God-given authority over creation at cross-purposes with God. For example, referring to these cosmic agents, Athenagorus argued that, while some "free agents . . . continued in those things for which God had made and over which He had ordained them," others "outraged both the constitution of their nature and the government entrusted to them."[49] These agents thus now use their authority to corrupt "natural" processes. Similarly, Origen argued that famines, scorching winds, and pestilence were not "natural" in God's creation: they were rather the result of fallen powers bringing misery whenever and however they were able.[50] These rebel forces were also "the cause of plagues, . . . barrenness, . . . tempests, . . . [and] similar calamities."[51]

Tertullian similarly argued that "diseases and other grievous calamities" were the result of demons whose "great business is the ruin of mankind." When "poison in the breeze blights the apples and the grain while in the flower, or kills them in the bud, or destroys them when they have reached maturity" one can discern the work of these rebellious spirit-agents.[52] For these and other early church fathers, the reason creation doesn't consistently reflect the goodness of its beneficent and omnipotent Creator was because it has been, and is yet being, corrupted by malevolent cosmic powers. An "enemy" has sown tares among the wheat of God's good creation, and until harvest time comes, they must be allowed to grow together (Matt 13:24–30).

Following the teachings of the New Testament, these early theologians all understood that the leader of the rebel army that now ravages nature was Satan, and also in keeping with the New Testament, they uniformly understood him to possess an astounding degree of authority. For example, according to Athenagoras, Satan was "the spirit" originally entrusted with "the control of matter and the forms of matter."[53] In his view, the entire material creation was supposed to be overseen by this highest ranking cosmic agent. Unfortunately, this "spirit" used its free will to rebel against God. Hence, Athenagoras concludes, he now exercises his tremendous cosmic authority against God and abuses "the government entrusted to [him]." "The prince of matter," Athenagoras writes, "[now] exercises a control and management contrary to the good that is in God."[54] And this, he argued, is why nature does not consistently reflect the benevolent character of the Creator.

---

49. Athenagorus, *Plea for the Christians*, 2, 142.

50. Origen, *Against Celsus* 8.31.

51. Origen, *Against Celsus* 1.31 (409).

52. Tertullian, *Apology*, 22 (36).

53. Athenagoras, *Plea for the Christians*, 2, 142.

54. Athenagoras, *Plea for the Christians*, 2, 142–43.

Clearly, for these early Christian thinkers, everything in nature that *looks* contrary the Creator's goodness appears that way because it *is* contrary to "the good that is in God." In their view, the dark side of nature didn't arise from the design of the Creator. It was rather due to the design and activity of an evil "ruling prince" and of "the demons his followers."[55] When these early thinkers confronted diseases, famines, and other "natural" evils, they did not ascribe this to the mysterious hand of God: they said, "An enemy has done this."

If we apply the perspective of the New Testament and early church to the process of evolution, it is not hard to conceptualize evolution as an on-going conflict between the all-good Creator, on the one hand, and Satan and the powers, on the other. In this view, the Creator creates, Satan and the powers then corrupt what the Creator created, but God always wisely finds a way to bring good out of evil and to turn the enemy's corruption to God's advantage by using it to advance the evolutionary process.

On this note, it is significant that an increasing number of evolution theorists over the last several decades have been arguing that the ruthless competition for survival that Darwin believed drove the evolutionary process only tells part of the story. These theorists argue that the evolutionary process also progresses as living organisms develop mutually-beneficial symbiotic relationships with other organisms.[56] When the cooperation among organisms becomes sufficiently complex, the collective produces emergent properties that transcend the capabilities of the individual organisms, and this constitutes a leap forward in the evolutionary process. Not only this, but the higher up the evolutionary tree one looks, the more these mutually beneficial symbiotic relationships begin to look like what we would call *love*. Contrary to Richard Dawkins's claim that evolution is driven by "the selfish gene,"[57] many are now arguing that the ubiquitous phenomena of emergence, convergence, and cooperation in nature suggest a force is moving evolution in an other-oriented direction.

In this light, one can easily understand the Creator to be the force driving evolution in the direction of cooperation, and ultimately of love, with the goal of arriving at human beings who possess for the first time the capacity to love in a way that directly reflects the loving character of the Creator. Conversely, it is not hard to understand Satan and the rebel powers to be forces that perpetually work to corrupt the Creator's creation. Everything in creation that fails to reflect the loving character of the Creator must ultimately

---

55. Athenagoras, *Plea for the Christians*, 2, 142–43.

56. See, e.g., Morris, *Deep Structure of Biology*; Coakley, "Providence," 179–93; Creegan, *Animal Suffering*, 110–26.

57. Dawkins, *Selfish Gene*.

be traced back to this corruption. If there are "tares" in the farmers wheat field, it is only because an "enemy" has planted them there!

From this perspective, the fact that God managed to arrive at agents who are made in God's image and are capable of reflecting his loving character in all their relationships, despite working with corrupted material and facing opposition at every turn, bears witness to the unfathomable wisdom of God. The God who decisively outwitted Satan and caused his kingdom to implode by offering up his life on the cross for the redemption of humankind and of the whole of creation has been outwitting Satan for at least the last half billion years in order to finally arrive at the creation of humankind, who were to be enthroned as the viceroys of God's creation (Gen 1:26–28).

All who have been freed by Christ's saving work are now invited to regain their original position as God's viceroys on this planet and to partner with God's work of bringing God's *shalom* to the whole of creation by means of the sacrificial love that was perfectly revealed on the cross (Col 1:19–20). Whereas every square inch of the cosmos is presently caught in a cosmic battle, as Lewis noted, God's promise is that someday every square inch of the cosmos will reflect God's perfect *shalom* (wholeness, harmony, peace). And the mission of the church is to partner with God to further this process by striving to bring about God's will "on earth as it is in heaven" (Matt 6:10) in every area of life. To reference Jesus' parable of the wheat and tares once again, we are called to uproot whatever weeds we find in the field of God's creation.

To do this, however, we must be able to distinguish between wheat and tares, for until God's kingdom comes in fullness at the end of the age, we are told that the two will grow together. When we come upon tares—things in creation that do not reflect the loving character of God that was definitively revealed on Calvary, such as diseases, deformities, parasites, viruses, predation, etc.—we must acknowledge that "an enemy has done this." And insofar as it is possible, we are called to do whatever we can to uproot these enemy-sown weeds, to alleviate suffering, and to thereby bring creation more in line with God's original ideal for creation than it was before.

In this light, I believe we must consider all efforts to eradicate misery-inflicting physical diseases such as COVID-19, as well as chaos-creating social diseases such as racism, to be as much a part of the call of the gospel as is evangelism.

# Bibliography

Arnold, Clinton E. *Powers of Darkness: Principalities and Powers in Paul's Letters*. Downers Grove, IL: InterVarsity, 1992.

Athenagoras. *A Plea for the Christians*. In *Fathers of the Second Century*, edited by Alexander Roberts et al., 129–48. Translated by Benjamin Plummer Pratten. Vol. 2 of *The Ante-Nicene Fathers*. Buffalo, NY: Christian Literature Company, 1885. Online. https://oll-resources.s3.us-east-2.amazonaws.com/oll3/store/titles/1970/1333.02_bk.pdf.

Barth, Karl. *Church Dogmatics: The Doctrine of Creation*. Edited by G. W. Bromiley, and T. F. Torrance. Edinburgh: T&T Clark, 1961.

Basinger, David. *Divine Power in Process Theism: A Philosophical Critique*. Albany: State University of New York Press, 1988.

Berkhof, Hendrik. *Christ and the Powers*. Translated by John H. Yoder. Scottdale, PA: Herald, 1962.

Boyd, Gregory A. "Evolution as Spiritual Warfare." In *Creation Made Free: Open Theology Engages Science*, edited by Thomas J. Oord, 125–45. Eugene, OR: Pickwick, 2009.

———. *God at War: The Bible and Spiritual Conflict*. Downers Grove, IL: InterVarsity, 1997.

———. *Satan and the Problem of Evil: Constructing a Trinitarian Warfare Theodicy*. Downers Grove, IL: InterVarsity, 2001.

———. *Trinity and Process: A Critical Evaluation and Reconstruction of Hartshorne's Di-Polar Theism Towards a Trinitarian Metaphysics*. New York: Peter Lang, 1992.

Brunner, Emil, and Olive Wyon. *The Christian Doctrine of Creation and Redemption*. Vol. 2 of *Dogmatics*. London: Lutterworth, 1952.

Coakley, Sarah. "Providence and the Evolutionary Phenomenon of 'Cooperation': A Systematic Proposal." In *Providence of God*, edited by F. A. Murphy and P. G. Zielger, 179–93. Edinburgh: T&T Clark, 2009.

———. *Sacrifice Regained: Reconsidering the Rationality of Christian Belief*. Cambridge: Cambridge University Press, 2012.

Cobb, John B., and David Ray Griffin. *Process Theology: An Introductory Exposition*. Philadelphia: Westminster, 1976.

Coetzee, J. C. "Christ and the Prince of This World in the Gospel and the Epistles of St. John." *Neotestamentica* 2 (1968) 104–21.

Creegan, Nicola Hoggard. *Animal Suffering and the Problem of Evil*. New York: Oxford University Press, 2013.

Cross, Frank Moore. *Canaanite Myth and Hebrew Epic*. Cambridge, MA: Harvard University Press, 1973.

Darwin, Charles. "Letter 49." Letter from Charles Darwin to J. D. Hooker, July 13, 1856. In vol. 1 of *More Letters of Charles Darwin*, edited by Francis Darwin and A. C. Seward. Online. https://www.gutenberg.org/files/2739/2739-h/2739-h.htm.

———. "Letter 2814." Letter from Charles Darwin to Asa Gray, May 22, 1860. *Darwin Correspondence Project*. Online. https://www.darwinproject.ac.uk/letter/DCP-LETT-2814.xml.

Davaney, Sheila Greeve. *Divine Power: A Study of Karl Barth and Charles Hartshorne*. Philadelphia: Fortress, 1986.

Davies, W. D. *Paul and Rabbinic Judaism*. 1948. Reprint, Philadelphia: Fortress. 1980.

Dawkins, Richard. *The Selfish Gene*. 2nd ed. New York: Oxford University Press, 1990.

Deane-Drummond, Celia. *Christ and Evolution: Wonder and Wisdom*. Minneapolis: Fortress, 2009.

Derrett, J. D. M. "Fig Trees in the New Testament." *Heythrop Journal* 14 (1973) 249–65.

Dunn, James D. G. *Romans 1–8*. Word Bible Commentary 38A. Waco, TX: Word, 1988.

Ferguson, Everett. *Demonology of the Early Christian World*. New York: Mellen, 1984.

Forsyth, Neil. *The Old Enemy: Satan and the Combat Myth*. Princeton: Princeton University Press, 1987.

Fretheim, Terence E. *Creation Untamed: The Bible, God, and Natural Disasters*. Grand Rapids: Baker Academic, 2010.

Gokey, Francis X. *The Terminology for the Devil and Evil Spirits in the Apostolic Fathers*. Washington, DC: Catholic University of America Press, 1961.

Görg, Manfred. *Mythos und Mythologie: Studien zur Religionspeschichte und Theologie*. Wiesbaden: Harrassowitz, 2010.

Gregory. *Dialogues*. Vol. 39 of *The Fathers of the Church: A New Translation*. Translated by O. J. Zimmerman. Washington, DC: Catholic University of America Press; New York: Fathers of the Church, 1959.

Griffin, David Ray. *God, Power, and Evil: A Process Theodicy*. Philadelphia: Westminster Press, 1976.

Gruenler, Royce Gordon. *The Inexhaustible God: Biblical Faith and the Challenge of Process Theism*. Grand Rapids: Baker, 1983.

Gunkel, Hermann. *Schöpfung und Chaos in Urzeit und Endzeit: Eine religions-geschichtliche Untersuchtung über Gen 1 und Ap Job 12*. Göttingen: Vandenhoeck and Ruprecht, 1895.

Haught, John. *Deeper Than Darwin: The Prospect for Religion in the Age of Evolution*. New York: Westview, 2003.

Heirs, R. H. "Not the Season for Figs." *Journal of Biblical Literature* 87 (1968) 394–400.

Kallas, James. *The Significance of the Synoptic Miracles: Taking the Worldview of Jesus Seriously*. New York: Seabury, 1961.

König, Adrio. *New and Greater Things: Re-Evaluating the Biblical Message on Creation*. Pretoria: University of South Africa, 1988.

Kovacs, Judith L. "'Now Shall the Ruler of This World Be Driven Out': Death as Cosmic Battle in John 12:20–36." *Journal of Biblical Literature* 114 (1995) 227–47. Online. http://library.mibckerala.org/lms_frame/eBook/now%20shall%20the%20ruler.pdf.

Levenson, Jon D. *Creation and the Persistence of Evil: The Jewish Drama of Divine Omnipotence*. San Francisco: Harper & Row, 1988.

Lewis, C. S. *Christian Reflections*. 1967. Reprint, Grand Rapids: Eerdmans, 2014.

———. *The Problem of Pain*. New York: Macmillan, 1962.

Linzey, Andrew. *Animal Gospel: Christian Faith as Though Animals Mattered*. London: Hodder & Stoughton, 1998.

Messer, Neil. "Natural Evil after Darwin." In *Theology after Darwin*, edited by Michael Northcott and R. J. Berry, 139–54. Carlisle: Paternoster, 2009.

Moltmann, Jürgen. *Science and Wisdom*. Minneapolis: Fortress, 2009.

Morris, S. Conway, ed. *The Deep Structure of Biology: Is Convergence Sufficiently Ubiquitous to Give a Directional Signal*. West Conshohocken, PA: Templeton, 2008.

Murphy, Nancy, and George F. R. Ellis. *On the Moral Nature of the Universe: Theology, Cosmology, and Ethics*. Minneapolis: Fortress, 2009.

Murray, Michael. *Red in Tooth and Claw: Theism and the Problem of Animal Suffering*. Oxford: Oxford University Press, 2008.

O'Brien, Peter T. "Principalities and Powers: Opponents of the Church." *Evangelical Review of Theology* 16 (1992) 353–84.

Origen. *Against Celsus.* In *Fathers of the Third Century: Tertullian, Part Fourth; Minucius Felix; Commodian; Origen, Parts First and Second,* edited by Alexander Roberts et al., 395–669. Translated by Frederick Crombie. Vol. 4 of *Ante-Nicene Fathers.* Buffalo, NY: Christian Literature, 1885. Online. https://oll-resources.s3.us-east-2.amazonaws.com/oll3/store/titles/1976/1333.04_bk.pdf.

Polkinghorne, John, ed. *The Work of Love: Creation a Kenosis.* Grand Rapids: Eerdmans, 2001.

Rolston, Holmes, III. "Does Nature Need to Be Redeemed?" *Zygon* 29.3 (1994) 205–29.

———. "Kenosis and Nature." In *The Work of Love: Creation and Kenosis,* edited by John Polkinghorne, 43–65. Grand Rapids: Eerdmans, 2001.

Russell, Jeffrey Burton. *Satan: The Early Christian Tradition.* Ithaca, NY: Cornell University Press, 1981.

Russell, Robert John. "The Groaning of Creation: Does God Suffer with All Life?" In *The Evolution of Evil,* edited by Gaymon Bennett et al., 120–42. Göttigen: Vanderhoeck & Ruprecht, 2009.

Scully, Matthew. *Dominion: The Power of Man, the Suffering of Animals, and the Call to Mercy.* New York: Saint Martin's, 2002.

Shaw, Mark R. "Ichneumonidae: Life Cycle of Parasitoids in Provence." *Filming VarWild,* 2013. Online. http://www.filming-varwild.com/p-ichneumonidae.html.

Shuster, Marguerite. *The Fall and Sin: What We Have Become as Sinners.* Grand Rapids: Eerdmanns, 2003.

Southgate, Christopher. *The Groaning of Creation: Evolution and the Problem of Evil.* Louisville: Westminster John Knox, 2008.

Suchocki, Marjorie Hewitt. *The End of Evil: Process Eschatology in Historical Context.* Albany: State University of New York Press, 2008.

Tattersall, Ian. *Becoming Human: Evolution and Human Uniqueness.* Orlando: Harcourt, 1998.

Tertullian. *Apology.* In *Latin Christianity: Its Founder, Tertullian,* edited by Alexander Roberts et al., 17–60. Translated by Sydney Thelwall. Vol. 3 of *Ante-Nicene Fathers.* Buffalo, NY: Christian Literature, 1885. Online. https://oll-resources.s3.us-east-2.amazonaws.com/oll3/store/titles/1971/1333.03_bk.pdf.

Waal, Frans de. *Our Inner Ape: The Best and the Worst of Human Nature.* London: Granta, 2005.

Wakeman, Mary K. *God's Battle With the Monster.* Leiden: Brill, 1973.

Watson, Lyall. *Dark Nature: A Natural History of Evil.* New York: HarperCollins, 1995.

Whitehead, Alfred North. *Process and Reality.* 1929. Corrected ed. New York: Free Press, 1978.

Whitney, Barry L. *Evil and the Process God.* New York: Edwin Mellen, 1995.

Wink, Walter. *Engaging the Powers: Discernment and Resistance in a World of Domination.* Minneapolis: Fortress, 1992.

———. *Naming the Powers: The Language of Power in the New Testament.* Philadephia: Fortress, 1984.

———. *Ummasking the Powers: The Invisible Forces That Determine Human Existence.* Philadelphia: Fortress, 1986.

Wright, J. Stafford. "The Place of Myth in the Interpretation of the Bible." *Journal of the Transactions of the Victorian Institute* 88 (1956) 18–30.

# Why Creation Groans

*Responding to Objections to the Corruption of Nature (CON) Hypothesis*

—Gregory A. Boyd

Many of the essays in this volume have argued for the plausibility of the thesis that nature as we now find it has been corrupted by rebel spirit-agents, which is why nature now is "red in tooth and claw," and produces a multitude of organisms that afflict both humans and animals with disease, and sometimes brings about "natural" disasters.[1] In this essay I will refer to this perspective as "The Corruption of Nature (CON) Hypothesis." The CON-Hypothesis is deeply grounded in Scripture and the church tradition, and it is my contention that, whatever merits other hypotheses may have concerning why nature is "red in tooth and claw," it is only by accepting that nature has been corrupted at a fundamental level that we can adequately reconcile nature as we now find it with the belief in a loving and kind Creator. If there are tares in the good farmer's wheat field, it is because an "enemy" planted them there (Matt 13:24–30).

Not surprisingly, there are a number of objections that have been raised against this view, its strengths notwithstanding. The goal of this present essay is to respond to the five objections that are most common and/or that I consider to be the most forceful.[2]

---

1. As in my previous essay, I will place quotation marks around "natural" when speaking of "natural" evil to remind readers that, in my view, there is actually nothing natural about so-called "natural" evil.

2. For other objections not treated here, see Murphy, *Nature Red in Tooth & Claw*, esp. 96–106.

# Objection 1. Modern Western People Simply Cannot Any Longer Believe in the Devil

Undoubtedly, the most common objection against the CON-Hypothesis is simply that modern Western people can no longer seriously entertain the possibility that invisible agents like "Satan," "principalities and powers," or "demons" actually exist. We can understand why people in ancient times believed in such things because, as Van Harvey put it, these people were "naïve and mythologically minded folk without any conception of natural order or law. They lived in a mythological time in which unusual events of nature and history were attributed to supernatural beings of all kinds."[3] By contrast, we are told, modern Western people understand the world scientifically and have therefore embraced a "naturalistic worldview." And whether they are aware of it or not, there simply is no place for belief in spirit-agents or supernatural occurrences within this worldview. As Rudolf Bultmann famously stated almost eighty years ago: "We cannot use electric lights and [radios] and, in the event of illness, avail ourselves of modern medical and clinical means and at the same time believe in the spirit and wonder world of the New Testament."[4]

Now, if the scholars making these claims simply meant that modern people can no longer accept the stereotyped mythological depictions of Satan or other malevolent spirit-agents that have been handed down to us from medieval times, their claims would be uncontroversial. But these scholars are claiming much more than that. They are claiming that modern Western people can no longer believe in spirit-agents as such.

The most curious thing about this claim is that it *simply is not true*. All indications are that the majority of Western people continue to believe in God, Satan, angels, demons, and miracles.[5] In this light, it is apparent that when Western scholars (primarily) boldly make claims about what Western people supposedly can no longer believe, what they are actually claiming is that Western people *shouldn't* any longer be able to believe in spirit-agents or supernatural occurrences—though the masses apparently are not smart enough to realize this fact. Robert Funk makes the arrogance implicit in this claim explicit when he argues: "The notion that God

---

3. Harvey, *Historian and the Believer*, 10.

4. Bultmann, *New Testament and Mythology*, 4.

5. For example, a 2005 Baylor Religion Survey found that 75 percent of Americans believe in Satan, while 73 percent believe in demons. See Baker, "Who Believes in Religious Evil?," 211; Newport, "Most Americans"; "More Americans"; Gallup and Castelli, *People's Religion*.

interferes with the natural order from time to time in order to aid or punish is no longer credible, *in spite of the fact that most people still believe it.*"[6] If most people continue to believe this notion, then it is false, *by definition*, to claim it is "no longer credible."

What is it then that prevents so many Western academics from taking seriously the belief in spirit agents, malevolent or otherwise? Have there been some new scientific discoveries that have proven the non-existence of these agents? There are none. Indeed, it's hard to imagine how any scientific discovery could conceivably have a bearing on the question of the existence of these agents. Alternatively, are there irrefutable philosophical arguments against the existence of spirit-agents or supernatural occurrences? If there are, I have yet to encounter them.[7]

What, then, grounds the current academic skepticism toward the existence of spirit agents? C. S. Lewis addresses this question when he writes: "The doctrine of Satan's existence and fall is not among the things we know to be untrue: it contradicts not the facts discovered by scientists but the mere, vague, 'climate of opinion.'"[8]

It is apparent that the current "climate of opinion" regarding the disbelief in spirit-agents is nothing more than an assumption shared by a relatively small cadre of Western scholars. And on Lewis's reckoning, assumptions that are grounded in nothing but the current "climate of opinion" only serve to close minds and impede intellectual curiosity.[9]

On that note, it is highly significant that the naturalistic worldview, with its *carte blanche* dismissal of spirit-agents, has not been shared by the vast majority of people on the globe throughout history. If we accept the post-modern claim that all worldviews are social constructs, the myopia of the academic "climate of opinion" becomes particularly problematic. For it means that this "climate of opinion" is arguably both *chronocentric* and *ethnocentric* inasmuch as it is premised on the assumption that the *modern* Western academic interpretation of reality is *superior to* the interpretation of people in the *past* as well as to contemporary people *outside of the West* who continue to believe in the existence of spirit-agents.[10]

---

6. Funk, "Twenty-One Theses," 8 (emphasis added).

7. For several responses to naturalistic arguments against spirit-agents and supernatural occurrences, see Lewis, *Miracles*; Geivett and Habermas, *In Defense of Miracles*; Eddy and Boyd, *Jesus Legend*, 37–90. The most insightful and comprehensive historical case for supernatural occurrences is Keener, *Miracles*.

8. Lewis, *Problem of Pain*, 134.

9. Lewis, *Problem of Pain*, 138.

10. For a fuller treatment of this charge, see Eddy and Boyd, *Jesus Legend*, 67–78.

Interestingly enough, since Western culture has taken a "post-modern turn," an increasing number of Western scholars are acknowledging that their own naturalistic worldview has no right to claim superiority over other world-views. Peter Berger, a father of the sociology of knowledge school of thought, states the point clearly: "We may agree, say, that contemporary consciousness is incapable of conceiving of either angels or demons. We are still left with the question of whether, possibly, both angels and demons go on existing despite this incapacity of our contemporaries to conceive of them."[11]

As a result, some of these scholars—especially in the fields of anthropology, sociology, and ethnography—are now arguing that one can only truly understand the worldview of other people groups by "going native" and experiencing these non-Western worldviews *from the inside*. The Western scholar must therefore suspend her own assumptions about the world, as much as this is possible, so as to enter as deeply as possible into the worldview of the group she is studying. Hence, in sharp contrast to the way Western scholars in these fields used to attempt to explain away or simply dismiss accounts of encounters with spirit-agents or of supernatural occurrences, these post-modern scholars are now arguing that Western scholars need to take these accounts seriously and as potential challenges to their own naturalistic assumptions.[12]

The results of this paradigm shift have been startling. A surprising number of the scholars have discovered that non-Western ways of looking at and experiencing the world often disclose aspects of reality that remain hidden within the naturalistic Western worldview. More specifically, some of these Western academics report having actual encounters with spirit-agents and/or of witnessing some other sort of supernatural occurrence.[13] In this light, not only do we have no compelling reasons for rejecting belief in spirit-agents and supernatural occurrences; these eye-witness reports from Western scholars who have "gone native" arguably provide support for the belief in their reality.

There are other reasons for affirming the reality of spirit-agents as well. First and foremost, Jesus clearly believed in the reality of Satan and other spirit-agents. Since I have compelling historical, philosophical and experiential reasons for concluding that the historical Jesus was "Yahweh

---

11. Berger, *Rumor of Angels,* 52–53.

12. Editors' Note: For accounts of African worldviews, see chapter 13, "A West African Perspective on God and Disease," and chapter 14, "An East African Perspective on God and Disease."

13. One ground-breaking example of this is Turner, *Experiencing Ritual.* For a sampling of such cases, see Eddy and Boyd, *Jesus Legend,* 67–73.

embodied," as N. T. Wright puts it,[14] I feel compelled to affirm the existence of spirit-agents on Jesus' authority.

Against this, some scholars have argued that the belief in spirit-agents was simply part of the cultural package that Jesus inherited by virtue of being incarnated in first-century Jewish culture, in which belief in Satan and other spirit-agents was a given. Since Jesus was fully human, these scholars argue, the fact that he shared this belief should be considered no more binding on modern people than other mistaken first-century beliefs that Jesus shared, such as the assumption that people have vision because light proceeds *out of* their eyes (Matt 6:22–23) or that the mustard seed is the smallest of all seeds (Mark 4:31).[15]

I grant that, as a full human being, Jesus undoubtedly appropriated some of the mistaken assumptions of the first-century Jewish culture he was embedded in.[16] But while he may have shared some of his culture's mistaken *assumptions*, Jesus himself claimed to only *teach* what he "heard from the Father," according to the Gospel of John (John 7:16–17; cf. 8:38; 14:24). Jesus may have *assumed* that light came out of the eye and that the mustard seed was the smallest of all seeds (although in this instance Jesus may have simply been speaking hyperbolically), but he *explicitly taught* that Satan was "the ruler of this world" (John 12:31; 14:11; 16:11) and an ever-present source of temptation (e.g., Matt 5:37).

Moreover, Jesus' teaching on Satan's authority sets the context in which his over-all ministry must be understood.[17] He came to destroy the works of the devil (1 John 3:8; cf. John 12:31; Heb 2:14), as I argued in my previous essay, "An Enemy Did This." This is precisely what we see Jesus doing throughout his healing and deliverance ministry, and we see it most decisively on the cross, which is presented in John's Gospel as Jesus' culminating exorcism of the prince of this world (John 12:31). If we can't trust Jesus on this foundational teaching, it's hard to know what teaching of his we *can* trust.

Not only this, but while Jesus and the Gospel authors share much in common with the prevailing thinking of the time about spirit-agents, they also have a good deal to say about these agents—and especially about Satan—that

14. Wright, *Jesus and the Victory of God*, 642, 653. My historical reasons for believing in Jesus are spelled out in Eddy and Boyd, *Jesus Legend*.

15. See, for example, Walton and Walton, *Demons*.

16. That is to say, I hold to an orthodox version of kenotic Christology, on which see Boyd and Eddy, *Across the Spectrum*, 118–23.

17. On the centrality of Satan and demons in Jesus' ministry, see Boyd, *God at War*, 171–237; Twelftree, *Jesus the Exorcist*; Hiers, "Satan," 33–47; Kallas, *Jesus and the Power of Satan*; *Significance of the Synoptic Miracles*.

goes significantly beyond the thinking of their contemporaries. Most importantly, the scope and authority ascribed to Satan in the New Testament, as well as the depiction of the kingdom of darkness as a unified army headed up by Satan, is without parallel. This is not what one would expect if Jesus' belief in spirit-agents simply reflected his cultural conditioning.

Beyond the authority of Jesus, I would argue that the cross-cultural experience of demon possession and exorcism supports belief in the reality of spirit-agents.[18] Around the globe and throughout history, continuing up to the present time, we find reports of people being "demon possessed" and "exorcized."[19] Despite the fact that these reports come from widely divergent cultures, they share a surprising amount in common, including supernatural features. For example, across cultures we find eyewitness reports of people levitating, of things flying through the air on their own, of bodies contorting in ways impossible to explain on natural terms, of people possessing knowledge they could not have acquired by any natural means, or of people speaking in languages they never learned.[20] Closely related to this, around the globe and throughout history, we find people claiming to have encountered spirit-agents, whether they be good or (more frequently) malevolent. It could be argued that the significant trans-culture commonality of these reports, combined with the supernatural elements found in these reports, supports the conviction that these unrelated reports are each dealing with the same supernatural reality.

Of course, we cannot naively assume all or even most of these reports are credible. But neither is there any reason, other than the prevailing "climate of opinion" in certain circles, to dismiss all these reports as hearsay, exaggeration, or deception. They should instead be evaluated on a case-by-case basis. It's also worth mentioning that, for contemporary people such as myself who have actually witnessed some of the supernatural phenomena commonly associated with demon possession and exorcism, it is not at all difficult to accept the veracity of some of these reports.[21]

---

18. On how widespread the belief and experience of "spirit possession" is within primordial cultures, see Bourguignon, "Spirit Possession," 19. For other sources, see Eddy and Boyd, *Jesus Legend*, 67–73.

19. See, e.g., Keener, *Miracles*.

20. A number of anthropologists, for example, have admitted to witnessing phenomena, commonly associated with spirit possession rituals, that defy naturalistic explanations. See, e.g., Bulatao, "Local Cases of Possession," 424–25; Houk, *Spirits, Blood, and Drums*, 4, 123–24.

21. For several contemporary accounts, see Peck, *Glimpse of the Devil*; Kiely, *Dark Sacrament*; Martin, *Hostage to the Devil*; Betty, "Growing Evidence," 13–30; Gallagher, "Case of Demonic Possession," 22–32.

In light of these considerations, I contend that it is not only false that Western people can no longer believe in spirit-agents; we actually have compelling reasons to do so, notwithstanding the current prevailing "climate of opinion" in Western academic circles.

## Objection 2. The Corruption of Nature Hypothesis Implies Dualism

A second common objection to the CON-Hypothesis is that, by attributing to Satan and other spirit-agents the potential to corrupt fundamental aspects of God's creation, including the corruption of natural processes and structures leading to disease or the process of evolution, the CON-Hypothesis comes dangerously close to Dualism.[22] This is the belief that God and Satan (or some similar figure) are equal in power and are eternally at war with one another, and the cosmos is their perpetual battleground. One form of this dualistic teaching that the early church had to confront was called Manicheanism, and it has been uniformly condemned by the church as a heresy.[23]

Is the CON-Hypothesis guilty of this heresy, as some detractors have suggested? There is no denying that the CON-Hypothesis shares with Manicheanism the belief that the conflict between God and God's cosmic opponents is woven into the very fabric of the cosmos. As we saw C. S. Lewis put it in my previous essay, "every square inch, every split second, is claimed by God and counterclaimed by Satan."[24] But instead of concluding from this that the CON-Hypothesis is dualistic and therefore wrong, I rather contend that this suggests that Manicheism, despite being wrong and heretical for considering evil to be eternal and equal to God, nevertheless *got something right*. They correctly captured the New Testament truth that we live in a "wheat and tares universe" in which the conflict between good and evil pervades everything.[25]

To illustrate, as "natural" as the law of entropy is to us, for this is all we've ever known, the New Testament associates the inevitable process of decay and death with God's cosmic enemy, the devil (Heb 2:14; John 8:44). Indeed, Paul explicitly teaches that the current creation's "frustration" (or

22. See, for example, Giberson and Collins, *Language of Science and Faith*.

23. For a comprehensive overview and history of the Manichean heresy, which later morphed in expression within the so-called Cathar heresy, see Stoyanov, *Other God*.

24. Lewis, *Christian Reflections*, 41.

25. The "wheat and tares universe," based on Jesus parable of the wheat and tares (Matt 13:24–30), comes from Creegan, *Animal Suffering*.

futility) and "bondage to decay" is evidence of its fallen state (Rom 8:20–21). If the law of entropy, which is one of the foundational laws of contemporary physics, reflects satanic corruption, we can only conclude that this corruption affects creation down to the core. It was for reasons such as this that C. S. Lewis confessed that, "next to Christianity, Dualism is the manliest and most sensible creed on the market."[26]

It is evident that the spirit-agents who have corrupted creation are remarkably powerful, according to the CON-Hypothesis. Yet, for all the remarkable authority the New Testament and early post-apostolic church ascribed to Satan and other rebel spirit-agents, they nevertheless departed radically from every form of Dualism by insisting that God alone is eternal and that this eternal God is the Creator of all things, including the spirit-agents who now oppose God.

Hence, whereas Dualism posits two co-eternal and co-equal deities to explain why we live in a "wheat and tares" world, the early post-apostolic church rather appealed to the free will of created spirit-agents.[27] So too, whereas Manicheanism could only promise ultimate victory over evil for certain divinely elected human individuals, not for the cosmos as a whole, the early church promised an ultimate unending victory for the entire cosmos, when God will finally be "all in all" (Acts 3:21; 1 Cor 15:28; Eph 1:10; Col 1:15–20; Rev 21:1–3). In this light, I trust it is clear that the allegation that the CON-Hypothesis is dualistic or in danger of becoming dualistic is without merit.

## Objection 3. The CON-Hypothesis Must Give Some Account of How and When Nature Was Corrupted

A third objection that has been raised against the CON-Hypothesis is that, since it is making a claim about the history of the cosmos—namely, that it became corrupted at some point—it is incumbent upon defenders of this hypothesis to provide some plausible suggestions as to how and when this corruption occurred.[28] More specifically, defenders of the CON-Hypothesis must demonstrate how the "story" of the corruption of nature fits in with the "story" of the evolution of the cosmos that is told by science. And among the problems these defenders face, according to this objection, is that the scientific "story" of the cosmos is a self-contained story. This entails that all

26. Lewis, *Mere Christianity*, 49.

27. Boyd, *Satan*, 39–49.

28. For the following, see Dunnington, "Problem," 265–74.

the "natural" evil that the CON-Hypothesis attempts to explain by appealing to the corrupting work of spirit-agents can be fully explained simply by appealing to the laws of nature.

In this light, it could be argued that the CON-Hypothesis fails "Occam's razor," which basically states that the simplest explanation is the mostly likely to be true. On top of this, inasmuch as the CON-Hypothesis appeals to Satan and other spirit-agents to protect God's impunity in the face of "natural" evil, it could be argued that the CON-Hypothesis is "egregiously ad hoc."[29]

In response, it must first be acknowledged that to date, no recognized theologian, philosopher, or scientist has ventured anything like a comprehensive and detailed account of how the story of nature's corruption fits with the story of the evolution of the cosmos and of life that is told by science.[30] In a sense, one could interpret some of the essays in this present volume to be initial forays in this direction,[31] though I suspect all the contributors to this volume would acknowledge that these are only initial baby steps.

Does this lacuna present a valid objection to the CON-Hypothesis? I do not believe that it does. Consider that theologians, philosophers, and scientists have only recently begun to wrestle with the question of how we should understand *God's* involvement in the world in light of modern science.[32] Given that the Enlightenment turned the "climate of opinion" among Western academics against the belief in Satan and other spirit-agents, I do not think it surprising that reflection on how spirit-agents might have been involved in the corruption of nature is lagging a little behind.

Second, I'm not sure it is fair to insist that defenders of the CON-Hypothesis provide an account of when and how the cosmos became corrupted. While this hypothesis is deeply rooted in Scripture, Scripture provides

29. Murray, *Nature*, 100.

30. Though he is not a widely recognized scholar in science or theology, Lawrence Burkholder blends the theological story of creation's corruption with science in an interesting, if somewhat quirky, way in *The Leviathan Factor*. Editors' Note: Missiologist Ralph Winter wrote and spoke often on the topic of "prehistory," hypothesizing that both "young earth" and "old earth" perspectives were credible, giving timelines up to the present. For a condensed version of his thinking see Winter, "Prehistory." For more detail, including a chart, see Winter, "Story of Our Planet," 249–70; "Theologizing Prehistory," 12–23.

31. Editors' Note: See, e.g., chapter 2, "The Biblical Story"; chapter 3, "A Theology of Creation"; chapter 4, "Early Church Perspectives on the Cosmic Conflict"; and chapter 15, "A Scientist's Perspective on Disease and Death."

32. For a sampling see Polkinghorne, *Quarks*; *Quantum Physics*; *Trinity*; Dodd, *Unlocking Divine Action*; Russell et al., *Chaos and Complexity*; Worthing, *God, Creation, and Contemporary Physics*; Miller, *Perspectives on an Evolving Creation*.

nothing that would have any bearing on this question. Hence, by necessity, any attempt to provide an answer to the question of when and how spirit-agents corrupted creation is going to be highly speculative, and any attempts at relating such an account to the story of evolution of the cosmos as told by science is going to be even more so.

A defender of the CON-Hypothesis could perhaps speculate that the corruption of the cosmos began seven and a half billion years ago when the mysterious force known as "dark energy" began to propel galaxies away from one another at an ever-accelerating speed. Alternatively, one could perhaps speculate that the corruption of the cosmos began around the time of the Cambrian explosion, when we first find evidence of predation. Then again, perhaps the corruption of the physical cosmos began prior to the big bang, as Lawrence Burkholder has argued.[33]

As for how the spirit-agents introduced violence into the animal kingdom, perhaps there is something to Norman Williams's speculation that there exists a "World Soul" or "life force" that served as the primogenitor of all living things and that this "life force" became corrupted which is why all the life that springs from this source is also corrupted, to one degree or another.[34] Or perhaps we should consider Burkholder's suggestion that Satan used his God-given authority, intelligence, and freedom to tweak foundational variables that affect information flow and negative feedback loops, thereby altering for the worse how the cosmos would unfold.[35]

Perhaps, but nothing more. For we simply don't have access to the information that would be necessary to provide such an account. The most I suspect we can hope for is for defenders of the CON-Hypothesis to demonstrate that this hypothesis doesn't *conflict* with any of the known facts of science. This doesn't imply that the CON-Hypothesis is baseless, however, for as I've said, there are other compelling reasons for accepting the CON-Hypothesis, beginning with the authority of Jesus, the New Testament, and the post-apostolic church. It simply implies that the story of the evolution of the cosmos that is told by science is not among these compelling reasons.

Third, I think it is entirely misguided to argue that the CON-Hypothesis fails Occam's Razor. This could only be the case if the CON-Hypothesis was trying to explain something that was already adequately explained by appealing to the laws of nature. But this is not what the CON-Hypothesis is attempting to do. While scientific explanations presuppose the laws of

33. Burkholder, *Leviathan*.

34. Williams, *Idea of the Fall*.

35. Burkholder, *Leviathan*, 261–88.

physics as we now find them, the CON-Hypothesis attempts to explain why the laws of nature as we now find them fail to reflect the loving kindness of the Creator. This is not a question science can address, which is why the CON-Hypothesis cannot be charged with adding any unnecessary complexity to what science is already telling us.

The allegation that the CON-Hypothesis is ad hoc, constructed simply to protect the Creator's impunity in the face of nature's terrors, has even less merit, in my opinion. Belief in the existence of Satan and other spirit agents wasn't conjured up in an ad hoc manner to help solve the problem of "natural" evil. To the contrary, going back to the earliest stages of Israel's theological development, God's people have always believed that God faces opposition from spirit-agents as God seeks to establish God's will "on earth as it is in heaven" (Matt 6:10). Whether these spirit-agents were conceptualized as a raging sea, or as sea monsters, or as principalities and powers, or as Satan and his fallen angels, belief in God has always been accompanied by the belief in opposing spirit-agents and powers.

Now, it *turns out* that belief in spirit-agents is also helpful when it comes to understanding why nature fails to consistently reflect the loving and kind character of the Creator. But this belief was not generated for this purpose, which is why it is completely misguided to charge the CON-Hypothesis with being ad hoc.

## Objection 4. If God Is All-Powerful, the CON-Hypothesis Is Superfluous

The fourth objection I'll address argues as follows: If God is all-powerful, God has the power to stop Satan (and *a fortiori*, all other spirit-agents) if God so choses. Hence, if God chose not to prevent Satan from corrupting creation, this can only be because God *didn't want to* prevent Satan from corrupting creation. Moreover, on the orthodox assumption that everything God chooses to do is good, we have no choice but to conclude that it was somehow good that God chose to allow Satan to corrupt creation. Hence, it is argued that even if one were to accept the CON-Hypothesis, it would accomplish nothing in terms of reconciling the violence and suffering in nature with the loving kindness of the Creator.

This is an important issue, for it was primarily this line of logic that eventually led Augustine to the dreadful conclusion that every horrendous thing that Satan does in history is ultimately for the good, as is every evil decision made by other spirit-agents as well as by humans. The assumption is that the all-powerful God could intervene and stop Satan from corrupting creation any time God wanted to. While it may initially sound counterintuitive, I will now argue that this assumption is, in fact, false.

Consider what it means for God to give an agent free will—or, more precisely, libertarian free will,[36] I submit that, whatever else free will might entail, an agent is free if and only if it is *up to them* to resolve *possible* courses of action into one single *actual* course of action. Stated as simply as possible, an agent is free if it lies within their own power to decide between going *this* possible way or *that* possible way. Hence, if God gives an agent free will, this *means* God has given them the ability to resolve for themselves whether they will go *this* way or *that* way.

But now suppose that God gave an agent I'll name Cedric the ability to decide for himself whether he will chose to go *this* way or *that* way but then intervened to prevent Cedric from going *that* way because God disapproved of it. Were God to do this, it would simply reveal that God *didn't* actually give Cedric the ability to go this way *or that way*. Stated otherwise, if God genuinely gave Cedric the ability to go this way *or that way*, then God *has no choice* but to allow Cedric go *that way*, despite the fact that God disapproves of it. The possibility of Cedric going *that* way, against God's will, was simply the risk God took when God endowed Cedric with the free will to decide for himself whether to go this way *or that way.*

This means that free will is, *by definition*, irrevocable.[37] God can no more revoke free will, once given, than God can create a round triangle, a square circle, or a married bachelor. It's not a question of how powerful God is. I grant that God is all-powerful. It's rather a question of *what kind of world the all-powerful God decided to create.* If God decides to create a world in which a certain specific area is fully contained within a triangle, God *can't* decide to simultaneously have that same area enclosed by a circle. So too, if God decides to create a world containing free agents, that world cannot be the kind of world in which God can intervene any time a free agent, whether human or angelic, is going to choose things God disapproves of.

Our capacity to resolve possible courses of action into a single actual course of action constitutes our "say-so" in how the future unfolds. We

---

36. Philosophers commonly distinguish between "libertarian" (or "incompatiblistic") free will, which holds that agents are free because they are *not* exhaustively determined by antecedent causes (including God's will), and "compatiblistic" free will, which holds that agents are free, despite being exhaustively determined by antecedent causes, so long as they are able to do what they want to do. For several helpful defenses of libertarian freedom from a variety of perspectives, see O'Conner, *Agents*; Ginet, *On Action*; Nozick, *Philosophical Explanations*, 291–388.

37. For a more comprehensive defense, see Boyd, *Satan*, 178–206.

might therefore say that, to the degree that God gives "say-so" to created agents, human or otherwise, to that same degree God has to set aside God's right to unilaterally exercise "say-so" over how the future unfolds. Hence, to the degree God has endowed created agents with free will, or "say-so," God *must* allow them to go down the path they choose regardless of how much God wishes they would do otherwise.

This doesn't mean that God must simply sit by and watch as people and spirit-agents make a mess of things. Scripture depicts God as an ever-present active Spirit who has always been working in every human heart to turn people from darkness to light, insofar as this is possible (e.g., Acts 17:26–28). But because God must honor the personhood—the "say-so"—of the agents God creates, God operates by means of influential love, not by means of coercion. Hence Paul declares that the cross, which is the most perfect revelation of God's self-sacrificial love, is the power of God (1 Cor 1:18, 24). God's power, in short, is synonymous with God's self-sacrificial love, and we are told that this cruciform love is at work throughout creation to reconcile everything to God and to each other and to thereby bring peace to the whole of creation (Col 1:19–20). It is this same cruciform love that draws, but never coerces, people to God. Hence, referring to his impending crucifixion, Jesus declares, "And I, when I am lifted up from the earth, will draw (*helkō*) all people to myself" (John 12:32).[38]

Not only this, but while God cannot unilaterally prevent an agent from making a fateful free decision once God has given them the freedom to do so, God *can* influence others who are receptive to God's promptings to use their God-given "say-so" to intervene and possibly prevent this person from making this fateful decision. In such cases, whether the person is stopped or not will depend, at least in part, on the degree to which other people were open to sensing and responding to God's promptings.

In this light, the reason the Creator didn't unilaterally intervene to prevent Satan and other spirit-agents from corrupting creation was not because God saw that their corruption of nature contributed to the beauty of the cosmos as a whole, as Augustine supposed. God rather didn't unilaterally intervene to prevent this corruption simply because, given God's prior decision to entrust these agents with "say-so" over aspects of the creation, God *couldn't*. Consequently, the remarkable potential for good that Satan and other spirit-agents had, to use their "say-so" to bless creation for ages, is

---

38. Calvinists have sometimes argued that *helkō* implies a strong force and could even be translated as "drag" or "pull." Yet, the Gospel of John presents people as capable of resisting God's will and as needing to freely choose to come to Christ. See Osborne, "Soteriology in the Gospel of John," 243–60. This entails that, whatever strength is implied by *helkō*, it stops short of anything like coercion.

now manifested as a remarkable potential to afflict creation for ages. And this, ultimately, is why we currently live in a "wheat and tares universe" that includes physical and societal chaos and disease.

Finally, there is an ancient maxim going back to Heraclitus (c. 535–475 BCE) and reappearing frequently in history that holds that people's choices become their habits; their habits, if persisted in, become their character; and their character, once solidified, becomes their destiny.[39] In short, we become the choices we make. We might say that our "say-so" in how the future unfolds is ultimately our "say-so" in *what kind of agents we will become.* C. S. Lewis makes this observation well: "Every time you make a choice you are turning the central part of you, the part of you that chooses, into something a little different from what it was before. And taking your life as a whole, with all your innumerable choices, all your life long you are slowly turning this central thing either into a heavenly creature or into a hellish creature."[40]

This means, among other things, that our "say-so" is limited, both in time and space. It exists during this probationary epoch, when each human is gradually determining whether they will become "a creature that is in harmony with God . . . other creatures . . . and with itself," or a creature "that is in a state of war and hatred with God, with its fellow creatures, and with itself."[41] Similarly, while the "say-so" that Satan and other spirit-agents have over creation is massively greater than that of humans both in scope and duration, it is nevertheless *finite.* God must honor the "say-so" of these agents, just as God does with humans. But the "say-so" of every agent God endowed with free will, including Satan, eventually runs out as the agent becomes increasingly solidified in their character.

It is only because the free will of every created agent, including Satan, is limited in time and scope that God can promise that this "wheat and tares" cosmos will not always be this way. In stark contrast to all forms of Dualism, the Bible proclaims that a time is coming when all the weeds in God's wheat field will be uprooted and destroyed (Matt 13:24–30). Nature will then no longer be "red in tooth and claw," but will instead perfectly reflect the loving character of its Creator.

We have no more of a clear idea as to how God will ultimately de-corrupt creation than we have of how and when creation became corrupted in the first place. What we must know, however, is that we are not merely to wait for the deliverance of the cosmos; we are to instead *participate* in its deliverance. And we do this by partnering with the Spirit to come against

39. For a discussion, see Boyd, *Satan,* 185–204.
40. Lewis, *Mere Christianity,* 86.
41. Lewis, *Mere Christianity,* 86.

everything in our life, in society, and in the creation that is contrary to the loving character of the Creator and the fullness of life God intends for us and the plant and animal kingdom. This includes avoiding, addressing, and eliminating diseases wherever possible.

## Objection 5. The "Fragility Objection"

The final objection that I'll consider was put forth by Michael Murray. According to the CON-Hypothesis, Murray correctly notes, "natural evil is ultimately rooted in moral evil." But this creates a problem, he believes. "In order for moral wrongdoing to leave such catastrophic consequences in its wake it must be the case that God created things so that the integrity of the natural order was, in some important sense, initially *dependent upon* the integrity of the moral order." The trouble with this, Murray contends, is that, "If God were omniscient, he would surely know that the natural order was fragile in this way." Hence, he argues, "Unless there is some reason why the fragility of nature is necessary, or why making it fragile in this way makes possible certain outweighing goods, the fragility of nature itself seems to be a puzzling defect in creation."[42]

According to Murray, this leaves us with "the vexing question of why God would create a universe which was subject to such catastrophic corruption on the occasion of a Fall of this sort?"[43]

Rather than directing the objection at the alleged defective nature of creation, one could raise this same objection by questioning the wisdom of God in giving Satan and other spirit-agents so much authority over creation that they could corrupt creation to the degree that the CON-Hypothesis suggests they have. After all, it is the authority entrusted to these spirit-agents that renders nature "fragile" to their decision-making. In any case, whether directed at the fragility of nature or at the wisdom of God in entrusting so much authority to spirit-agents, I believe there are three things that can be said to alleviate the weight of this objection.

First, it is not clear to me how the Creator could have created morally responsible free agents, whether human or angelic, without rendering nature vulnerable to their free decisions, to one degree or another. An agent's free will is morally significant only because they can choose to use their "say-so" to benefit or to harm people, animals, and the environment.[44] The suggestion

42. Murray, *Nature*, 83; cf. 92–93.

43. Murray, *Nature*, 101.

44. On the necessary connection between moral responsibility and the potential to benefit or harm sentient beings, see Frankena, *Ethics*, 113.

that the Creator should have restricted the "say-so" of morally responsible agents such that they lacked the capacity to harm people, animals, and the environment is thus equivalent to suggesting that the Creator should not have created morally significant free agents in the first place.

Against this, I would argue that morally responsible free will, which is the precondition for agents having the capacity to love, is an intrinsic good.[45] Indeed, if we accept that one of the ultimate goals of creation was to eventually have humans, and with them the whole creation, eternally participating in the perfect love of the triune Creator, then morally responsible free will must be considered a supreme good. Hence, the Creator cannot be faulted for creating such agents, despite the fact that the "say-so" of these agents renders creation fragile.

Still, one might wonder why an all-wise Creator would invest spirit-agents with so much "say-so" that they could corrupt even some of the laws of nature and thereby bring about so much horrific suffering throughout the evolutionary process? My second response to the fragility objection attempts to respond to this question.

As I see it, the potential that free spirit-agents have to bring about harm is simply an inverse reflection of the potential these agents have to bring about good. I have elsewhere labeled this "the principle of proportionality."[46] All other things being equal, a free agent's potential for good is also their potential for evil.[47] The more potential an agent has to use their "say-so" for good, the more potential that agent has to use their "say-so" for evil. This principle is articulated well by C. S. Lewis when he notes that "the higher a thing is, the lower it can descend."[48] And again,

> The better stuff a creature is made of—the cleverer and stronger and freer it is—then the better it will be if it goes right, but also the worse it will be if it goes wrong. A cow cannot be very good or very bad; a dog can be both better and worse; a child better or worse still; an ordinary man, still more so; a man of genius, still more so; a suprahuman spirit best—and worst—of all.[49]

---

45. For a discussion on free will as the precondition for love and on issues surrounding the concept of free agency, see Boyd, *Satan*, 50–115.

46. Boyd, *Satan*, 169–77.

47. I say "all other things being equal" because in any given moment there are innumerable contingent variables that influence an agent's God-given potential for good or evil, including the free decisions of other agents that directly or indirectly impact this agent.

48. Lewis, *Great Divorce*, 124.

49. Lewis, *Mere Christianity*, 53.

The Creator clearly took a huge risk endowing Satan and other spirit-agents with the "say-so" to bless or curse nature to the degree that God did, according to the CON-Hypothesis. But this is simply a macro-example of the risk God took when God entrusted humans with the "say-so" to bless or harm each other as well as the Earth and animal kingdom (Gen 1:26–27). As the saying goes, "Nothing ventured, nothing gained." Of course, the Creator could have risked less and thus rendered creation less vulnerable to the free decisions of agents, whether human or angelic. But for every increase in creational invulnerability, there would have had to be a decrease in agents potential for good, and ultimately for love.

In this light, can it be argued that the Creator should have placed a more restrictive cap on the potential of spirit-agents for good and evil? I, for one, do not see how any human could ever be in a position to know this. The omniscient Creator alone knows all that would need to be known to decide this matter. Only God knows how much good could have been brought about had Satan and other spirit-agents chosen to use their God-given authority in accordance with God's will rather than in opposition to it. Similarly, only the Creator could know ahead of time just how much potential for evil these agents have as well as how much good God could bring out of their evil should one or some or all of these spirit-agents choose to rebel. Hence, only the Creator is in a position to know whether the level of risk God took, in endowing spirit-agents and humans with as much "say-so" as God did, was worth it.

If the CON-Hypothesis is correct, the Creator obviously deemed the potential for good that these agents could contribute to creation worth the risk of the potential for evil that necessarily accompanied this potential for good. And since we humans lack the requisite knowledge to judge otherwise, I submit that our only recourse is to trust that the all-wise God always makes the wisest decisions, even when the risk God took turns out badly.

My third and final response to the fragility objection is to concede that trusting the wisdom of the Creator isn't always easy, for whenever a significant risk turns out badly, it *feels* like the risk was *not* worth it. And it feels this way because, at least in the short run, the failed risk *wasn't* worth it. But I would like us to see why it is misguided to judge the wisdom of the Creator on the basis of this notion of *feeling*.

Wherever God might have placed the parameters of creaturely "say-so"—which is to say, whatever level of risk the Creator might have been willing to take in endowing agents with "say-so"—it would feel to us like the parameters were too broad and the risk too great whenever agents actualized their potential for evil in ways that approach this parameter. The most extreme examples of goodness impress us, and the corresponding extreme examples of evil horrify us, precisely because they are *extraordinary*. And this would hold true regardless of how broad or narrow the "ordinary" of our God-created universe might have been.

For example, if God had decided to create a less vulnerable world in which the greatest good humans could possibly attain was being kind to a cat, we would naturally consider torturing a cat to death to be a supreme evil. And precisely because this act would reflect the parameters of any human's potentiality for evil in this less vulnerable world we are imagining, it would feel like the Creator had risked too much were someone to actualize this macabre potential. We would naturally wonder why the Creator would create a world in which cats were so vulnerable to the "say-so" of humans.

My point is that the fragility objection could be raised against the Creator in any possible world endowed with free agents that God could have created, and this implies that the fragility objection carries no force in the actual world that God decided to create. In light of the massive suffering brought about by the corruption of creation, it feels like God overplayed God's hand and risked too much, because in the short run we experience only loss.

Yet, it is a fundamental tenet of the Christian faith that "the short run" does not have the last word. Indeed, Paul has the audacity to declare that all the suffering in this corrupted, decaying creation that we find ourselves in, including suffering associated with disease, can't be compared to the glory that God has in store for us and the entire creation (Rom 8:18–25; cf. Col 1:15–20; Eph 1:9–11). Since we are in no position to judge otherwise, I again submit that our only recourse is to trust that the all-wise God knew God could deliver on this promise when the Creator decided to endow human and spirit-agents with the degree of "say-so" that we find them exercising in the cosmos as we currently find it.

I thus conclude that, as out of academic vogue as it may currently be, the belief that nature has been corrupted by Satan and other spirit-agents, including corruption related to disease, is biblical, coherent, rational, and is able to withstand the objections of its critics.

## Bibliography

Baker, Joseph. "Who Believes in Religious Evil? An Investigation of Sociological Patterns of Belief in Satan, Hell, and Demons." *Review of Religious Research* 50 (2008) 211.

Berger, Peter L. *A Rumor of Angels: Modern Society and the Rediscovery of the Supernatural.* Garden City, NY: Doubleday, 1969.

Betty, Stafford. "The Growing Evidence for 'Demonic Possession': What Should Psychiatry's Response Be?" *Journal of Religion and Health* 44 (2005) 13–30. Online. https://doi.org/10.1007/s10943-004-1142-9.

Bourguignon, Erika. "Spirit Possession Belief and Social Structure." In *The Realm of the Extra-Human: Ideas and Actions*, edited by Agehananda Bharat, 17–26. Paris: Mouton, 1976.

Boyd, Gregory A. *God at War: The Bible and Spiritual Conflict.* Downers Grove, IL: InterVarsity, 1997.

———. *Satan and the Problem of Evil: Constructing a Trinitarian Warfare Theodicy.* Downers Grove, IL: InterVarsity, 2001.

Boyd, Gregory A., and Paul Eddy. *Across the Spectrum.* 2nd ed. Grand Rapids: Baker Academic, 2009.

Bulatao, Jamie. "Local Cases of Possession and their Cure." *Philippine Studies* 30 (1982) 424–25.

Bultmann, Rudolf. *The New Testament and Mythology.* Translated and edited by Schubert M. Ogden. Fortress: Philadelphia 1984.

Burkholder, Lawrence. *The Leviathan Factor.* Eugene, OR: Wipf & Stock, 2017.

Creegan, Nicola Hoggard. *Animal Suffering and the Problem of Evil.* New York: Oxford University Press, 2013.

Dodds, Michael J. *Unlocking Divine Action: Contemporary Science and Thomas Aquinas.* Washington, DC: Catholic University of America Press, 2017.

Dunnington, Kent. "The Problem With the Satan Hypothesis: Natural Evil and Fallen Angel Theodicies." *Sophia* 57.2 (2018) 265–74.

Eddy, Paul, and Gregory A. Boyd. *The Jesus Legend: A Case for the Historical Reliability of the Synoptic Tradition.* Grand Rapids: Baker Academic, 2007.

Frankena, William K. *Ethics.* 2nd ed. Englewood Cliffs, NJ: Prentice Hall, 1973.

Funk, Robert W. "Twenty-One Theses." *The Fourth R* 11.4 (1998) 8.

Gallagher, Richard E. "A Case of Demonic Possession." *New Oxford Review* 75 (2008) 22–32.

Gallup, George, Jr., and Jim Castelli. *The People's Religion: American Faith in the 90s.* New York: Macmillan, 1989.

Geivett, R. Douglas, and Gary R. Habermas. *In Defense of Miracles: A Comprehensive Case for God's Action in History.* Downers Grove, IL: InterVarsity Academic, 1997.

Giberson, Karl W., and Francis Collins. *The Language of Science and Faith: Straight Answers to Genuine Questions.* Downers Grove, IL: InterVarsity, 2011.

Ginet, Carl. *On Action.* Cambridge, UK: Cambridge University Press, 1990.

Harvey, Van A. *The Historian and the Believer: The Morality of Historical Knowledge and Christian Belief.* Philadelphia: Westminster, 1966.

Hiers, Richard H. "Satan, Demons, and the Kingdom of God." *Scottish Journal of Theology* 27 (1974) 33–47.

Houk, James. *Spirits, Blood, and Drums: The Orisha Religion in Trinidad.* Philadelphia: Temple University Press, 1995.

Kallas, James. *Jesus and the Power of Satan.* Philadelphia: Westminster, 1968.

———. *The Significance of the Synoptic Miracles: Taking the Worldview of Jesus Seriously.* New York: Seabury, 1961.

Keener, Craig S. *Miracles: The Credibility of the New Testament Accounts.* Grand Rapids: Baker Academic, 2011.

Kiely, David. *The Dark Sacrament: True Stories of Modern-Day Demon Possession and Exorcism*. New York: HarperOne, 2008.

Lewis, C. S. *Christian Reflections*. 1967. Reprint, Grand Rapids: Eerdmans, 2014.

———. *The Great Divorce*. New York: Macmillan, 1946.

———. *Mere Christianity*. New York: Macmillan, 1996.

———. *Miracles: A Preliminary Study*. New York: Harper One, 2015.

———. *The Problem of Pain*. New York: Macmillan, 1962.

Martin, Malachi. *Hostage to the Devil: The Possession and Exorcism of Five Living Americans*. New York: Reader's Digest, 1976.

Miller, Keith B., ed. *Perspectives on an Evolving Creation*. Grand Rapids: Eerdmans, 2003.

"More Americans Believe in the Devil than Darwin." *Reuters*, November 29, 2007. Online. https://www.reuters.com/article/us-usa-religion-beliefs/poll-finds-more-americans-believe-in-devil-than-darwin-idUSN2922875820071129.

Murray, Michael J. *Nature Red in Tooth and Claw: Theism and the Problem of Animal Suffering*. Oxford: Oxford University Press, 2008.

Newport, Frank. "Most Americans Still Believe in God." *Gallup*, June 29, 2016. Online. https://news.gallup.com/poll/193271/americans-believe-god.aspx.

Nozick, Robert. *Philosophical Explanations*. Cambridge: Harvard University Press, 1981.

O'Conner, Timothy, ed. *Agents, Causes, and Events: Essays on Indetermininism and Free Will*. Oxford: Oxford University Press, 1995.

Osborne, Grant R. "Soteriology in the Gospel of John." In *The Grace of God, The Will of Man*, edited by Clark H. Pinnock, 243–60. Grand Rapids: Zondervan, 1989.

Peck, M. Scott. *Glimpse of the Devil: A Psychiatrists Personal Accounts of Possession*. New York: Simon & Shuster, 2005.

Polkinghorne, John. *Quantum Physics and Theology: An Unexpected Kinship*. New Haven: Yale University Press, 2008.

———. *Quarks, Chaos, and Christianity*. New York: Crossroads, 1996.

———, ed. *The Trinity and an Entangled World: Relationality in Physical Science and Relationality*. Grand Rapids: Eerdmans, 2010.

Russell, Robert John, et al., eds. *Chaos and Complexity: Scientific Perspectives on Divine Actions*. Notre Dame: University of Notre Dame Press, 1995.

Stoyanov, Yuri. *The Other God: Dualistic Religions From Antiquity to the Cathar Heresy*. New Haven: Yale University Press, 2000.

Turner, Edith. *Experiencing Ritual: A New Interpretation of African Healing*. Philadelphia: University of Pennsylvania Press, 1992.

Twelftree, Graham H. *Jesus the Exorcist: A Contribution to the Study of the Historical Jesus*. Peabody, MA: Hendrickson, 1993.

Walton, John H., and J. Harvey Walton. *Demons and Spirits in Biblical Theology*. Eugene, OR: Cascade, 2019.

Williams, Norman P. *The Idea of the Fall and of Original Sin*. London: Longmans, Green, 1927.

Winter, Ralph D. "Pre-History Compiled Article." n.d. Online. https://static1.squarespace.com/static/5b3157f3b40b9d21a8096625/t/5c33a7361ae6cfb0999887e9/1546889016413/5g+Prehistory+compiled%2C+edited.pdf.

————. "The Story of Our Planet." In *Frontiers in Mission: Discovering and Surmounting Barriers to the Missio Dei*, edited by Ralph D. Winter, 249–72. 4th ed. Pasadena, CA: William Carey International University Press, 2008.

————. "Theologizing Prehistory: Implications for Mission." In *Frontiers in Mission: Discovering and Surmounting Barriers to the Missio Dei*, edited by Ralph D. Winter, 12–23. 4th ed. Pasadena, CA: William Carey International University Press, 2008.

Worthing, Mark W. *God, Creation, and Contemporary Physics*. Minneapolis: Fortress, 1996.

Wright, N. T. *Jesus and the Victory of God*. Minneapolis: Fortress, 1996.

# Epilogue

—Daniel W. O'Neill

This world is an amazing place, filled with beauty, grace, and wonder, and this includes the human being, the Creator's crowning glory. Yet, as the contributors to this book have expressed, it does not take much to see that *all creation groans*. There is no one person or nation who does not feel the weight of the cursed and corrupted Earth, subjected to decay. It becomes highly personal when it affects the integrity of our own bodies and those we know and love. Brokenness encroaches on our thoughts, memories, and feelings—affecting behavior and impairing relationships. Corruption is also experienced in many systems, even those which are intended for good, such as families, governments, churches, organizations, and healthcare, all of which impair human flourishing when corrupted. Exploring deep upstream causes and informing hope-filled solutions to be applied throughout the world has been the purpose of this collective work.

This creational groaning is global, so the solutions must be global. Yet these solutions must be locally applied and owned at the community level. Since *all* creation groans, it is our prayer that this book provokes you and your organization or congregation to be *all-inclusive* regarding the implications of such a challenging state of affairs on the Earth.

## Consider All the Data

We hope you will consider *all the biblical, scientific, and historical data* on the topic of disease/death and healing/life in order to know enough to apply the best of the balm of Gilead to the sickness of the world. Based on

Aquinas's view of grace and nature, Francis Schaeffer wrote of two stories in the modern world: 1. An upper story where supernatural and metaphysical meaning is found through faith, spirit, forms, and universals, and 2. A lower story where we live our earthly lives each day in material reality, particulars, empirical evidence, and rationality.[1] Both modernism and postmodernism have rendered these two stories mutually exclusive, with the upper story being completely subjective, private, culture-bound, and optional; and the lower story being where "truth" can be autonomously demonstrated with ostensible certainty. Can we maintain a fluid staircase between these two stories so that truth can be derived from both for an integrated reality? Can we live as if there is only one house in practice?

## Listen to All Christian Voices

We hope that listening intently to *all voices* from various denominational and ecclesiological traditions will help inform a more robust understanding of the fullness of the gospel and the diversity of Christ's universal body. Unity around the high value of the holy Scriptures brings us closer to a wisdom perhaps deeper than we had before imagined from within the tents of our particular encampments. This orientation can help us re-evaluate our understanding of broad reality, and can give us an uncompromising trinitarian understanding of the God who both heals and saves.

## Hear Songs from All Nations

We hope to hear new songs from *all nations* who experience God's healing presence. "Sing to the Lord a new song, his praise *from* the ends of the earth" (Isa 42:10). As the culture-shaping gospel has spread far and wide throughout the world, a broader perspective has emerged collectively, and continues to emerge. A globalized Christianity requires listening intently to these multi-cultural voices from the increasingly ethnically diverse family of God. As each people group finds profound meaning in the revealed word of God through the Holy Spirit, each applies this transforming grace to local problems with creative solutions in their own language and melody.

---

1. Shaeffer, *Escape from Reason*, 13–15.

## Be Challenged by All Perspectives

It may be a challenge for some to hear *all theological perspectives*, even those which do not entirely comport with their pre-conceived philosophical or theological constructs. These challenges or areas of disagreement could include:

- The timing and process of creation events
- Divine sovereignty in relation to human and angelic free will
- The degree to which spirit-agents can affect the created material world
- The priority of proclamation over or against demonstration
- Understandings of the distinctions of moral and natural evil
- Eschatological particulars for the world's future events and states of being.

Though we might disagree on some of these ideas, we hope the contents of this book elicit a healthy tension of belief, while still maintaining a generous and robust unity of action—a compelling harmony.

## Emphasize God's Work of Reconciling All of Creation

We hope to emphasize God's work of reconciling *all of creation*. With both a return to a creation-centered hermeneutic and taking into account emerging scientific data on complex ecosystems, we can avoid an overly anthropocentric or exploitative understanding of dominion or stewardship of God's world. We also want to avoid an overly dualistic spiritualized view of salvation. These are inadequate responses which are gaining increasingly less traction in the contemporary world. This is especially important to emerging generations sensitized to ecological and geo-political crises and driven to enact justice in tangible ways in a multi-cultural world marked by suffering. The redemption of all of creation includes the plant, animal, fungal, monera, and protozoal kingdoms as well as all the "kingdoms" of men and women. *Shalom* is the ultimate goal in the restoration of harmonious, life-giving, loving relationships, and in tangible ways it can begin now. This entails the active eschewing of evil—a praxis of "driving out" corruption—bodily, materially, systemically, environmentally, morally, and spiritually.

## Acknowledge Redemption within All Spatial Dimensions

We acknowledge God's sovereign work of redemption within *all spatial dimensions*. This ranges from the microscopic battle ground of pathogens and biochemical processes revealed in the last one hundred fifty years, to the macroscopic world of human affairs experienced and recorded from ancient times, to the cosmic realm encompassing prehistory and extending into the *eschaton*. Renewal and healing of a rebellious and corrupted creation is a cohesive metanarrative that comports with both the biblical and natural sciences, while still maintaining some mystery—never quite plumbing the depths of wonder. Any approach to global health must take into account realities that are historical and contemporary, physical and metaphysical, and global realities from the "four winds" (eastern, western, northern, and southern). All this still leaves us humbled in our limitations, more aware than ever of the need to fully trust the God who knows all.

## Include All Members of the Universal Church

*All members of the universal church* are blessed to be a blessing for the healing of nations. God's vicarious work of healing through his redeemed children takes many shapes. It is not relegated to just professionals or medics, nor just to pastors or priests, but also to a mobilized and empowered deployment of millions of lay leaders, community health workers, family nurturers, community activists, artists, and truth tellers. This is a vision for the whole church, including those healing communities yet to be planted in the global frontiers and in areas of extreme chaos or deprivation where they are needed most.

## Prioritize Justice

We must be ever-mindful of the weight of the moral imperative to prioritize justice toward *all the marginalized, oppressed, impoverished, displaced, fatherless, forgotten, and forsaken.* All ethno-linguistic people groups experiencing the pain of disease and the corruption of nature are awaiting a full revelation of the majestic saving glory of Jesus the Messiah within their unique cultural contexts. "The creation waits in eager expectation for the children of God to be revealed" (Rom 8:19). This revelation requires the church to be formed, planted, and developed to express God's character well. This includes demonstrating God's healing desire, his love for the poor, his uncompromising pursuit of justice, and his pursuit of a people for rescue, comfort, and protection. The church's demonstrations of God's character must be marked by various tangible expressions of compassion and mercy in continuity with the well-documented character and ongoing work of the Savior who sets the captives free.

## Appreciate All Facets of Healing Practice

We must appreciate *all the facets of healing practice* through which God blesses the world, and in which all his people can participate.

- From words of rebuke, affirmation, or hope aptly spoken at the community level, to sophisticated therapeutic orders written in hospitals.

- From local natural plants with healing properties locally cultivated, to pharmaceuticals creatively designed in laboratories to inhibit processes that lead to early death.

- From a reflexive congregation of nurture, health promotion, and discipline, to dedicated professionals trained in the science and art of medicine and nursing in clinics.

- From public health measures for the common good and prevention of disease, to focused curative care for the afflicted individual.

- From the pursuit of removing material etiologies through empirical scientific inquiry in the academy, to the bold casting out of evil spirit-agents in churches and homes.

- From advocating for the poor in local municipalities, to witnessing to the powers in governments and multilateral organizations.

- From preaching and teaching a life-giving message in the local congregation or parish, to paradigm-shifting scholarly publications on the high healing value of faith and the gospel for policy-makers

These gifts, limited though they may be, and themselves subject to corruption, can be received as gifts from the God who heals (Exod 15:26). Their shortcomings can be mended by God's supervening grace and improved upon by new levels of human social responsibility.

A theology of disease is not true to the biblical and historical witness if it excludes or avoids the corrupting effect on the natural world of the sin and misaligned dominion of both spirit agents and human beings. Such a truncated, materialist view is obstructive to faith in God and irrelevant to the majority world. Narrow views inform insufficient solutions. It is uncontroversial that disease causation can be traced to corruptions in the material world, such as mutated DNA sequences, disordered gene expressions, microorganism mutations that confer destructive and evasive characteristics, or invasion of the purity of sacred anatomic spaces. But causation must be expanded to include corruptions in systems, be they family dynamics, community relations, ecological balances, or governments, as well as unseen principalities and powers. Consideration for etiologies beyond the material world and against our materialist and reductionist tendencies from the West informs a more cohesive and collaborative approach to prevention and treatment in global health which a well-informed Christian community can uniquely bring.

## Contemplate All Reflections on the Current Pandemic

The world is currently being shaken deeply through the pandemic of CO-VID-19. A simple RNA betacoronavirus, with 30,738 base pairs, which continues to evolve at two mutations per month, SARS-CoV-2 has, as of this writing, infected over thirty-one million people and caused over a million deaths in all 188 countries, and the toll continues to rise.[2] There are disabilities for some survivors, and even for those not infected there is resultant mental health pathology, increases in domestic violence and substance abuse, despair-generating social isolation, stunted education, and a 5.2 percent downturn in the global economy in 2020, with millions of people being pulled back into extreme poverty.[3]

For people of the Christian faith, this global crisis, in a short time, has provoked renewed theological reflection on the nature of disease, human social and economic inequities, ecological imbalance, natural evil, and questions of God's purposes and presence. Some have taken it as an opportunity to put forth new apologetics of the Christian faith. Professor John Lennox was quick in the pen to write that seeing pandemics and disasters as being a direct judgment of God is a "very crude response that causes a lot of unnecessary hurt."[4] Yet after not once mentioning in his book that Satan is a force to contend with, he is "left with many ragged edges and issues

2. "Coronavirus Resource Center." Editors' Note: This website updates daily with the most recent statistics.

3. "COVID-19 to Plunge Global Economy."

4. Lennox, *Where Is God*, 22

on which I would like to have more clarity."[5] Could this book, *All Creation Groans*, assist in that sincere endeavor?

On the other hand, John Piper contends that this pandemic is not outside God's sovereign will as a form of "bitter providence,"[6] revealing the ubiquity of our offense to God and serving as a wake-up call to repentance. The secret of "sorrowful, yet always rejoicing" (2 Cor 6:10), he writes, is this: "knowing that the same sovereignty that could stop the coronavirus, yet doesn't, is the same sovereignty which sustains the soul in it." Though he recognizes the activity of Satan in our suffering, he emphasizes his limitations under God's sovereign hand, and that Satan serves God's judgments unwittingly.[7] "Sin, in fact, is why all physical misery exists."[8] Yet he shares renewed hope that this pandemic would foster faith in God, and propel God's people to new levels of justice, service, and mission in the world despite or even because of this bitter providence.

In a third theological reflection, N. T. Wright's welcome response to the pandemic is to critique some common responses by Christians such as assuming this is a sign of the end times, fostering escapism, blaming others, ascribing it to the sin of victims, receiving it as a newfound opportunity for evangelism, or ascribing it to "ancient pagan theories" of retributive destructive acts of an angry deity.[9] He traces the Deuteronomic biblical story of Israel and God's "healing, rescue, restoration, and new creation following after a time not only of judgment but of despair," which was manifest in the example of the Babylonian captivity followed by the regathering. This story line is carried through into the central story of Jesus' healing and redeeming work culminating in his resurrection. Wright recognizes the deeper story of the good creation and the "dark power that has from the start tried to destroy God's good handiwork," but remains agnostic toward that unknowable dark power. Instead he proposes a pastoral "lament . . . complain . . . state the case . . . and leave it with God" approach.[10] He cautions against looking back at hypothetical causes, instead following Jesus' kingdom-oriented approach which was to start with tears and groans of lament, then to look forward to see what God is going to do about it—then courageously and sacrificially *joining* with God (*synergeo*, Rom 8:28) in bringing it about in the here and

5. Lennox, *Where Is God*, 62.

6. Piper, *Coronavirus*, 37.

7. Piper, *Coronavirus*, 65.

8. Piper, *Coronavirus*, 61.

9. Wright, *God and the Pandemic*, 6.

10. Wright, *God and the Pandemic*, 14.

now.[11] This kingdom-mindedness "is all about restoring creation the way it was meant to be." Wright explains that God does this globally through "loyal human beings," bringing Christ's healing presence.[12]

## Contribute to the Healing of All Nations

But where do we begin? How can we engage in this restoring work of God's? N. T. Wright's recent call to "genuine new possibilities, new ways of working which will regenerate old systems and invent new and better ones,"[13] must include the prayerful discernment of deep upstream causes of disease, even if there is uncertainty in the pursuit, and provided we do not hold too tightly to our particular theories. Instead of remaining agnostic of evil powers, there is the call for wise discernment of spirits (Acts 19:15; 1 John 4:1–2) and active casting out in the powerful name of Jesus (Mark 3:15). Likewise, engagement needs to include, but be much more than, a chaplaincy role of lamenting and comforting the afflicted while passively waiting for redemption. By exploring deep physical intermediaries at the cellular and molecular level through emerging scientific inquiry, a praxis of truth-telling in the matrix of a testable universe can become a worthy alignment with God's healing desire. In addition, applying complex systems thinking in the realm of human social relationships and systems in order to find innovative ways to foster equity, peace, and justice is a praxis of thinking God's thoughts after him. Through our actions we can collaborate and anticipate all that God is doing in the world for global health. This advances further the vision both Ralph Winter and Daniel Fountain proposed toward fighting the works of evil and aligning with God's unchanging healing intentions in suffering communities throughout the world.

Creative collaborations will combine compassionate hand holding, risk-taking, care-giving (especially during pandemics), honest lament, heart-felt intercessory prayer, witnessing to the powers in the spiritual realm which manifest in the physical realm, and correctly diagnosing (naming) and eradicating (casting out) disease and corruption in its many forms. This requires a call for a change of mind (*metanoia*) which expels harmful myths and webs of lies which oppress and de-animate, freeing many to experience new life in the risen Savior-Healer. Doing so is a form of doxology, passionately following Jesus' inseparable ways of preaching,

11. Wright, *God and the Pandemic*, 16–17.
12. Wright, *God and the Pandemic*, 32.
13. Wright, *God and the Pandemic*, 75.

teaching, and healing with a vision for a new creation. Before his ascension Jesus promised, "I am with you always, to the very end of the age" (Matt 28:20). Jesus also promised that his disciples would do even greater things than he had done (John 14:12). But more than utilizing a scalable capacity-building method or ethical code-of-conduct, his disciples *embody* Christ, the hope of glory (Col 1:27), guided and empowered by the Holy Spirit, for his kingdom to come on Earth as it is in heaven.

Out of all the people of the Earth, Abraham was blessed to be a blessing (Gen 12:2), and out of all the families of the earth, Israel was chosen to show YHWH's grace and glory to the nations (Isa 2:1–5). We must keep central the greatest blessing for global health in the (singular) Seed (Gal 3:16), who is the Messiah, the righteous Healer-King from the line of David, promised to Eve from Genesis to be the One who would ultimately crush the striking serpent's head, and set the captives free. When his life-giving presence is made available to all the families of the Earth as the supremely worthy object of saving/healing faith, sin is forgiven, abundant life emerges, *shalom* is restored, and corruption flees in the light of his glory and grace. That is our prayer for the world.

> He will be the sure foundation for your times,
>
> a rich store of salvation and wisdom and knowledge;
>
> the fear of the LORD is the key to this treasure. . . .
>
> No one living in Zion will say, "I am ill";
>
> and the sins of those who dwell there will be forgiven (Isa 33: 6, 24).

## Bibliography

"Coronavirus Resource Center." *John Hopkins University of Medicine*, n.d. Online. https://coronavirus.jhu.edu/map.html.

"COVID-19 to Plunge Global Economy into Worst Recession since World War II." *World Bank*, June 8, 2020. Online. https://www.worldbank.org/en/news/press-release/2020/06/08/covid-19-to-plunge-global-economy-into-worst-recession-since-world-war-ii.

Lennox, John C. *Where Is God in a Coronavirus World?* Epsom, Surrey, UK: Goodbook, 2020.

Piper, John. *Coronavirus and Christ*. Wheaton: Crossway, 2020.

Schaeffer, Francis A. *Escape from Reason*. Downers Grove, IL: InterVarsity, 2006.

Wright, N. T. *God and the Pandemic: A Christian Reflection on the Coronavirus and Its Aftermath*. Grand Rapids: Zondervan, 2020.

# General Index

abiding, xxxiii, 27, 80, 84–85
addiction, xv, xx, 2, 128
Abraham, xxxi, 14, 15, 17, 20, 53, 182, 186, 243
Adam, xvi, xx, xxii, 15, 23, 41, 44, 45, 54, 167, 193n3, 201
advocacy, xxxiii, 95, 98, 177
Africa, xiv, xvii, xxxi, xxxiv, 2, 10, 11, 50, 141–55
*agape*, 81
agrarians, 69–71
AIDS (See HIV/AIDS)
ancestral spirits, 57, 142, 144, 145
angel(s), xvi, xxxii, 20, 25–26, 31, 37, 41, 42–44, 77, 176, 182, 185, 187, 202, 207, 217, 224, 225, 228, 230, 237
anthropology, 115–16, 117, 119–20, 217
animal health, xxxiii, 42, 63, 64, 65, 164–65,
animal suffering, 71, 73, 74, 75–76, 77, 187, 195–96, 199, 214, 228
antibiotics, 60, 176
Aquinas, Thomas, 5, 184, 236
Asamoah-Gyadu, J. Kwabena, 11
Athenagoras, 207–9
atonement, xxviii, 48, 82, 98, 103, 104, 108
authority, 15, 26, 58, 107, 142, 168n21, 183, 188, 197, 200, 202–4, 207–8, 218–19, 221, 223, 228, 230

bacteria, 52, 57, 59, 60, 67, 157, 162–64, 165, 176, 177, 185, 186, 188, 188n7
Babylon, 16, 33, 74, 135, 203, 241
Balthasar, Hans Urs von, 123
baptism, 102, 121
Benedict XVI, 119n17
Berger, Peter, 217
Berry, Wendell, 64, 67–68, 70
Bevans, Stephen, 145
Black Plague, xvn6, 66–67, 164
blessing, xix, xxx, xxxi, 15–17, 18, 25, 45, 46, 54, 66, 77, 145, 177, 182, 185, 186, 238, 243
body of Christ, xxviii, xxx, xxxvi, 236, 238
Bruckner, James, 9, 45n23, 174, 178
Brueggemann, Walter, 73, 75
Burkholder, Lawrence, 222n30, 223

Caird, George B., 178
Calvin, John, 6, 17, 184, 226n38
Campolo, Tony, 23
cancer, xxi, xxiii, xxviii, 28, 54, 55, 61, 92, 110–12, 113n56, 161, 162, 166–67
casting out, 10, 111, 174, 206, 239, 242
Chan, Simon, 11
chaos, xxxi, 8, 9, 10, 20–29, 40, 41, 80, 136, 174, 201, 202n28, 210, 227, 238

# Scripture Index

## Genesis

| | |
|---|---|
| 1:1–4a | 20, 22, 26 |
| 1:2 | xxxi, 24, 25, 28, 201 |
| 1:11–12 | 76, 198 |
| 1:20–31 | 71–72, 77, 230 |
| 1:26–28 | 22, 201, 207, 210 |
| 1:28 | xxxii, 3, 28, 174, 185 |
| 1:29–30 | 196, 200 |
| 1:31 | 169 |
| 2:1–3 | 73 |
| 2:15 | 77, 201 |
| 3 | 166 |
| 3:1 | 35, 56 |
| 3:4 | 173 |
| 3:6 | 35 |
| 3:10 | 35 |
| 3:15 | 27 |
| 3:17–19, 24 | 200–201 |
| 6:5 | 14 |
| 8:1 | 196 |
| 12:1–3 | 15, 17, 243 |
| 12:17 | 183 |
| 18:18; 22:18 | 15 |
| 26:4 | 16 |
| 28:14–15 | 16 |
| 41:38 | 15 |
| 45:4–5 | 15 |

## Exodus

| | |
|---|---|
| 3:13–14 | 69 |
| 5:10 | 24 |
| 15:26 | 54, 239 |
| 19:6 | 23 |
| 20:8–11 | 72–73 |
| 22:22 | 135 |
| 23:4–5, 12 | 196 |
| 23:9 | 93, 135 |
| 23:10–11 | 72–74, 135 |
| 34:6–7 | 93 |

## Leviticus

| | |
|---|---|
| 11:19–24 | 130 |
| 13:47–58 | 130 |
| 19:33–34 | 135 |
| 25:1–7 | 73–74 |
| 25:8–24 | 74 |
| 26 | 54 |

## Numbers

| | |
|---|---|
| 14:18 | 47 |
| 32:22, 29 | 201 |